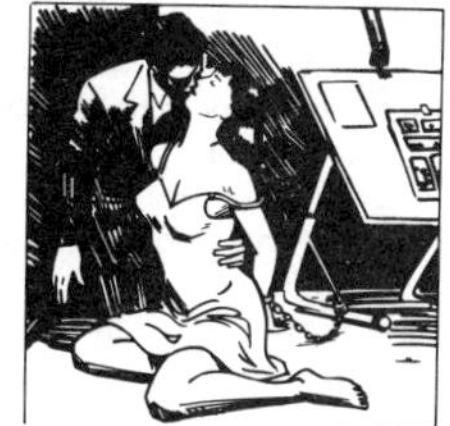

TWISTED SISTERS

A COLLECTION OF BAD GIRL ART

Edited by Diane Noomin

PENGUIN BOOKS

Thanks for help and encouragement to Bill Griffith, Aline Kominsky-Crumb, David Stanford, Janis Siegel, Linda Josefowicz, Helene Kaplan Wright, Bernard Gershater, Barbara Griffith, Jake Widman, Mitch Berger, Nancy Dorking, Joyce Zavarro, and Ron Turner.

PENGUIN BOOKS
Published by the Penguin Group
Viking Penguin, a division of Penguin Books USA Inc.,
375 Hudson Street, New York, New York 10014, U.S.A.
Penguin Books Ltd, 27 Wrights Lane,
London W8 5TZ, England
Penguin Books Australia Ltd, Ringwood,
Victoria, Australia
Penguin Books Canada Ltd, 10 Alcorn Ave., Suite 300,
Toronto, Ontario, Canada M4V 3B2
Penguin Books (N.Z.) Ltd, 182–190 Wairau Road,
Auckland 10, New Zealand

Penguin Books Ltd, Registered Offices:
Harmondsworth, Middlesex, England

First published in Penguin Books 1991

10 9 8 7 6 5 4 3 2 1

EDITOR'S NOTE

With a few exceptions, the comics included in this book are entirely fictitious. In the few which are based on actual events (pp. 180, 219, 228, 237), the characters have not been drawn to resemble anyone and, with the exception of incidental references to famous celebrities (pp. 180, 194, 209), the names and any distinguishing characteristics have been changed.

Printed in the United States of America
Cover design by Diane Noomin

Dedicated to Dori Seda

(1951–1988)

CONTENTS

SNAP

Betty and Veronica "Identity Crisis"

Photo: Aline Kominsky-Crumb

FOREWORD

In its original incarnation, *Twisted Sisters* was an underground comic book created by Aline Kominsky and myself in 1976, our "politically incorrect" response to some infighting going on at the time in the San Francisco based Wimmen's Comix Collective (remember, it *was* the seventies).

Now, fifteen years later, we've joined a dozen other "bad girl" cartoonists who have uncapped their simmering inkwells and allowed their fantasies, fears, and fictions to boil over into work that is personal, cathartic, and funny.

As editor, I've looked for an uncompromising vision reflecting a female perspective. This is frequently expressed in deeply felt, autobiographical narratives. Often the art graphically reflects inner turmoil. Sex is demystified, and romance is light years away from eternal bliss.

Some of us work in a very traditional comics medium, making it all the more startling when we peel away comforting illusions of women as soothing, earth mother nurturers to reveal anger, loneliness, and pain. Humor emerges from personal revelations, role reversals, and the tearing down of cultural stereotypes. These ladies are not sitting around, waiting for the phone to ring. They're more likely to throw it at you.

Sex, lies, and crosshatching vie for center stage with cellulite, alienation, and *TRUE LOVE*. From bubble baths to "The Mean Woman Blues," our paths diverge radically, only to reconnect on some subliminal plane, then veer off toward distinctly personal dreams and demons. Obsessive, excessive, and diverse, we're oddly in tune with one another.

We range in age from our midtwenties to our midfifties. We range in attitude from snidely whimsical to scathingly sardonic, with stops along the way for swipes at Motherhood, Marriage, and Machismo.

In our twisted, crazy quilt, the threads lead from puberty to "The Anatomy of a New Mom," from religion to PMS, sex-crazed housewives, and "Bimbos from Hell."

Do bad girls have more fun? Read this book.

—Diane Noomin

CAROL LAY

1952: Born in Whittier, California.

1955: Mom gives me such an impressive compliment on a drawing of a woman in high heels that I am doomed to be an artist.

1957: Fingerpainting. 'Nuff said.

1963: A popular vote sends Howard Endo to represent my fifth grade class in the schoolwide art show. I was the better artist, but there were more boys than girls and people vote along gender lines when they're ten. I appeal the decision to the school's art coordinator (named, appropriately, "Art Farmer") by saying I had "a friend" who felt she deserved to be in the show as well. He goes along with it.

1965: I win first place in the junior division of the Anaheim Art Show for a painting I copied from a picture my mom liked in *American Artist.* I win $25.00. (Insert cash register sound effects here.)

1970: I escape Orange County by entering UCLA's Fine Arts program. Other influences include sex, drugs, and Zap Comix.

1973: After one too many classes in conceptual art, I give up art altogether for two years and consider becoming a computer geek.

1976: A friend reintroduces me to comic books and I get my foot in the door by lettering some undergrounds.

1977–1990: One thing leads to another. Hanna Barbera comics, Western Publishing, DC Comics, Eclipse Comics, Cocaine Comix, Viper, Cannibal Romance, Wimmen's Comix, Zomoid Illustories, Weirdo, *Raw, LA Weekly, L.A. Reader*, storyboards for live-action feature films and animation, Mattel ("It's Swell"), Good Girls 1–5 with Fantagraphics, and, for two weeks during college, I paint the beaks on Jonathan Livingston Seagull pins for two bucks an hour.

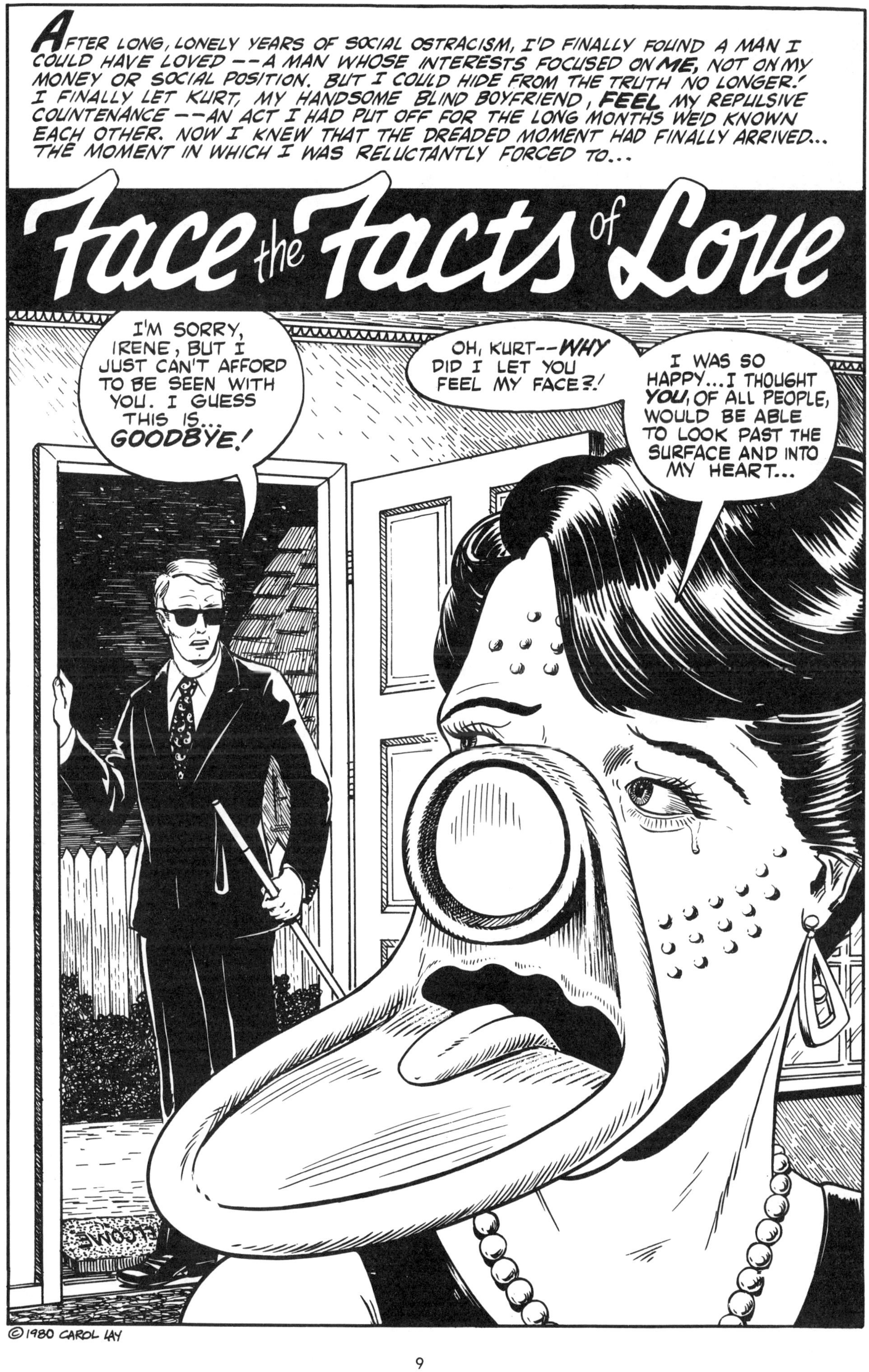

AFTER LONG, LONELY YEARS OF SOCIAL OSTRACISM, I'D FINALLY FOUND A MAN I COULD HAVE LOVED -- A MAN WHOSE INTERESTS FOCUSED ON **ME**, NOT ON MY MONEY OR SOCIAL POSITION. BUT I COULD HIDE FROM THE TRUTH NO LONGER! I FINALLY LET KURT, MY HANDSOME BLIND BOYFRIEND, **FEEL** MY REPULSIVE COUNTENANCE -- AN ACT I HAD PUT OFF FOR THE LONG MONTHS WE'D KNOWN EACH OTHER. NOW I KNEW THAT THE DREADED MOMENT HAD FINALLY ARRIVED... THE MOMENT IN WHICH I WAS RELUCTANTLY FORCED TO...

I'M SORRY, IRENE, BUT I JUST CAN'T AFFORD TO BE SEEN WITH YOU. I GUESS THIS IS... **GOODBYE!**

OH, KURT-- ***WHY*** DID I LET YOU FEEL MY FACE?!

I WAS SO HAPPY... I THOUGHT ***YOU***, OF ALL PEOPLE, WOULD BE ABLE TO LOOK PAST THE SURFACE AND INTO MY HEART...

BUT WHY SHOULD YOU BE ANY DIFFERENT?...
SLAM!
...WHEN NOT EVEN THE MOST MONEY-HUNGRY GOLDIGGER CAN BEAR TO LOOK ME IN THE FACE LONG ENOUGH TO TELL ME THE WORDS I LONG TO HEAR...

MY FACE IS TOO WEIRD FOR THESE MODERN MINDS. THAT WASN'T SO BACK IN AFRICA...

YES, LIFE WAS SIMPLER THEN... AS AN INFANT, I'D BEEN ORPHANED ABRUPTLY WHEN A TROOP OF BABOONS ATTACKED MY PARENTS' SMALL SAFARI. I DON'T REMEMBER WHY I WAS SPARED, BUT I WAS RESCUED FROM STARVATION OR WORSE BY SOME NATIVE HUNTERS WHO TOOK ME TO THEIR VILLAGE TO LIVE...

LUCKILY, I WAS ADOPTED INTO THE CHIEF'S CLAN AND THUS BEGAN MY EDUCATION IN THE WAYS OF THE BONGODIANS...

FACE-SHAPING IS COMMON AMONG THEIR WOMEN. I OFTEN DREAMT OF HOW I MIGHT SOME-DAY MATCH THEIR BEAUTY...

WHEN THE LONG PROCESS WAS FINALLY BEGUN, I ENDURED THE PAIN HAPPILY, KNOWING THE RE-SULTS WOULD BE WELL WORTH IT...
2

WHEN THE DANCING BEGAN, I WAS IGNORED BY THE MEN. IT IS A BAD SIGN TO BE LEFT OUT OF THE DANCE ON THE NIGHT OF INITIATION. CHIEF'S KIN ARE USUALLY COURTED BY MANY HUNTERS.

LIFE IS HARD ON UNMARRIED WOMEN OF MY TRIBE, FOR THEY ARE ALL EVENTUALLY DENOUNCED AS WITCHES AND BEATEN TO DEATH. SUDDENLY, MY FUTURE DID NOT LOOK SO GOOD.

THAT'LL BE ME IN A FEW YEARS IF I DON'T GET OUT OF HERE!

THEIR STORIES AND DESCRIPTIONS HADN'T QUITE PREPARED ME FOR WHAT I WAS TO SEE IN THE CITY. TO SPARE MY FEELINGS, THE TRADERS HAD NOT TOLD ME THAT THESE WOMEN DID NOT SHAPE THEIR FACES SO I TOOK THEM TO BE WEAKLING MALES AT FIRST. WHEN I SAW THAT THEY WERE, INDEED, WOMEN I WAS REPULSED-- SO UNACCUSTOMED WAS I TO GAZING UPON SUCH PLAIN, UNORNAMENTED FACES ON WOMEN...

IT WASN'T LONG, THOUGH, BEFORE I LEARNED IT WAS *I* WHO WAS REPULSIVE BY THEIR STANDARD OF BEAUTY.

EXPOSURE TO THEIR CULTURE MADE IT PAINFULLY CLEAR. THE EXAMPLES WERE PLENTIFUL, ESPECIALLY OF WHITES LIKE ME...

EVEN THE MOST WORLDLY MEN SEEMED TO PREFER THEIR PLAIN FACES OVER MY MASTERPIECE OF FACIAL ENGINEERING...

BUT NEWS CAME THAT MY FINGERPRINTS MATCHED THOSE OF THE LONG-LOST HEIRESS SO I IMMERSED MYSELF IN LEARNING THE LANGUAGE AND HISTORY OF THE PLACE THAT WOULD SOON BE MY HOME...

I LEFT AFRICA IN MY EIGHTEENTH SUMMER. IN ANOTHER TIME I MIGHT HAVE BEEN TAKEN IN CHAINS, BUT I WAS RIDING FIRST-CLASS, EN ROUTE TO THE LAND OF THE FREE AND A SUBSTANTIAL INHERITANCE...

REUNION WITH RELATIVES WAS STRAINED...DUE AS MUCH TO MY APPEARANCE AS TO MY THREAT TO THEIR FINANCIAL STATUS...

BUT THE NEWS MEDIA WELCOMED ME WITH FRONT-PAGE FEATURE STORIES WHICH SEEMED TO ENSURE MY SUCCESS IN THIS SOCIETY...

Los Angel

Sunday, Jul

Return of Heiress

African girl Faces Future of Fortune and Fame

By ROBERT GILLETTE
Times Staff Writer

Presumed dead for more than 16 years, Irene Van de Kamp arrived at LAX yesterday, turning many heads as she made her way towards the waiting limousine.

Face-shaping, achieved by scarification and insertion of lip and nose disks, was a popular way among certain tribes to discourage slave-trading. Now a

BEFORE LONG, MY CORPORATE ADVISORS RECOMMENDED THAT I FURTHER ESTABLISH MY POSITION IN HIGH SOCIETY BY MAKING A FORMAL DEBUT...

I WAS MADE OVER FROM DAWN TILL DUSK BY THE TOP DESIGNERS AND FASHION MOGULS WITH COACHING SESSIONS IN ETIQUETTE SANDWICHED IN BETWEEN...

THE BIG NIGHT FINALLY ARRIVED AND I DESCENDED INTO THE SOCIETY OF THE RICH TO THE APPLAUSE AND ADULATION OF ALL PRESENT--OR SO IT SEEMED AT THE TIME...

I WAS VERY SURPRISED WHEN ALL OF THE NICEST, HANDSOMEST YOUNG MEN CROWDED AROUND **ME** AND NOT THE OTHER PRETTY GIRLS--SURPRISED AND VERY PLEASED.

THAT NIGHT AS I LAY IN SLEEPLESS AGONY, I DECIDED TO ESCAPE FROM THESE PHONIES AND FORTUNE HUNTERS TO SOME PLACE WHERE I COULD FIGURE OUT WHAT TO DO WITH ALL THAT MONEY...

I BUSIED MYSELF FOR DAYS, BUYING THINGS AND DECORATING. SHOPPING HELPED FAMILIARIZE ME TO THE NEIGHBORHOOD.

I ALWAYS WENT OUT VEILED, BUT MADE FRIENDS ANYWAY AMONG THE LOCALS WHOSE CURIOSITIES WERE TEMPERED BY A NEED FOR DISTRACTION.
MATCHES
SUGAR DADDY
ZAGNUT

NEWS OF MY "DISAPPEARANCE" GRADUALLY FADED FROM EVEN THE BACK PAGES OF THE CHEAPEST TABLOIDS AND I FELT ODDLY AMBIVALENT ABOUT IT.

I'D BEEN LIVING THERE QUIETLY FOR A FEW MONTHS WHEN KURT SUDDENLY CAME INTO MY LIFE...
HEY, PAL-- WHICH WAY IS DOHENY?
TAP
TAP

Uh-- LET ME SEE...
Oh, YEAH...

...THAT WAY!
WHACK!

YOU'D BETTER CALL AN AMBULANCE. SHE LOOKS BAD!
OOPS!
DON'T WORRY, LADY--I'M OKAY... WHAT HIT ME?

I'M AFRAID I DID, MISS--WITH MY CANE. I'VE ONLY BEEN BLIND FOR A YEAR AND I'M STILL NOT USED TO THE EQUIPMENT.
ARE YOU ALL RIGHT? IF NOT, I'LL PAY FOR ANY DAMAGES.
NO - THAT'S OKAY. IT DOESN'T EVEN HURT ANYMORE.
BUT YOU-- YOU'RE GORGEOUS!
7

WE DID MEET THE NEXT DAY... AND THE NEXT AND THE NEXT. AND EACH DAY I HAD TO STALL HIM OFF WITH NEW EXCUSES TO MAKE HIM KEEP HIS PAWS OFF MY FACE...

ALL THROUGH DINNER, KURT WAS ACTING VERY NERVOUS AND SUSPICIOUS. I KNEW THEN THAT I HAD DECEIVED HIM FOR TOO LONG AND I WOULD HAVE TO BARE MY FACE TO HIM *TONIGHT,* BUT I WAITED UNTIL *HE* BROACHED THE SUBJECT, SO RELUCTANT WAS I TO REVEAL MYSELF...

SORRY, IRENE, BUT IF I'M GOING TO GET BACK ON TOP, I'LL NEED THE KIND OF WOMAN WHO WILL HELP ME--NOT HINDER!
I UNDERSTAND, KURT. I WAS JUST... HOPING YOU'D BE... DIFFERENT.

NO, IRENE, I'M JUST LIKE EVERY OTHER AMBITIOUS GUY. IT'S A MONEY WORLD, IRENE, AND I CAN'T LET YOU KEEP ME FROM GETTING MY SHARE!

GOODBYE, IRENE!
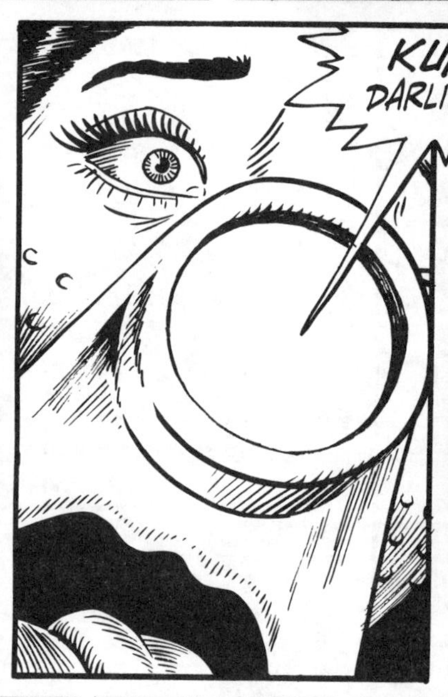
KURT-- DARLING...

Sigh
HE'S GONE NOW...

SNIF

...JERK...

MAYBE I SHOULD HAVE TOLD HIM I WAS RICH...
END

GRUNGE 361 / CAROL LAY

SHE WONDERED IF IT WAS GOING TO HURT. SHE WAS SURE IT WOULD IN ONE WAY OR ANOTHER, BUT SHE KNEW SHE HAD TO GO THROUGH WITH IT.

THE "DOCTOR" CAME IN AND GAVE HER A PILL. "THIS WILL MAKE THE PAIN BEARABLE," SHE SAID, GIVING HER SOME WATER SO SHE COULD WASH IT DOWN.

BEFORE LONG, SHE FELT QUITE RELAXED. SHE'D NEVER EXPERIENCED A DRUG BEFORE AND IT MADE HER FEEL VERY DIFFERENTLY ABOUT A LOT OF THINGS BESIDES JUST THE PHYSICAL NUMBNESS.

HER FEAR OF THE OPERATION SUBSIDED, HER REASONS FOR HAVING IT DONE SEEMED TRIVIAL, AND THE ANXIETY OF BEING CAUGHT AND TRIED DISAPPEARED.

THE SMILING FACE OF THE PRESIDENT BEAMED AT HER FROM THE T.V. SET WHILE SHE WAITED FOR THE DOCTOR TO BEGIN THE OPERATION.

HE LOOKED JUST AS YOUNG AND VAPID AS HE DID WHEN HE FIRST CAME TO OFFICE FIVE TERMS EARLIER. MAYBE HE'D HIRED A BETTER PLASTIC SURGEON OR SOMETHING.

OR, SHE THOUGHT, HE COULD EVEN BE DEAD NOW AND IT'S ALL DONE BY TECHNICIANS WITH SOPHISTICATED COMPUTER EQUIPMENT.

HE NEVER WAS MORE THAN A FACE ANYWAY, SHE THOUGHT ...BEFORE SHE FORGOT HOW TO THINK ENTIRELY.

WHEN SHE CAME TO, SHE FOUND HER-SELF SURROUNDED BY RIGHT-LIFERS. HER ANXIETY ABOUT BEING CAUGHT THAT HAD BEEN QUELLED BY THE DRUG CAME BACK IN ONE HORRIFIC RUSH.

SHE SAW THE DOCTOR BEING DRAGGED AWAY, THE RIGHT-LIFERS KICKING AND BEAT-ING HER WITH OBVIOUS RELISH.

"YOU HAVE THE RIGHT TO REMAIN SILENT," BEGAN ONE OF THE ENFORCEMENT MEN.
SHE DIDN'T REALLY HEAR THE REST...

THE DRUG WORE OFF QUICKLY AS SHE WAS HUSTLED INTO A VAN OCCUPIED BY TWO
OTHER PREGNANT WOMEN.

THE OFFICERS TREATED HER GENTLY AS MEN TREAT THEIR PREGNANT WOMEN BUT MADE SURE THE CUFFS FIT SNUGLY.

WEEKS LATER AT THE TRIAL, SHE WAS FOUND GUILTY.

SHE WAS SENTENCED TO SERVE THE REMAINDER OF HER PREGNANCY AT THE SYBIL BRAND INSTITUTE UNTIL SHE BORE THE CHILD ...WHICH SHE DID.

THEN SHE WAS TAKEN OUTSIDE AND SHOT.

CONFESSIONS OF A WOULD-BE GOLDDIGGER...
The Prince and the ArtGiRL
'ALLO, CAROL? THIS IS BOZAINA IN NICE! ... 'OW ARE YOU, BABEE?
BOZ! HI!!
BOZAINA IS A LIVE WIRE I MET ON A SCREWY FRENCH COMPUTER NETWORK. WE BECAME INSTANT FRIENDS AND STAYED SO EVEN AFTER THE FRENCH PHONE POLICE NAILED HER WITH AN $8,000.00 PHONE BILL. (IT WAS FREE FOR YANKS BUT THAT'S ANOTHER STORY.)
©1989 CAROL LAY

HERE'S A PICTURE OF BOZAINA AND ME IN ENSENADA BUT THAT'S ANOTHER STORY AS WELL...
WHAT SHE'D CALLED FOR WAS TO TELL ME THAT AN ENGLISH STUDENT OF HERS, AN ARABIAN PRINCE, WAS ON HIS WAY TO L.A.

HE HAS A PACKAGE FOR YOU FROM ME ... CAN YOU MEET HIM?
OK... I DON'T SEE WHY NOT...

AND DON'T WORRY ABOUT HIM... HE IS VERY GENTLEMAN, HE IS VERY VERY RICH, HE IS VERY HANDSOME, AND SO SWEET AND FUNNY.
I'M SURE HE WILL TAKE YOU TO A VERY NICE RESTAURANT AND AFTERWARDS IF YOU WANT TO GO TO THE BED WITH HIM I WILL NOT MIND...

I DIDN'T KNOW ABOUT THAT, BUT I WAS CERTAINLY READY FOR A DECENT MEAL AFTER LIVING ON FROZEN DINNERS AND TAKE-OUT FOOD FOR A WEEK...
DIET MAYONNAISE
SALSA
I WONDER IF I COULD EAT CAT FOOD WITHOUT BARFING IF I REALLY HAD TO...?

THE PRINCE CALLED THE VERY NEXT MORNING...
ALRIGHT... I'LL MEET YOU THERE AT 7:30

I SPENT MOST OF THE DAY DUPING TAPES AND COLLECTING A PACKAGE OF THINGS FOR BOZ...
CONTENTS:
4 TAPES (PERUVIAN FOLK TUNES, JAPANESE POP VOCALISTS, RUSSIAN JAZZ FROM THE '20'S, NOVELTY TUNES FROM OLD 78'S), THE LATEST CALVIN & HOBBS (HER FAVORITE CARTOON)
2 WEIRDOS
A NEAT STUFF
A PHOTO OF SOME NAKED MEN, SOME EARRINGS, A PHOTO OF MY NEW DIGS & A LONG LETTER.
THEN I WALKED AROUND LAKE HOLLYWOOD TO WORK UP A REAL GOOD APPETITE.

DURING DINNER, I FOUND THAT HIS INTERESTS INCLUDED BANKING, FRENCH WINES, REAL ESTATE, YACHTING, GOURMET FOOD, AND TRAVELING.

HAVE YOU BEEN TO PARIS?

NOT YET BUT I WANT TO... THERE'S A LOT OF ART I'D LIKE TO SEE THERE.

OH. I DO NOT KNOW ANYTHING ABOUT ART.
OH.
WHAT KIND OF MUSIC DO YOU LIKE?

I AM DEAF TO MUSIC, BUT IF SOMEONE TELLS ME OF SOMETHING GOOD THEN I CAN SEE THE GOOD IN IT.
OH.

CONVERSATION SLOWED DOWN A BIT...
YOU HAVE A VERY NICE FIGURE FOR A GIRL SO TALL... VERY NICE.
THANK YOU.
I, OF COURSE, DISAGREE BUT I DON'T ARGUE IT.

THE PRINCE'S NEXT STOP WAS BOSTON FOR A FEW DAYS. HE ASKED ME IF I WOULD LIKE TO COME ALONG TO DO SOME SIGHTSEEING AND KEEP HIM COMPANY.
I WAS TEMPTED... I WAS CURIOUS TO SEE BOSTON...
...OCTOBER LEAVES... HISTORIC SITES...
...BUT COMMON SENSE PREVAILED AND I TOLD HIM I HAD A LOT OF WORK TO DO.
ACTUALLY, I WOULD HAVE CONSIDERED IT SERIOUSLY IF I COULD HAVE HAD A SEPARATE HOTEL ROOM...

WELL... THAT APPARENTLY WASN'T THE IDEA...
YOU ARE VERY NICE...
GROPE
UH-- YEAH... I GOTTA GO NOW!
I'M NO ANGEL BUT I FLEW OUT OF THERE FAST.

THE PRINCE CALLED A COUPLE OF NIGHTS LATER AT 11:30 P.M. AND TRIED TO TALK ME INTO GOING TO HIS HOTEL.
WHEN THAT FAILED, HE PESTERED ME SOME MORE TO GO TO BOSTON WITH HIM.
WELL, TO TELL YOU THE TRUTH, I DON'T WANT TO GO BECAUSE I THINK YOU WOULD WANT ME TO GO TO BED WITH YOU.
NO, I AM NOT THAT KIND OF CHEAP MAN. IF YOU WANTED TO GO TO BED WITH ME, THAT WOULD BE A SEPARATE THING.
OH BROTHER.

STILL, I HAD VISIONS OF LOBSTERS AND CHOWDER DANCING IN MY HEAD...
I WANTED ADVENTURE... TRAVEL ... SEAFOOD.

IN IDLE MOMENTS, MY IMAGINATION WAS CARRIED AWAY EVEN FURTHER...
GOSH... THANKS FOR THE FABULOUS COAT, PRINCE. I WAS GETTING A BIT CHILLED...
THE MOST EXPENSIVE IMITATION FUR MONEY CAN BUY.

...BUT MY FRIEND AUDRI BROUGHT ME BACK TO EARTH.
THIS GUY HAS NOTHING TO OFFER BUT MONEY... AND YOU WERE GOING TO START A DIET ANYWAY.
I KNOW... I'M JUST INDULGING IN SOME FANTASIES...

BUT THE PRINCE KEPT CALLING ME AND I STARTED WONDERING...
CHRIS, WHY IS THIS GUY CHASING ME? I'M NO BEAUTY...
YOU HAVE THIS UNDERLYING SEXUALITY THAT OOZES OUT OF YOU IN THE MOST UNEXPECTED PLACES...

HUH? WHAT PLACES?
YOU KNOW... THE WAY YOU TALK OR MOVE... YOU TRY TO COVER IT UP BUT IT SHOWS THROUGH...

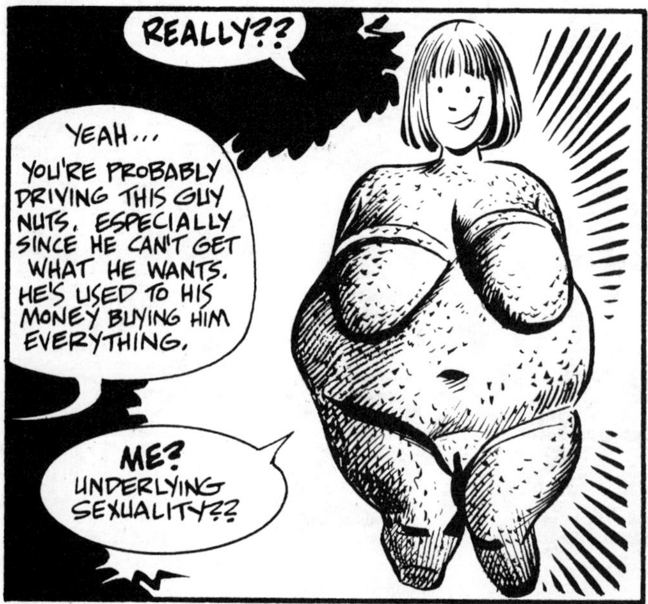
REALLY??
YEAH... YOU'RE PROBABLY DRIVING THIS GUY NUTS. ESPECIALLY SINCE HE CAN'T GET WHAT HE WANTS. HE'S USED TO HIS MONEY BUYING HIM EVERYTHING.
ME? UNDERLYING SEXUALITY??

THE EPISODE FINALLY ENDED WHEN HE MADE ONE LAST PLEA FOR ME TO GO TO BOSTON WITH HIM BEFORE HE TOOK OFF FOR THE AIRPORT...
I'M SORRY, BUT I REALLY HAVE A LOT OF WORK TO DO.
ALRIGHT-- I UNDERSTAND... JUST DO NOT PUT ME INTO ONE OF YOUR COMIC STORIES, OK?
THE END

PENNY MORAN VAN HORN

I was born in 1954 and raised in Rye, a suburb of New York City. When I was a kid, my father brought home a couple of comic books for me whenever he went to the local stationery store for cigarettes and the newspaper. *Little Lulu, Audrey, Dot and Iodine, Richie Rich*, and *Dennis the Menace*. I also enjoyed the funny papers and *Mad* Magazine.

In seventh and eighth grade, my friend and I did comics for each other called "Conversation Hour" based on our teachers and other students. They were incredibly cruel caricatures preying on their foibles, speech impediments, and human frailty in general. Unfortunately, these priceless masterpieces have been lost forever.

I majored in art in high school and college and had planned to do "fine art" (abstract painting and drawing). I moved to Manhattan. I shunned commercial art for years after college until, several secretarial jobs later, I caught myself jealously eyeing the drafting tables and art supplies in the art department of the publishing company in which I worked. I took a paste-up and mechanicals course which got me more involved in the print media. I found that I preferred the printed page to the gallery scene. I was interested in illustrating and, after many false starts and a move to Texas, began to have some success.

One day while leafing through *National Lampoon*, I saw Ron Hauge's strip, *Modern Problems*. It seemed to hit a nerve. I loved his work. I became obsessed with comics. I wrote fan mail and ordered self-produced comic books that were advertised in the editorial sections of comics. Dennis Worden's *Stickboy*, which is another favorite of mine, came to my attention in this way.

I was driven to make some of my own comics, and slowly began to undo years of neglect and denial: "No, I'm not interested in that 'cutting edge of graphics bullshit' " . . . or . . . "I can incorporate art into my life-style—I don't need to put it on paper," etc., etc. I had had a few scratchboard illustrations published, but I felt it would be stupid of me to attempt to do comics in that labor-intensive, time-consuming medium. "Only an idiot would take the time to do that," I thought. Soon I embarked on the project. Luckily, *Weirdo* was interested in my work and provided the initial encouragement for me to continue.

I enjoy reading, and feel that comics combine the best of both the written word and visual imagery. The difficult part of making comics for me is maintaining originality and humor and avoiding excessive cuteness. Now I am happily married and recently gave birth to my first child, a daughter. I live in Austin, Texas, and still do free-lance illustration.

A TRUE STORY

CATHOLIC SCHOOL

BY PENNY MORAN ©89

I ATTENDED CATHOLIC SCHOOL 1959-1966. WE WORE UNIFORMS.

THE NUNS WHO TAUGHT US WERE CALLED THE "SISTERS OF CHARITY."

THEY DEVOTED TOO MUCH OF EACH DAY TO TEACHING "RELIGION"

KNOW
LOVE
SERVE
ONCE, DURING DISTRIBUTION OF WEEKLY READERS,
YIPPEE!
I BECAME OVERLY EXCITED AND CHEERED.
I FELT MY HAIR YANKED FROM BEHIND.
GO UP TO THE FRONT OF THE ROOM...
I HAD "DISRUPTED THE CLASS".
AND APOLOGIZE TO THE BLESSED VIRGIN MARY!!!
I WAS SENT TO THE SHRINE OF THE B.V.M....
THERE WAS A SNAKE AROUND HER FEET
I WAS NOT SORRY
THE END

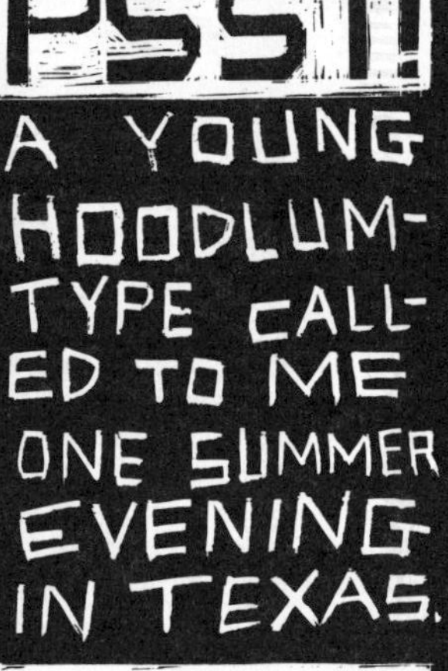

I TOOK A CHANCE & LISTENED TO WHAT HE HAD TO SAY.

"I FOUND A JOB... BUT I NEED A PLACE TO STAY."

HE WAS FROM THE SOUTH BRONX AND HAD A WICKED N.Y. ACCENT. I WAS ON MY WAY TO AN ART OPENING AND TOLD HIM HE MIGHT AS WELL COME ALONG. BUT HE FELT SO ILL-AT-EASE THERE THAT HE JUST GLARED AT ALL THE WINE-SWILLING YUPPIES

THINGS PROCEEDED WAY TOO QUICKLY. AS SOON AS WE LEFT THE SHOW, DOWN ON THE GROUND WE WENT. AND HE WAS WAITING FOR ME THE NEXT DAY, CLAD IN LEATHER, WITH A GHETTO BLASTER CRANKED UP.

SOON MY LITTLE PICKUP HAD SOMEHOW BECOME MY BOYFRIEND. I LET HIM STAY AT THE CO-OP I LIVED IN UNTIL HE "GOT HIS FEET ON THE GROUND." BUT HE REALLY ABUSED MY GENEROSITY.

HE NURSED A SECRET **DRINKING PROBLEM** UNTIL IT BLOSSOMED INTO A BURDEN TO THE ENTIRE HOUSEHOLD.

THE CARPENTRY AND HOME REPAIR JOBS WE LET HIM DO INSTEAD OF PAYING RENT WERE **BECOMING AWFULLY SCARCE...**

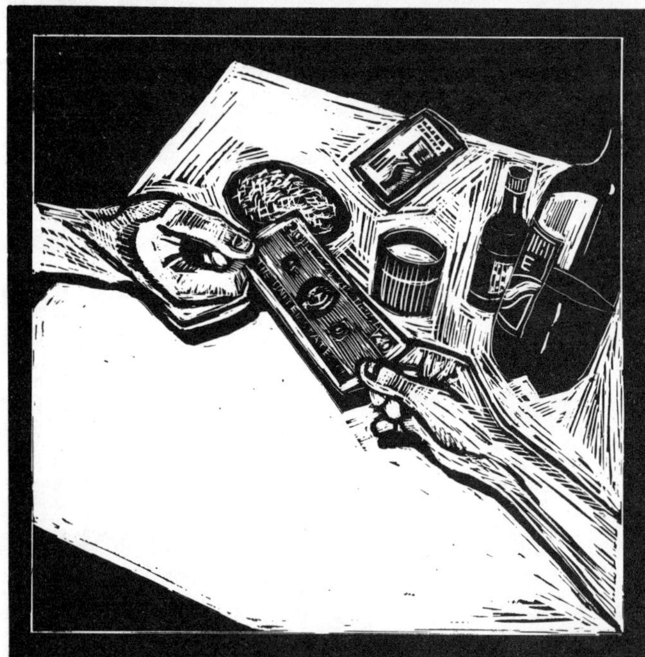

I FOOLISHLY LENT HIM MONEY AGAIN THAT AWFUL DAY-- "FOR FOOD," HE TOLD ME...

HE CAME BACK FROM THE CORNER STORE WITH **TWO SIX-PACKS**, FILLED A COOLER WITH ICE, AND PROCEEDED TO GET

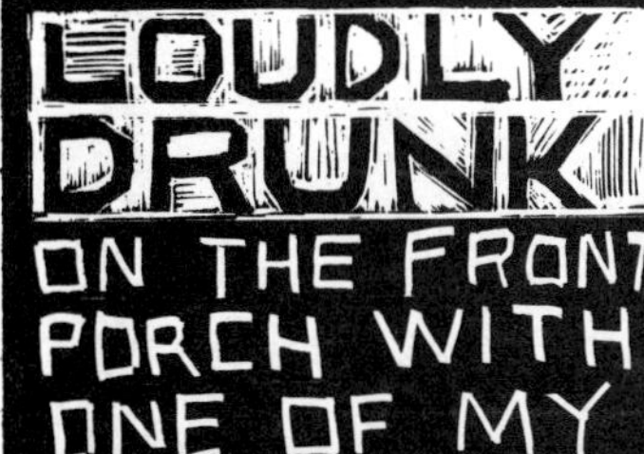

ON THE FRONT PORCH WITH ONE OF MY HOUSEMATES. I EAVESDROPPED, AND HEARD HIM SAY,

"PENNY'S JUST ANOTHER UPPER MIDDLE/ LOWER UPPER-CLASS BITCH ENTERING EARLY MIDDLE AGE. THEY'RE A DIME A DOZEN."

I WENT OUT AND UPTURNED THE COOLER FULL OF BEER AND ICE ON HIS HEAD.

HE SAT THERE GASPING WITH THE COOLER OVER HIS HEAD FOR A MINUTE, THEN TRIED TO HAVE THE LAST WORD.

HE LEFT ME WITH HIS BLACK LEATHER JACKET, BY WAY OF APOLOGY.

TEXAS CHARACTERS
'MIZ FLAK'
A TRUE STORY BY PENNY MORAN ©89
I TELL YA... THEY JUST COME DRAGGIN' IN ANY OLE TIME...
I WORKED IN AN OFFICE WITH AN OLDER WOMAN NAMED "MIZ FLAK."
HER MAIN JOB SEEMED TO BE MONITORING OUR LATENESS TO WORK.
WELL I WORK MY 8 HOURS A DAY!!
SHE WAS BOTH EVIL WITCH...
BIG DEAL 15 MINUTES
THAT'S SOME BLISTER, YOUNG MAN! HAND ME THAT THERE FIRST AID KIT.
...AND KINDLY GRANDMOTHER
NOW, WHO LEFT THAT STAIN ON THE CARPET OVER YONDER?
MIZ FLAK WAS OBSESSED WITH CLEANING...
LET'S CHECK THOSE SHOES FOR TAR
THOUGH IT WAS REALLY NOT IN HER JOB DESCRIPTION.

DID YOU JUST USE THAT BACK BATHROOM?
NO-- WHY?!
IN PARTICULAR, SHE WAS FIXATED ON "BATHROOM THINGS."
WELL..... SOMEONE DID -- AND THEY LEFT THEIR BUSINESS!
TSK!
SHE CONFRONTED ME AS IF I WERE SOMEHOW TO BLAME!
HEY, PENNY.. I FOUND THIS NOTE IN THE BATHROOM... IT SAYS, "JUST FLUSH IT- IT WILL GO AWAY."
THE NOTE WAS IN MIZ FLAK'S WRITING
"DO NOT COMB HAIR OVER SINK"
"DO NOT PUT HAND TOWELS IN TOILET"
CHECK THESE OUT!
"MEN'S WALL LATRINE LEAKS"
WE HAD ALREADY STARTED A COLLECTION OF THESE NOTES.
HEY MIZ FLAK, GUESS WHAT?
I GOT A NEW CAR!!! IT'S A 1968 VOLVO.
BUT PERHAPS THE MOST ENDEARING THING ABOUT HER
!? ?
DID Y'ALL HEAR?... BARBARA'S FINALLY GOT HER-SELF A VULVA...
?
!
?
WAS HER SPOKEN WORD...

WELL, I GAVE DON A PIECE OF MY MIND...
CHUCKLE CHUCKLE
SOMEHOW, MIZ FLAK'S WORD MIXUPS...

AND HE ATE ME OUT GOOD !!!!
SHE MEANT "CHEWED OUT"
ALWAYS DEALT WITH FEMALE GENITALIA.

OH, DEAR— YOU PUT ON WEIGHT!
BOINK!
MIZ FLAK HAD NO TACT.

Y'AINT GOT MUCH UP TOP, HAVE YA?

AT LEAST SHE HAD GOOD TASTE IN CARS.
IT'S ONLY BEEN OUTSIDE THE CITY LIMITS ONCE IN ITS THIRTY YEARS!
THE END

TEN DOLLARS FOR TWO MINUTES

A TRUE STORY BY PENNY MORAN©

EARLY ONE WINTER MORNING I AWOKE TO FIND THE LOOMING FIGURE OF MY LANDLORD IN MY TRAILER. HE HAD LET HIMSELF IN. "I NEED TO CHECK THE ROOF FOR LEAKS," HE LIED. QUICKLY HE GOT TO THE POINT: "HEY," HE SAID, "YA WANNA 'PLAY FOR PAY'?"

"I'LL GIVE YOU 10$ FOR 2 MINUTES." I REFUSED HIS OFFER. I WAS TRAPPED BENEATH THE COVERS WITHOUT ANY CLOTHES.

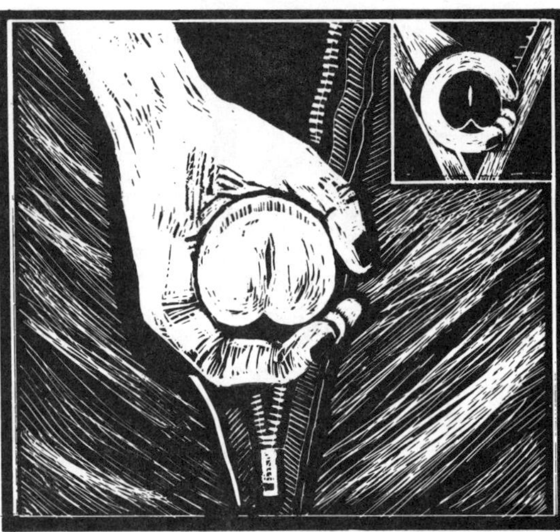

HIS PROPOSITION SOON BECAME A CHANT: PLAY FOR PAY / 10 FOR 2... HE PRANCED ABOUT ZIPPING AND UNZIPPING HIS PANTS. "WHAT AM I GONNA DO?" I ASKED MYSELF. SUDDENLY, HE FLUSHED, GRIMACED,

AND FELL TO THE FLOOR WITH A THUMP. "THANK GOD," I THOUGHT. I ASSUMED HE HAD FAINTED. I DRESSED AND WENT OVER TO FETCH

HIS WIFE. "HE SHOULDN'T BE SHOVELING SNOW OFF THOSE ROOFS," SHE WHINED, "NOT WITH HIS HEART!" SHE KNELT BY HIS SIDE. WHEN WE REALIZED HE WAS DEAD, SHE WAILED

IN HER GERMAN ACCENT, "HE WAS SUCH A GOOD MAN!!!" ON THE WAY TO THE HOSPITAL IN THE AMBULANCE SHE CRIED ON MY SHOULDER. I FOUND MYSELF WONDERING IF HE'D DIED WITH HIS ZIPPER UP OR DOWN.

AN INTERESTING FOOTNOTE: A COUPLE OF YEARS LATER, ONE OF MY FRIENDS SENT ME A NEWSPAPER CLIPPING ABOUT THE TWO OF THEM. THE HEADLINE READ: "ANGRY WIDOW FIGHTS TO CLEAR HUSBAND'S NAME." APPARENTLY, HE HAD BEEN CONVICTED OF TREASON DURING A RECENT WAR. "ON HIS DEATHBED," THE ARTICLE BEGAN, "MRS. X PROMISED HER HUSBAND SHE WOULD NOT REST UNTIL HIS NAME HAD BEEN CLEARED OF THE UNJUST TREASON ACCUSATION..."

END

DOMESTIC BLISS

"HONEY, I'M HOME!" I BLEAT HAPPILY...

Q-TIPS IN HIS EARS & SINUSES ABLAZE,

HE SULKS HOPEFULLY, PROFESSING HUNGER.

"LET'S GO OUT TO EAT" IS MY SUGGESTION.

I TAKE A MOMENT TO ANSWER THE PHONE

IN WHICH TIME HE GOBBLES LEFTOVERS

IMAGINE MY CHAGRIN, THEN, WHEN HE ENTICES ME OUT INTO THE YARD

ONLY TO COMPLETELY DOUSE ME WITH THE GARDEN HOSE

A TRUE STORY

PENNY MORAN '89 ©

MY FRIEND ONCE WORKED AS A COCKTAIL WAITRESS IN A DISCOTEQUE.

THE DISC JOCKEY AT THE DISCO BECAME INFATUATED WITH HER.

HE FLIRTED WITH HER USING HIS MICROPHONE IN BETWEEN SONGS.

SHE WAS EMBARRASSED BY HIS PUBLIC DISPLAYS.

YOO-HOO... I LOVE YOU... DO YOU LOVE MEEEE?

ONE EVENING WHILE SHE WAS RELAXING AT HOME, SHE HEARD A CAR PULL UP AND A VOICE CALL OUT IN SING-SONG, DRUNKEN TONES...

YO, HO! HIC! BLOW THE MAN DOWN
JEEZ, DON-- JUST HOLD ON!
PANT
BELCH
GASP
THE D.J.'S BREATHING WAS FAMILIARLY ERRATIC...

---THE HALTING GASP OF ONE ABOUT TO VOMIT.

AS SOON AS THE CAR STOPPED, HE FELL ON ALL FOURS ON THE LAWN.

HAVE SOME COFFEE.
THE TWO OTHERS WENT INTO THE HOUSE.

THE D.J. EVENTUALLY STAGGERED IN
SPORTING PUKE DRIP-PING FROM HIS MUSTACHE

AND BIRD PARTS AND FEATHERS IN HIS BEARD.

PHOEBE GLOECKNER

I was born in Philadelphia in 1960 of teenage parents. They got divorced pretty soon and my mother, my sister, and I went to live with my grandparents. My grandfather is one of those types who can barely utter a serious word and I suspect that he's one of the reasons I ever did comics at all.

I spent Saturdays with my dad at Dirty Frank's bar downtown. I drank Coke and played shuffleboard with my sister while he sat in the back drinking beer and punching out "Secret Agent Man" over and over on the juke box. He kept a stack of sticky dimes by his beer to use for this purpose.

We moved to San Francisco without my dad when I was tenish. My sister and I learned the particulars of sex around this time, when we found the copies of *Zap Comix* my mother hid under her mattress. We especially enjoyed the story of "Joe Blow" because it had kids in it.

I bought a copy of the now-classic original *Twisted Sisters* by Aline Kominsky and Diane Noomin when I was still in junior high. The book made such an impression on me that I wrote a fan letter to Aline. I was so elated to get a response that I began to entertain fantasies of running away from home to live with Aline and R. Crumb on their secluded, pastoral plot of land up near Sacramento. However, I had started "experimenting with drugs" and falling in love with gay teenage boys and ended up running away to Polk Street in San Francisco instead. I lived in a little boys' brothel, decorated completely in powder blue, until my mother tracked me down with the aid of a sympathetic tranvestite named Brandy, who spilled the beans. My first comics were about this period in my life.

By the time I became eighteen, I was so afraid of becoming an indigent that I decided to go to college. After many years of study and psychic torment, I completed a master's degree in medical illustration. I'd like to take this opportunity to warn you that there are doctors who actually make jokes about patients after they've been "put under." I witnessed this while observing an elective augmentation mammoplasty (breast enlargement procedure). My advice is to learn to like the way you are or get a padded bra.

MAGDA MEETS THE LITTLE MEN IN THE WOODS
CHOO-CHOO CHARLIE WAS AN ENGINEER, STUCK HIS FINGER UP HIS MOTHER'S--
BY PHOEBE GLOECKNER ©1989

?

HOWDY! I'M GOING TO BE YOUR HUSBAND IN TEN YEARS!

YOU'RE LITTLE AND CUTE!
SO ARE YOU! I'VE GOT A LOT OF TROUBLES & YOU'RE GOING TO TAKE CARE OF ME! WE'LL HAVE SOME KIDS!

LOOK, HERE YOU ARE, ONLY 17 YEARS OLD AND PREGNANT!
ME?
I GUESS SO.
WE HAVE TO GET MARRIED, DON'T WE?

I'VE GOT BEAUTIFUL LONG HAIR!
I'M GOING TO LIE TO YOU A LOT!

BYE SUGAR! I'M GOING OUT TO LOOK FOR A JOB!
OK DEAR-WHEN 'LL YOU BE HOME?
OH, I'LL BE HOME IN TIME FOR DINNER! HA HA!!!

BUT REALLY, SEE, I'M GOING TO GET DRUNK WITH MY FRIENDS + I WON'T COME HOME UNTIL 3:00 AM!! YOU'LL BE CRYING AND I'LL TRY TO HAVE SEX WITH YOU!!

I HATE YOU! YOU MEAN LIAR!
HEY SIS, DON'T GET HOT! YOU'LL LEAVE ME IN GOOD TIME!
MY RICH FATHER WILL PAY CHILD SUPPORT!!

HUMMPH!
CIAO SUGAR-PIE! SEE YOU AROUND!!
TOOT
TOOT

WHAT A STUPID FREAK!

?
HI! I'M GOING TO BE YOUR HUSBAND IN 13 YEARS!
OH YEAH? WELL, THAT'S NOT ME YOU'RE WITH!
WELL, THAT'S TRUE, BUT SEE, WE HAVE AN OPEN MARRIAGE!
WHAT'S THAT MEAN?
IT MEANS THAT I PROVE MY LOVE BY SLEEPING WITH OTHER WOMEN, BUT ALWAYS COMING BACK HOME TO YOU!! GET IT?

AND LOOK AT YOU! I'LL TELL YOU HOW TO DRESS!
I'M MUCH OLDER + MORE INTELLIGENT THAN YOU AND I'LL MAKE YOU GO TO COLLEGE!

AND I'LL DISCIPLINE YOUR CHILDREN BECAUSE YOU DON'T KNOW HOW!!
HEY! DON'T TOUCH THOSE BABIES!!

I HATE YOU TOO!
BOO HOO
GIVE ME A CHANCE! I WAS ONLY TRYING TO DO WHAT'S BEST FOR YOU!!

IT'S COLD AND I'M AFRAID

OH NO!!
I'M GONNA BE YOUR BOYFRIEND IN 17 YEARS!

WE'LL HAVE FUN! I'LL MOVE IN WITH YOU AND WE'LL DRINK ALOT + I'LL SLEEP WITH YOUR DAUGHTER! I SELL REAL ESTATE!

POW

MOMMY! I DON'T EVER WANT TO GROW UP!

BOO HOO!
OH HONEY, DON'T BE SILLY! YOU'LL GROW UP AND FIND A NICE MAN AND GET MARRIED AND HAVE CHILDREN AND LIVE HAPPILY EVER AFTER!

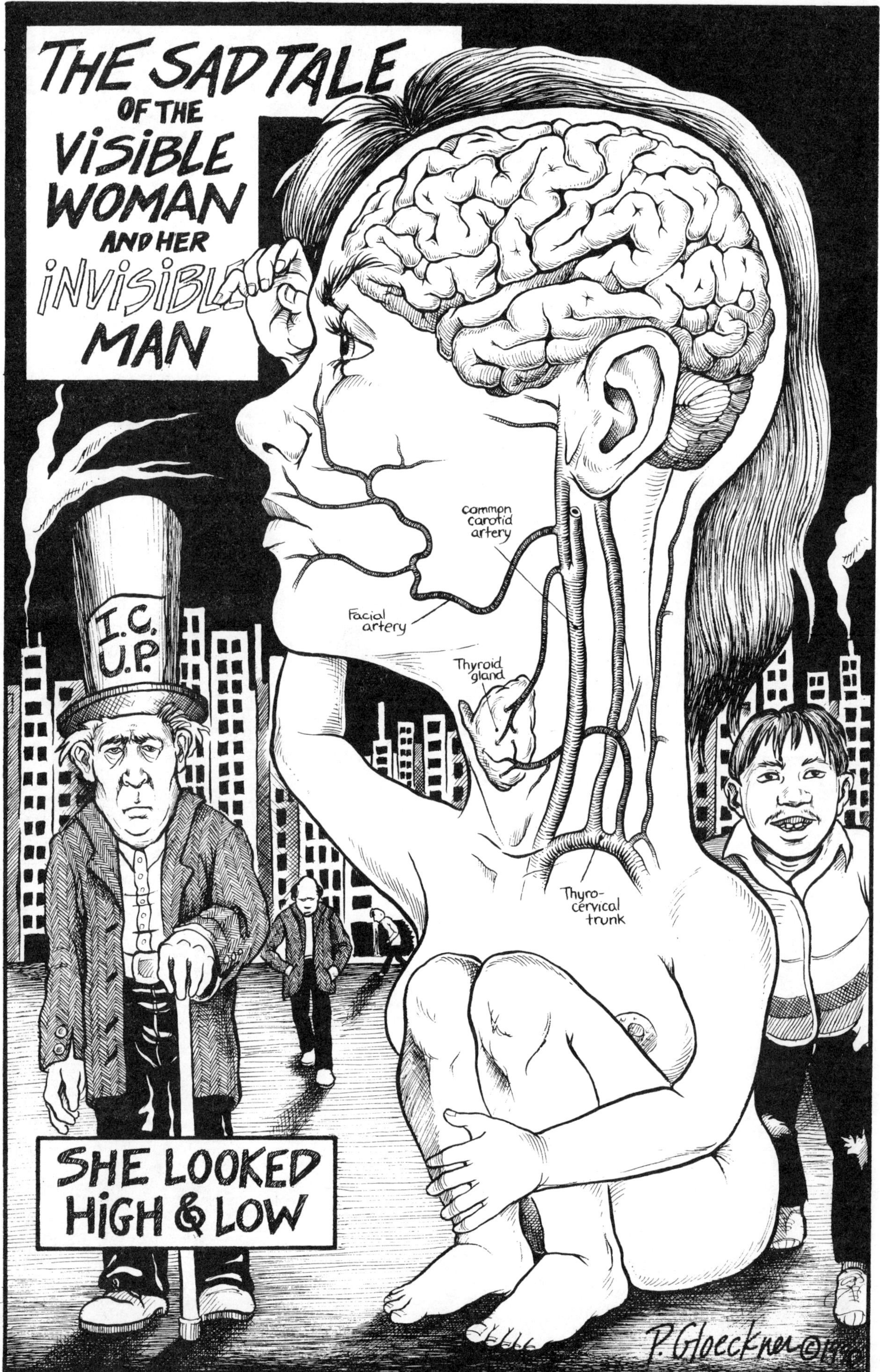
THE SAD TALE OF THE VISIBLE WOMAN AND HER INVISIBLE MAN
I.C. U.P.
common carotid artery
Facial artery
Thyroid gland
Thyro-cervical trunk
SHE LOOKED HIGH & LOW
P. Gloeckner ©1990

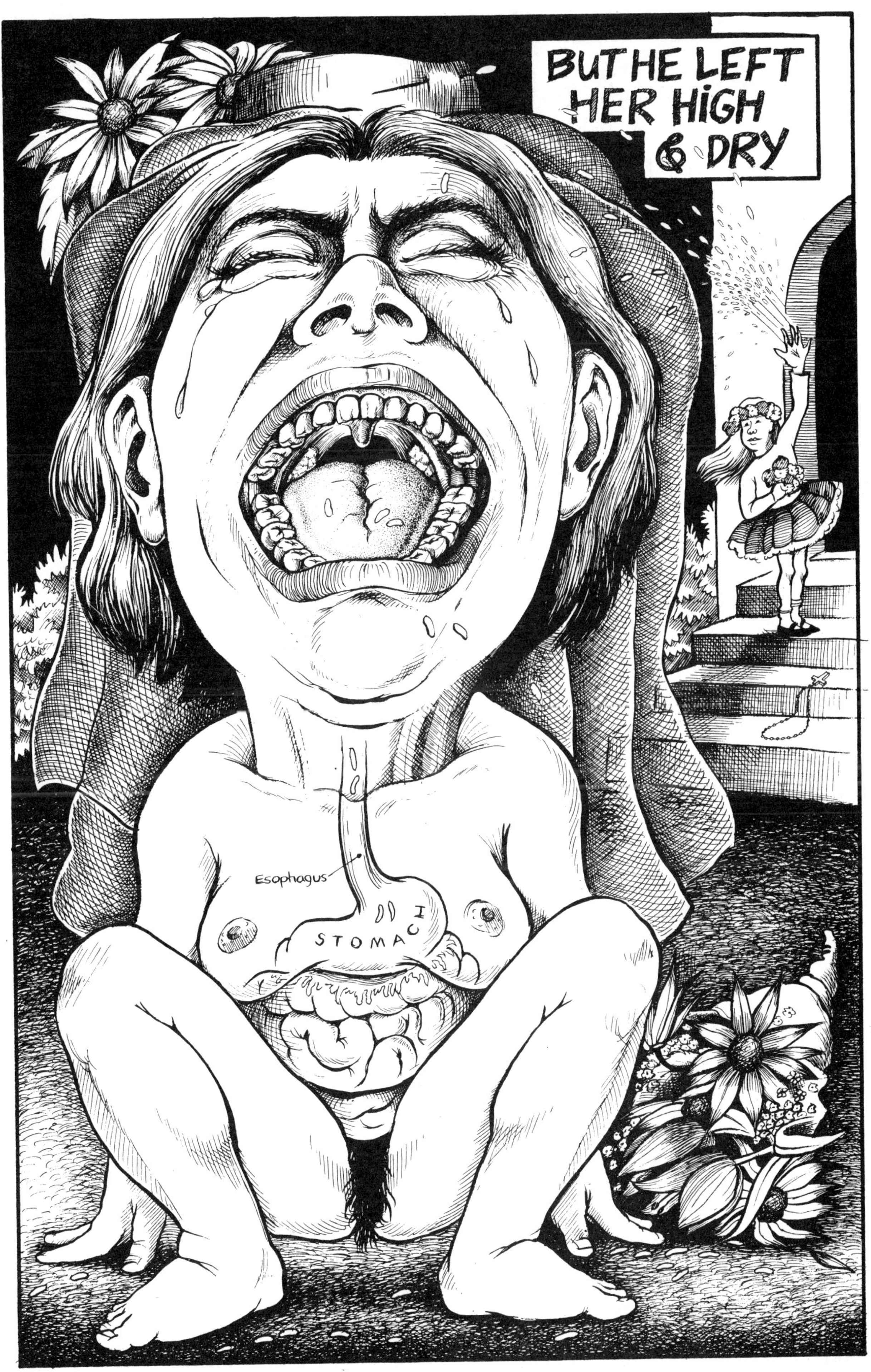
BUT HE LEFT HER HIGH & DRY
Esophagus
STOMACH

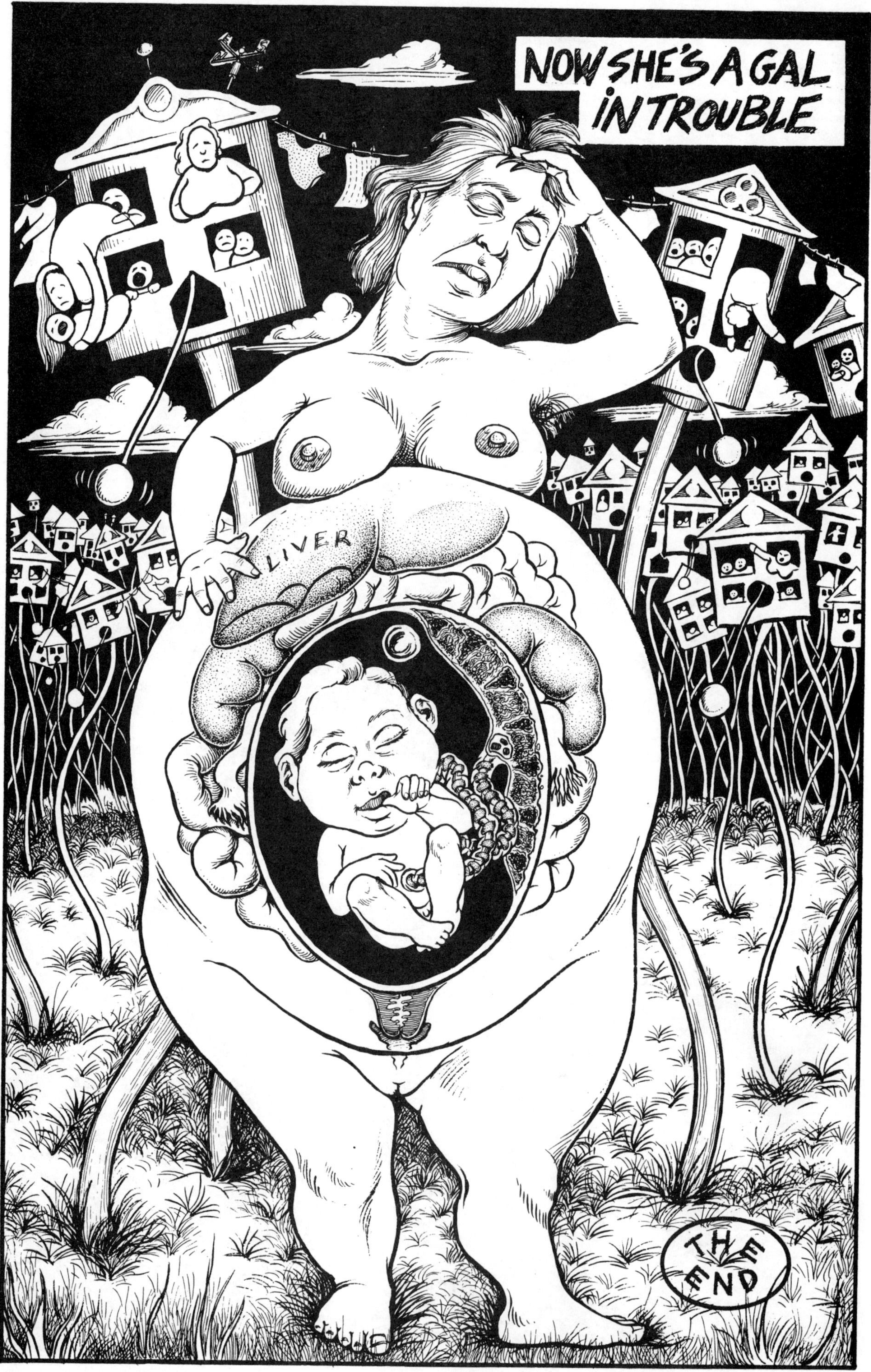
NOW SHE'S A GAL
IN TROUBLE
LIVER
THE
END

THE CONDOM IS PLACED ON AN ERECT PENIS
KVĚTEN 1990
WE FIND OUR HEROINE, 25-YEAR OLD JANA DVOŘÁKOVÁ, AT HOME WITH HER WIDOWED MOTHER, THE FAMOUS CZECH ART HISTORIAN, DR. ANNA DVOŘÁKOVA. EXISTING IN SEPARATE STATES OF ALIENATION, LIFE FOR THEM IS MADE UP OF NEVER-ENDING BITTER ARGUEMENTS ABOUT MONEY AND DISHES. BUT THEY JUST CAN'T SEEM TO ESCAPE EACH OTHER.
TESLA
BY FIFI GLICKMAN ©1990
Start 20 CIGARET
AN EVENING IN PRAGUE
HAVEL NA HRAD
IT'S BEEN A WEEK SINCE YOU PROMISED TO CLEAN THE KITCHEN, LITTLE MISSIE- WOULD YOU MIND LIFTING A FINGER TONIGHT?
I'M SORRY MOM, BUT I'VE GOT PLANS FOR THIS EVENING- BIG PLANS.

BRANICKÁ
KADERNICTVÍ MODA
POTRAVINY
JANA WAS ALWAYS A BAD, BAD GIRL.... SINCE THE REVOLUTION, ALL SHE WAS INTERESTED IN WAS GETTING MONEY + HAVING FUN FUN FUN.
A GIRL WITH ONLY DIFFUSE MOTIVATION TO IMPROVE HER CONDITION, SHE HAD BLAMED HER DEGENERACIES ON THE COMMUNISTS- BUT NOW, SHE + HER PUNKISH PALS WERE REBELS RUN OUT OF EXCUSES.

U KAFKU
PIVNICE
HOVNIC PRAHA
U KAFKU... A DARK BAR IN THE STAROMESTSKÉ DISTRICT, THE HAPPENING HANGOUT OF PRAGUE...

IRLS GIRLS SWEET + LOVELY GIRL
JANA!!!

HA!! ASSHOLE!!
OF
HEY YA LITTLE CUNT!! LET'S GET OUTTA HERE!

U KAFKU
IV SKUPINA
PIVNICE
LET'S GO SMOKE SOME SHIT!!
COOL!!

OBUV
DAM
SKÉ P
OTR
HEY! WAIT UP!

I'VE GOT A GAME- YOU GOT ANY MONEY?

YOU LOSE
UNFORTUNATELY
YOU LOSE
TOO BAD.
YOU LOSE
TRY AGAIN
YOU LOSE
BAD LUCK
YOU LOSE
THAT'S TOUGH
YOU LOSE
OH BOY
YOU LOSE
THE BREAKS.
YOU LOSE
PAINFUL
YOU LOSE
AW HECK.
YOU LOSE
FUCK
YOU LOSE
FUCK
YOU LOSE
FUCK

I'M ALL CLEANED OUT!!
I'D BE HAPPY TO BUY YOU A DRINK!

WE'LL GO TO A LITTLE OPEN-AIR BAR I KNOW
GOD I'M HORNY AS HELL!!
ME TOO

HUM BABY!!
SKODA

WOOOO
WOOOOOOO
VB

I REALIZE THAT THE REVOLUTION HAS GOT YOU KIDS ALL EXCITED, BUT DO YOURSELVES A BIG FAVOR + TAKE YOUR FUN + GAMES INDOORS!!!!
SURE OFFICER!

COME ON! HERE'S THE BAR!!!

LOOK- WE'LL BE BACK IN A MINUTE-
HEH! I'LL GET A TABLE!
HMMM.. SHOULD WE TRANSLATE THE FUTURIST COOKBOOK FROM THE ORIGINAL OR GO FROM YOUR ENGLISH TRANSLATION INTO CZECH??
UH-OH!!!

GOOD EVENING LADIES! MAY I SHARE YOUR TABLE?
WELL, I DON'T THINK-
OH ANNE! DON'T LET'S BE OLD FUDDIE-DUDDIES!

NO ONE'S LOOKING!
NOT HERE! SOMEONE WILL SEE US!

JUST WAIT 'TIL THEY GET HOME!

Periodic Fantasy
girls drowsy littl egg cells growi blossoming in breasts develo like a flower a covered with hair
by Phoebe Gloeckner ©1989
A GIRL'S BODY
MOM, CAN I GET THIS TRAINING BRA? ALL THE OTHER GIRLS HAVE THEM.
WHY MINNIE! YOU'RE JUST A TINY CHILD! YOU NEED TO DEVELOP YOUR ASSETS A BIT MORE... WHEN YOU BEGIN MEN-STRU-A-TING, YOU'LL GET A BRA.
Girls are me truating earlier nowadays. Scientist say that since the in vention of electricity girls are exposed to more light, causing the pituitary gla to secrete.
SO... IF I LEAVE THE LIGHTS ON WHILE I SLEEP, I'LL DEVELOP EVEN FASTER!
MAYBE I'LL GET RESULTS BY MORNING!
I CAN'T PLAY LACROSSE WITH THE OTHER GIRLS TODAY, MISS HESS... YOU SEE, I'M MEN-STRU-A-TING.
WELL, MINNIE, GIRLS YOUR AGE OFTEN FIB, SO YOU'LL HAVE TO TAKE OFF YOUR CLOTHES TO PROVE YOU'RE DEVELOPED ENOUGH TO MEN-STRU-ATE.
ISN'T THAT CUTE... SHE'S AFRAID OF THE DARK. I'LL TURN THE LIGHTS OFF.
WHAT BLOSSOMING!! SUCH A FIGURE IS A GREAT FORTUNE! AND FOR A GIRL ONLY EIGHT YEARS OLD! I WISH SOME OF THE OTHER LITTLE GIRLS COULD DUP-LICATE YOUR PROGRESS!!
BUT THAT MORNING...
NO RESULTS! AND THE LIGHTS ARE OUT!
MOM! WHY DID YOU TURN THE LIGHTS OFF? I WAS TRYING TO DEVELOP SOME VALUABLE ASSETS BY STIMULATING MY PECUNIARY GLAND!
WHY MINNIE!
End

Quaker School Q-Ties

-in-

"Plan Against the Boys"

A PHILADELPHIA STORY

MEAN STREET FRIENDS

RANGER RICK HAD A SIX-FOOT DICK AND HE SHOWED IT TO THE GIRL NEXT DOOR--

SHE THOUGHT IT WAS A SNAKE SO SHE HIT IT WITH A RAKE AND NOW IT'S ONLY FIVE-FOOT FOUR

A TRUE CHILDHOOD TALE WITH NO MORAL

BY PHOEBE GLOECKNER © 1989

PSYCHE OUT STUPID!
THE LAST ONE'S LEAVING!
CLOAK CLOSET
GOOD! TAKE THESE FILTHY CLOAKS OF THEIRS!
THEN QUICK! TO THE FORT!
PHILS
GIANTS
Phillies
PIRATES
BLUE JAYS
CHARGERS

WHAT IF THEY SEE US?
SO THIS GUY SAYS, "WHAT DO YOU CALL A PAIR OF NUTS ON THE WALL, BITCH?" AND SHE SAYS, "WALL NUTS?"
YEAH..?
GIRL'S A FØRT

"YOU AIN'T SO STUPID AFTER ALL, BITCH!," HE SAYS, "SO WHAT DO YOU CALL A PAIR OF NUTS ON YOUR CHEST?"
GET IN THE FORT AND PUT THOSE STINKIN' GARMENTS IN THE PILE, ALICE!
SHUT UP YOU TWO!
HEE HEE!
J-5

NOW WE DIG A HOLE...
AND SHE SAYS, "CHEST NUTS?"

"ALL RIGHT, BITCH," HE SAYS, "IF YOU'RE SO SMART, WHAT DO YOU CALL A PAIR OF NUTS ON YER CHIN?
AND STUFF THE JACKETS IN...

YEAH!
AN' PISS ON 'EM!!

"ON YER CHIN? HMM. I DON'T KNOW.... CHINNUTS?"

LOOK! SHE'S GOT HAIR!!
BLACK IS BEAUTIFUL
COME ON ALICE! YOU BETTER DO IT TOO!!

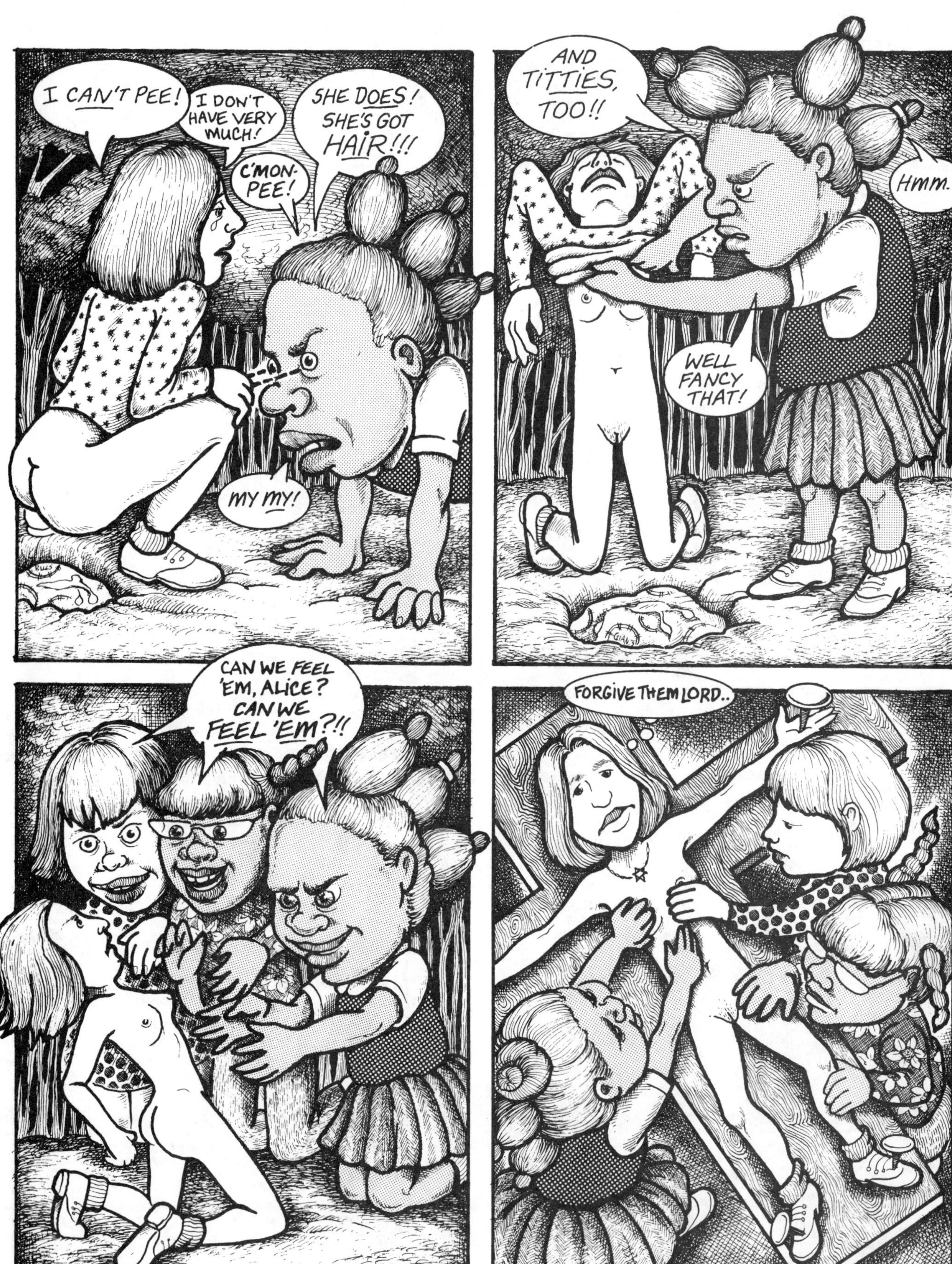
I CAN'T PEE!
I DON'T HAVE VERY MUCH!
C'MON-PEE!
SHE DOES! SHE'S GOT HAIR!!!
MY MY!
AND TITTIES, TOO!!
Hmm...
WELL FANCY THAT!
CAN WE FEEL 'EM, ALICE? CAN WE FEEL 'EM?!!
FORGIVE THEM LORD..

A
GIRL'S FORT
HEY! I THINK I HEAR THE BOYS!
QUICK! COVER THE HOLE!
GET OUT
THE COAST IS CLEAR...
SHHHHH!
YUCK! IT SMELLS LIKE PEE PEE IN HERE!!
BOO HOO!
WHAT YOU BEEN DOIN'?
AND ALICE IS ALL BARE!
WE'RE TELLIN'!!
SHE'S GOT BIG TITS!
YEAH, 'N YOU GOT A SMALL BAT, JERK!
GET THAT THANG OUTTA MY FACE!
GET OUT OF HERE, YOU PIGS! YER JUST SMELLIN' YOURSELVES!
EPILOGUE
AND TO THINK THAT NINE-YEAR OLD GIRLS COULD ENGAGE IN SUCH WILLFULL PERVERSION!
WAS IT WILLFULL OR ARE THEY VICTIMS OF SOCIETAL PRESSURES WE AREN'T AWARE OF?
SHOULD WE PUNISH THEM?
AND POOR ALICE MUST GO TO THE PSYCHIATRIST!!
IS THERE SYMBOLIC VALUE IN THE FACT THAT THEY PUT THE BOYS' ITEMS IN THEIR HOLE?
WHAT ARE THEY TALKIN' ABOUT?
SO HE SAYS, "CHIN NUTS?!!" NO, BITCH! YOU WON'T BE CALLIN' 'EM NOTHIN CAUSE MY DICK WILL BE IN YOUR MOUTH!
SO WHAT'S THE END OF THE JOKE?
HA!!
END

DIANE NOOMIN

Born in Brooklyn, New York, in 1947.

Grew up on Long Island, a "Red Diaper Baby" gone suburban.

Moved back to Brooklyn (Canarsie) in 1960.

Saved from clear vinyl slipcovers and total white-lipsticked, teased hair, teen slutdom by the High School of Music and Art. Took the Fred Braun shoes, status shopping bags, long-haired MOMA Member, Abstract Expressionist option instead.

Dropped out of college (art major) in the late sixties. Took a lot of drugs and got married . . . walked down the aisle of a Long Island Country Club in a mini skirt to "Hey Jude." Left Brooklyn and my husband and came out to San Francisco in the early seventies.

Met Aline Kominsky through a cosmic Upper-West-Side-Jewish-Dentist connection. She invited me to the first Wimmen's Comix Collective meeting. I was lucky enough to "learn while I earned" my twenty-five cents an hour drawing underground comics.

In 1973 I created DiDi Glitz. DiDi is both an exorcism of and a wallowing in my Canarsie "roots." She enthralls and repels me . . . and yes, I keep a Blonde Bubble Wig and fishnets in the closet, right next to husband number two's pinhead mask and polka-dotted muumuu.

In 1980, DiDi's Go-for-Baroque world of elaborately teased coiffes and suburban angst came to life in her favorite shades of hot pink and lime green, when Les Nickelettes, a San Francisco based theatre group, produced *I'd Rather Be Doing Something Else: The DiDi Glitz Story.*

As my alter ego, DiDi can host Rubberware parties, venture into gay bars and get "flocked" with impunity . . . and I get to draw it, a fabulously satisfying trade-off!

LIFE IN THE BAGEL BELT

WITH DIDI GLITZ

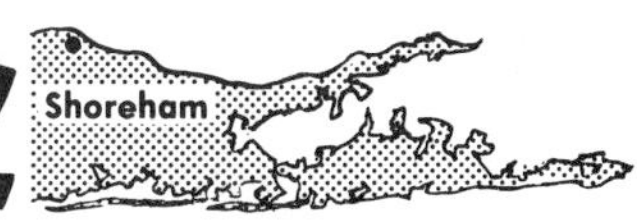

IMAGINE... SHE'S **ONLY** SCREWED HERBIE FOR HER ENTIRE LIFE.. WE'RE TALKING SERIOUSLY DEPRIVED, HERE!
C'MON.. MAYBE SHE'S HAPPY.. I MEAN WE CAN'T **ALL** HAVE SEXUAL HIT LISTS IN THE TRIPLE DIGITS... LORETTA!

MY GOD, DIDI, THE POOR GIRL DOESN'T EVEN KNOW WHAT SHE'S MISSING!!
NOT MUCH FROM MY POINT OF VIEW... THEY'RE ALL JERKS WHO ONLY WANT TO COME AND RUN!

YOU OFFER THEM A CUP OF COFFEE AND THEY'RE DOING YOU A BIG FAVOR IF THEY **DON'T** GET IT "TO GO"!
ON HER SOAP BOX

I'VE ALWAYS TOLD YOU DIDI... MEN ARE FINE IN **THEIR** PLACE... **NOT** YOURS! YOUR TROUBLE IS YOU START RE-DECORATING THEIR LIFE-STYLES ON THE FIRST DATE!!

WELL THANK YOU DEAR ABBY! NOT EVERYONE IS WILLING TO SETTLE FOR A FAST FUCK!

YOU LADIES ARE HAVING AN EXTREMELY ENLIGHTENING CONVERSATION... MAY I JOIN YOU?
YOU CAN GO DECORATE YOURSELF, SCUMBAG! I'M GOING TO THE LITTLE GIRLS ROOM!

LUM FONG EXIT

THAT NITE...
GO FOR BAROQUE
COFFEE TO GO BRUTE?
PLEASE ACCEPT THIS FABULOUS LIFETIME SUPPLY OF U.S. CURRENCY MISS GLITZ!

OOOH BRUTE... YOU ARE EVERSO ... SUAVE!!

TAKE THE SKINHEADS BOWLING..
TAKE THEM BOWLING!

CRYSTAL!

C'MON PLATO TRY IT ON YOU KNOW YOU'RE DYING TO... MOM WON'T MIND!!

FREA

SEX

BLOOD SIST

Vinyl

HI MOM... IT'S ABOUT TIME YOU GOT UP.. WE'RE LIKE STARVING! LOOK WHAT PLATO GOT ME FOR MY SWEET SIXTEEN!

IT'S A HICKEY NECKLACE! DO YOU LIKE IT MRS. GLITZ?

SLOPPY SECONDS

DISASTER

HICKOIDS

SPAWN

LIE

FAINTED!

MARCY HONEY, GET REAL!! YOU'VE GOT THE MRS. ROBINSON SYNDROME IN SPADES!!! WAKE UP TOOTS... IT'S TIME TO BROADEN YOUR HORIZONS!!

IT'S HARD TO BE A TEEN TODAY GALS... IT'S A ZOO OUT THERE! MY TIFFANY'S STEADY, SCOTT, GOT STABBED RIGHT IN THE HIGH SCHOOL CAFETERIA, BY A KID FROM A RIVAL FRAT!

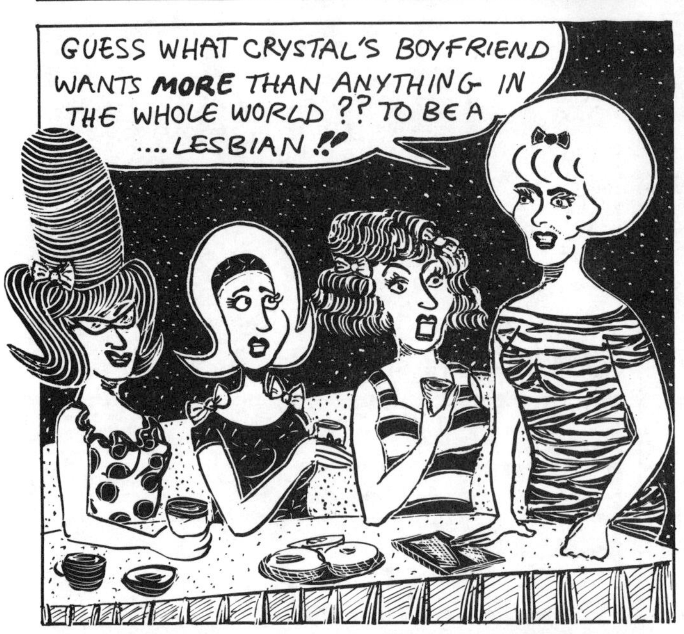
GUESS WHAT CRYSTAL'S BOYFRIEND WANTS MORE THAN ANYTHING IN THE WHOLE WORLD?? TO BE A ....LESBIAN!!
RING

THIS IS MS. BLISS AT MACYS, MRS. GLITZ... WE NEED TO VERIFY THAT A CRYSTAL GLITZ HAS YOUR PERMISSION TO CHARGE 200 TWENTY-FIVE DOLLAR GIFT CERTIFICATES TO YOUR ACCOUNT!
CAN I ASK YOU SOMETHING, HONEY... DO I SOUND LIKE SOME KIND OF A NUTCASE?! AT THIS POINT SHE'S LUCKY TO HAVE PERMISSION TO EXIST ON THIS PLANET!!

HOW COULD YOU CRYSTAL?! WHAT COULD BE SO IMPORTANT THAT YOU'D STEAL FROM YOUR OWN MOTHER?!!
SOB... I TOLD YOU I WAS SORRY, MOM!
YOU'RE GOING TO BE MUCH SORRIER, TOOTS!
HARM FARM
BIG
ATER
SOCIAL DISTORTION
SWAMP ZOMBIES
BLOODSISTER
THEATE OF

ALL RIGHT! I'LL TELL YOU... THE MONEY WAS FOR PLATO'S SEX-CHANGE OPERATION!!
UT
HE CHILLS
SLOPPY SECONDS
O-posiTIVE

MUCH LATER...
GLITZ-TO-GO... CAN I HELP YOU? GOLDEN VENUS SPA? I GOT THE JOB!?! FABULOUS... I'LL BE RIGHT OVER WITH MY SWATCH BOOK, HONEY!!

GOLDEN VENUS

THESE LOCKERS JUST GOTTA GET FLOCKED!
HI DIDI...
MARCY! HONEY! YOU'RE POSITIVELY GLOWING! WHO IS HE?!?

DIDI I WANT YOU TO MEET BABE... MY OWN PERSONAL TRAINER!
VERY PERSONAL!
AND I OWE IT ALL TO LORETTA... SHE TOLD ME TO BROADEN MY HORIZONS!!

I JUST DON'T GET IT LORETTA... IF EVERY OTHER COCKAMAMIE JELLO-BRAIN ON LAWNG GUYLIND CAN FIND TRUE LOVE... WHY CAN'T I ??
CHRIST, CRYSTAL.. THIS STOOPID VEIL ITCHES!
C'MON PLATO... IT HURTS TO BE BEAUTIFUL!!
!
?!
the end

MY GIRLFRIENDS WOULD GO ON AND ON ABOUT THEIR EXCITING LOVE AFFAIRS AND LATEST CONQUESTS UNTIL MY SHAME AND HUMILIATION BECAME SO UNBEARABLE THAT I WANTED TO SCREAM BECAUSE...

I Had to Advertise for Love

Diane Noomin © 1990

AND THEN SUDDENLY, I DARED TO HOPE... ONE LETTER STOOD OUT FROM ALL THE OTHERS LIKE A SHINING BEACON... BECKONING ME NEARER.. CALLING ME TO LOVE...

RUBBERWARE

©1985 DIANE NOOMIN

I WANTED TO HAVE A PARTY
WITH ONION DIP AND A JELLO MOLD..
BUT I SPENT MOST OF MY TIME WONDERING
HOW MANY SEXUAL AIDS I SOLD...

VIBRATORS CAN HELP WOMEN
TO HAVE **FUN** WITHOUT MEN...
YOU PLUG THEM IN...
THEY TURN YOU ON...
ORGASMS TILL YOU SAY WHEN

I LOVE TO USE MY CHARGE CARD
I ADORE HAVING MONEY TO SPEND
I BUY EVERYTHING FROM
CONVECTION OVENS TO DESIGNER CONDOMS
FOR MY HUSBAND...

I TELL YOU DIDI I BEEN THERE...
I DON'T NEED RUBBERWARE...
A VIBRATOR CAN RUN FOREVER
BUT MEN GIVE ME MORE PLEASURE!!

WE'VE GOT THAT RUBBERWARE FEELING... DEEP IN OUR HEARTS
FOR THOSE WHO NEVER STOP AND THOSE WHO DON'T KNOW HOW TO START!
WE'VE GOT THAT RUBBERWARE FEELING... DEEP IN OUR HEARTS
IT WILL PLACE YOUR POPULARITY AT THE TOP OF THE CHARTS!!

"A sociological study of primitive youth in western civilization."

COMING OF AGE IN Canarsie

WHEN WE MOVED FROM LONG ISLAND TO BROOKLYN IN 1960 I HAD JUST TURNED THIRTEEN... A VERY **YOUNG** THIRTEEN!

OVERNIGHT I WAS THRUST INTO THE JUNIOR HIGH SCHOOL WORLD OF MAKE-UP, MAKE-OUT PARTIES AND B-O-Y-S...

I GREW UP FAST...

BUT NOT QUITE FAST ENOUGH...

I LEARNED TO PRETEND I DIDN'T STUDY, TO ROLL UP MY SKIRTS, WEAR WHITE LIPSTICK, HANG OUT IN BOWLING ALLEYS AND SHOPLIFT...

AND I ACQUIRED ON MY FIRST DATE WITH A "COLLEGE MAN" THAT MUCH COVETED RED BADGE OF HONOR... THE HICKEY!!

Thanx & a tip o' the wig to Margaret Mead

Diane Noomin © 1989

1. Teen Smut Version: "Shut up and shove it up."

SHE MEANS IT!!
DON'T ASK
SHE REALLY DOES!
DiDi Glitz
Diane Noomin ©1988

"MOST DISASTROUS RELATIONSHIP"... NOW HERE'S A COSMO CONTEST YOU COULD WIN, GLITZ!
GLENDA IT'S YOU!
DON'T BE SO SURE LORETTA.. DID I EVER TELL YOU ABOUT MY FIRST HUSBAND?
THANKS EVERSO HONEY...
DON'T YOU THINK IT'S A LITTLE TIGHT?
COSMO
International House of Hair

AFTER I SPLIT UP WITH ALBERT, I LET HIM GUILT ME INTO SLEEPING OVER AT MY NEW PLACE...
YEH... YEH.. I'M ALL EARS! GO ON... GO ON... SO..
SORRY
OUCH!

SO THE NEXT MORNING (STILL GUILTY) I OFFER HIM SOME BREAKFAST...
I GOT EGGS,... O.J... OR I CAN MAKE PANCAKES...
NOTHING THANKS. I GOTTA RUSH HOME AND WASH THE KITCHEN FLOOR- ALISON ANDREWS IS COMING FOR LUNCH
NO NEED TO ADD HE'D NEVER WASHED THE FUCKIN' FLOOR IN FOUR FUCKIN' YEARS OF MARITAL BLISS!!

WELL MY FIRST BOY FRIEND WAS A PHARMACY STUDENT WHO TOOK ACID AND RAN OFF TO PARIS TO BE A POET...
"SUZANNE'LL TAKE YOU DOWN TO HER PLACE BY THE RIVER... SHE'LL FEED YOU TEA & ORANGES THAT COME ALL THE WAY FROM CHINA"
I WISH HE'D GO JUMP IN HER FERSHLUGGINER RIVER, ALREADY!
SHE'S PROBABLY A BLONDE WHO RIDES HORSES..
WHEN HE GOT BACK TO BROOKLYN HE ACTED LIKE I WAS GONNA TIE HIM TO A STAKE ON FLATBUSH AVENUE & FORCE-FEED HIM CHICKEN SOUP...

P.S. I MEET HIM 20 YEARS & 2 MARRIAGES LATER... HE'S A HIGH SCHOOL TEACHER, LIVING IN PHOENIX, MARRIED WITH KIDS AND HE'S SHTUPPING ONE OF HIS STUDENTS!

I SWEAR HE SOUNDED LIKE HE'D NEVER BEEN EAST OF THE MISSISSIPPI IN HIS LIFE!

I HAVE NO EXCUSE. I KNEW HE WAS A WORLD-CLASS ASS-HOLE... BUT ONE DAY HE DROPPED HIS GUARD AND WAS KINDA SWEET AND VULNERABLE AND WE DRANK CHAMPAGNE AND IT WAS O.K. NOTHIN' TO WRITE HOME ABOUT... SO FIVE YEARS LATER...

WELL, I GUESS YOU'RE RIGHT LORETTA... I WIN! DID I EVER TELL YOU ABOUT MELVIN?

ONLY 10,000 TIMES

OH NO! NOT THE MELVIN SAGA. AGAIN...

I WAS OBSESSED WITH MELVIN - I HAD JUST SPLIT UP WITH EDDIE & I WAS LOOKIN' FOR A NEW PLACE... MELVIN SHOWED ME THE APARTMENT - A 5th FLOOR WALK-UP.

HE LIVED ON THE SAME FLOOR!!

SO ONE DAY I'M AT HIS PLACE AND THIS GIRL COMES OVER AND STARTS CLEANING HIS OVEN...

I'M SO OBSESSED WITH THIS GUY, I GO TO SLEEP SINGING "MELVIN MY LOVE"... HE'S ALL I CAN THINK ABOUT OR TALK ABOUT... I START LEAPING UP TO PEEK OUT THE PEEP-HOLE EVERYTIME I HEAR STEPS!.. SOMETIMES I SEE HIM WITH OTHER GIRLS...

HE IGNORES ME FOR WEEKS AND THEN BRINGS ME FLOWERS AND POETRY... SOON HE'S GOT ME WRITING POETRY...

FINALLY I JUST CAN'T TAKE THE HOT AND COLD TREATMENT ANYMORE... I MOVE FAR AWAY...

I MET MELVIN YEARS LATER AT SOME CONVENTION... EVEN THO HE'D GOTTEN FAT HE STILL HAD THAT ATTITUDE... GIRLS WERE DANGLING OFF HIM... WE DANCED...

AND I GET A LETTER FROM MELVIN SAYING HOW NICE IT WAS TO SEE ME, AND HOW SORRY HE WAS THAT HE DIDN'T GET TO DANCE WITH MY BEST FRIEND, IRENE!

HEY GLITZ! RALPH'S ON THE PHONE! HE'S PISSED... YOU WERE SUPPOSED TO BE HOME AN HOUR AGO.. HE WANTS HIS SUPPER

MEET MARVIN MENSCH

MARVIN THINKS HE LOOKS LIKE RICHARD GERE... BUT IT'S MORE LIKE RICHARD BENJAMIN...

HE LIKES TO SEE AND BE SEEN

HE'S QUITE THE GOURMET...

MARVIN LIKES THINGS TO BE NEAT.

HE'S "INTO" WHITE.

HE'S TOO BUSY TO WATCH T.V.

MARVIN HAS A WAY WITH WOMEN...

HE'S RICH...

SUAVE...

TRENDY...

AND HE KNOWS HOW TO OPERATE...

A REAL MENSCH!

©1983 Diane Noomin

I'D HAD WORSE MORNINGS... MY EYES WERE CARRYING LUGGAGE... HEAVY LUGGAGE...

6 MINUTES LATER TROUBLE DROPPED IN... WELCOME AS A PIMP AT A PAJAMA PARTY...

6 HOURS LATER I HIT MIAMI... THE AIR WAS AS THICK AS THE MASCARA ON AN AGING DIVORCÉE...

6 SECONDS LATER, THE SOLUTION HIT ME LIKE A TON OF PANCAKE ON A PUBESCENT PIMPLE. SUDDENLY A POOL OF DARKNESS OPENED AT MY FEET.. I DIVED INTO IT... IT HAD NO BOTTOM

6 DAYS LATER I WAS DROWNING IN MY LIQUID ASSETS - AFTER 36 MAI-TAIS I WAS LIT UP LIKE A WHORE AT A HANNUKAH PARTY...

LESBO-A-GO-GO

with DiDi Glitz

©1990

Diane Noomin

GLITZ !! YOU'RE LATE!
SORRY LORETTA.. THE WEIRDEST THING JUST... GOD.. I NEED A DRINKY WINKY!

WHATS UP GLITZ?
I MET A WOMAN IN THE SAUNA...
YEAH...
I WENT TO HER PLACE FOR COFFEE...
YEAH...
SHE LIKED ME LORETTA!
YEAH, SO...
NO, I MEAN SHE **REALLY LIKED** ME...
SO...
SHE TOUCHED ME, LORETTA...
I THINK I LIKED IT...

OH LORETTA... I'M SO ASHAMED! MAYBE I'M A PREVERT...
DON'T KNOCK IT 'TIL YOU'VE TRIED IT!
YOU?

THAT NIGHT:

MARCY.. HAVE YOU EVER... YOU KNOW.. DONE IT WITH A WOMAN?
EE-YEW! DON'T TOUCH ME! HOW COULD YOU?

OH GOD... WHY **DID** I TOUCH HER... AM I A LESBO?

SIS... HOW CAN YOU TELL IF YOU'RE A LESBO? I'M SCARED.. WHAT'LL I TELL CRYSTAL.. SHE'S ONLY 13...
WHOA DIDI ONE FREAKOUT AT A TIME.. **FIRST**, BIG DEAL, WHO CARES WHAT TURNS YOU ON? **NEXT**, CRYSTAL CAN HANDLE IT.. JUST DON'T TELL MOM...

CRYSTAL, HONEY, WE NEED TO HAVE A TEENY WEENY CHAT... CRYSTAL!! TURN THAT CRAP DOWN... CRYSTAL!! OH NEVER MIND... GO BACK TO YOUR VIRGINITY ARREADY...
LIKE A VIR-GIN
TOUCHED FOR THE VERY FIRST TIME..

NO CHERRY... I GUESS I'M BETTER OFF... FUNNY, I DON'T FEEL BETTER OFF...

OOOH...OOOH.. YES!! UNH... THIS IS UTTERLY SEXIER THAN PLAYGIRL!
PLAYBOY
MASSAGE
PLAYGIRL

THAT NIGHT...

NEXT AM...

CHERRY... I WANT TO EXPLAIN ABOUT THE OTHER DAY... I WAS.. SCARED...
I UNDERSTAND DIDI... LET'S TAKE IT SLOW. OKAY?
OKAY.
I KNOW A REALLY FUN BAR... WANT TO MEET THERE TONITE?
OKAY.

Thanks and a tip o' the wig to Val, Sandy, Deb and Cheryl

The utter end...

The C Word[1]

Diane Noomin ©1990

The first year they made abortion legal in New York I got pregnant.

I was 22... stuck in a loveless marriage and...

...not sure who the father was.

I did what I had to do. It was easy.

Years later, my marriage over, I found myself in front of a painting at the Modern.

The pain and sense of loss I had long suppressed out of necessity flowed over me.

Now 20 years, a happy marriage and 4 miscarriages later, I am faced with infertility.

Looking back I'm grateful to that 22 year old for her strength.

I owe my life to her choice.

---

1. **choice** \'chois\ *n . adj., n.* **1:** act of choosing; SELECTION **2:** the right or power of choosing; OPTION **3:** an alternative *syn* CHOICE, ALTERNATIVE, OPTION, PREFERENCE all suggest the power of choosing between (2) things. CHOICE IMPLIES THE OPPORTUNITY TO CHOOSE.

KRYSTINE KRYTTRE

Born October 9, 1958, in San Francisco, California. A self-taught cultural misfit, I've been attracted to underground comix since childhood. I thought that being an outlaw cartoonist would be so . . . so . . . *romantic.* However, drawing comix *does* provide me with a nice, safe way to work out my urban-working-class-existential angst, *and* it keeps me out of trouble, too. Usually.

As a cheerful cynic, my life is plagued by conflicts with duality—both personal and in the world at large. I could just ignore it, but artists are *supposed* to suffer. Everyone knows that. If I *must* suffer, it might as well be over something intellectual.

A morose optimist at heart, I watched too many episodes of "The Addams Family" and "Dark Shadows" as a child.

I'm a romantic nihilist above all and since I can't live without art, and can't make art unless I'm alive, my art and life sometimes become tangled together in a sincere, but messy intercourse. Oh well.

My fellow cartoonists, friends, and family have referred to my being, art and/or whatever as: extreme, cryptic, wild, brooding, playful, morbid, spacy, manic, intense, kooky, spooky, honest, schizo, ethereal, paranoid, sedate, hideous, naïve, expressionistic, scary, interesting, a bad influence, a Caligari dream, undoubtedly bats, and maybe not necessarily beautiful, *but* kind of sexy.

BIMBOS FROM HELL!
IN 1984, I WAS A NEWCOMER TO THE UNDERGROUND COMIX SCENE IN S.F.
UPON FIRST MEETING DORI SEDA, I THOUGHT SHE WAS
TALL & SCARY!
COLOR FEATHERS PINK!
SOMEHOW, I KNEW SHE WAS AT LEAST AS TWISTED AS ME. I WAS AWESTRUCK BY WHAT A GREAT ARTIST AND STORYTELLER SHE WAS. OH, SHE LIKED ME A LOT, TOO!
KRYSTINE KRYTTRE ©1988
SEX AND DEATH
DOMESTIC BEASTIALITY
SNORT!
YOU KNOW, KRYSTINE, YOU'RE REALLY GOOD! YOU CAN REALLY DRAW! YOU'RE
GONNA BE REAL FAMOUS! NO ONE CAN DRAW LIKE YOU! YOU KNOW
HOW TO STYLIZE! AND YOU CAN SURE DRAW SOME DISGUSTING THINGS!
DON'T EVER STOP! I'M SO GLAD WE'RE BUDDIES!
HE JUST DIDN'T APPRECIATE YOU. HE HAD A BIG EGO, TOO. YOUR CARTOONING IS ONE THING THAT WILL NEVER EVER LEAVE YOU. DO A STORY ABOUT IT!*
* SEE TITS & CLITS #7 (Last Gasp).
DON HONEEE!! LOOK AT OUR HAIR!! AREN'T WEE BEEEOOOOTEEEEFUL!?
WE WON'T BE WALLFLOWERS ANYMORE, WILL WEE?!
BOYS WILL NOTICE US NOW!
OH YES. VERY BEAUTIFUL.
Mess Hairall PEROXIDE

MY WOMAN FROM SODOM LETS ME FUCK HER IN THE BOTTOM
YOU BETTER BE NICE TO KRYSTINE!
WAKE UP, ANN!
WE BROUGHT JR WILLIAMS HOME AS A PRESENT FOR YOU!
TELL HIM TO CALL ME TOMORROW.
BUT HE'S HERE RIGHT NOW!
I WASHED ALL MY MAKEUP OFF!
HE DOESN'T CARE! HE'S DRUNK!
ALIEN SEX FIEND
EVER GO TO A PARTY, AND YOUR BEST FRIEND IS WEARING THE SAME DRESS?
I HOPE YOU'RE WEARING UNDERWEAR!
WERE WE BAD GIRLS?
LET'S ASK RONZO!
RONZO! WHO LOOKS SLUTTIER?! ME OR KRYSTINE?!
WHY, YOU BOTH DO!*
DOG BOY
I HAD THIS DOG, AND HE HAD ECZEMA AND DISGUSTING OPEN SORES ALL OVER HIS BODY, AND HE SMELLED REALLY BAD...MY FRIENDS WOULDN'T COME OVER BECAUSE HE LIKED TO SHOVE HIS NOSE INTO THEIR CROTCHES, AND GO SNORT! SNORT! SNORT! OH, HE HAD WORMS, TOO, AN
AN OPEN BOOK!
WHO IS THIS WOMAN?
* THE ONLY RIGHT ANSWER!

SHE WAS HAPPY WHEN I LAST SAW HER.
I'M NOT ALONE...
LET'S NOT HAVE A SNIFFLE
LET'S HAVE A
BLOODY GOOD CRY
ALWAYS REMEMBER
THE LONGER YOU LIVE
THE SOONER YOU
BLOODY WELL DIE!
BUT I'M VERY ALONE.
BECAUSE WHEN SHE WENT—
—PART OF ME WENT, TOO.
I'M SORRY, KRYSTINE.
WE'RE BAD GIRLS, DORI! FUCK BEING SORRY!
OH! BAD GIRLS!
CLICK!
MY BEST FRIEND. ALWAYS.

ONE SUNNY DAY IN S.F., TWO CO-WORKERS TOOK THEIR LUNCH BREAK IN
DOLORES PARK
LOOK! THE PIGEONS LIKE MY BURRITO!
©1989 · KRYSTINE KRYTTRE
OH! THIS ONE HAS A STRING TIED TO IT'S LEG!
?
I'LL TAKE IT OFF—
POOR PIGEON!
!
HEY! C'MERE YOU!
AH HA!
I'VE NEVER SEEN A PIGEON WITH SUCH A BIG TAPEWORM!

HORNY BLOWS IT
© 1990
KRYSTINE KRYTTRE
$!
$?
#!

ON BEING TOO INTENSE
© 1987 KRYSTINE KRYTTRE
IT'S JUST AS WELL THAT WE BROKE UP... SHE SCARED ME! BESIDES, I'VE NEVER HAD A GIRLFRIEND FOR MORE THAN A YEAR, ANYWAYS.
SHE WAS JUST TOO WILD LOOKING FOR ME–
THOSE TEETH EARRINGS.
THAT RATTY HAIR.
THE WAY SHE WORE BLACK ALLA TIME.
THAT WEIRD SENSE OF HUMOR.
AND THOSE MORBID DRAWINGS...DISGUSTING!
THOSE EYES–THAT LOOK WAS SCARY! LIKE SHE WAS PUTTING A HEX ON ME OR SOMETHING!

RELATIONSHIPS FRIGHTEN ME!
I JUST DIDN'T WANT TO BE TIED DOWN.
SHE TOOK CARE OF ME WHEN I WAS SICK.
I SLYLY "FORGOT" OUR ONE-YEAR ANNIVERSARY.
SHE WAS ALWAYS SO PATIENT WITH ME... JUST A SAINT.
I SHOULDN'T HAVE BEEN WATCHING FOOTBALL WHEN WE MADE LOVE ON SUNDAY MORNINGS.
SHE WAS GOOD TO ME AND I WAS SUCH AN ASSHOLE! I WONDER IF SHE'D GIVE ME ANOTHER CHANCE -
HMM...NO ANSWER... I BET SHE'S OUT PAINTING THE TOWN RED.
BRRING!
BRANG!
END

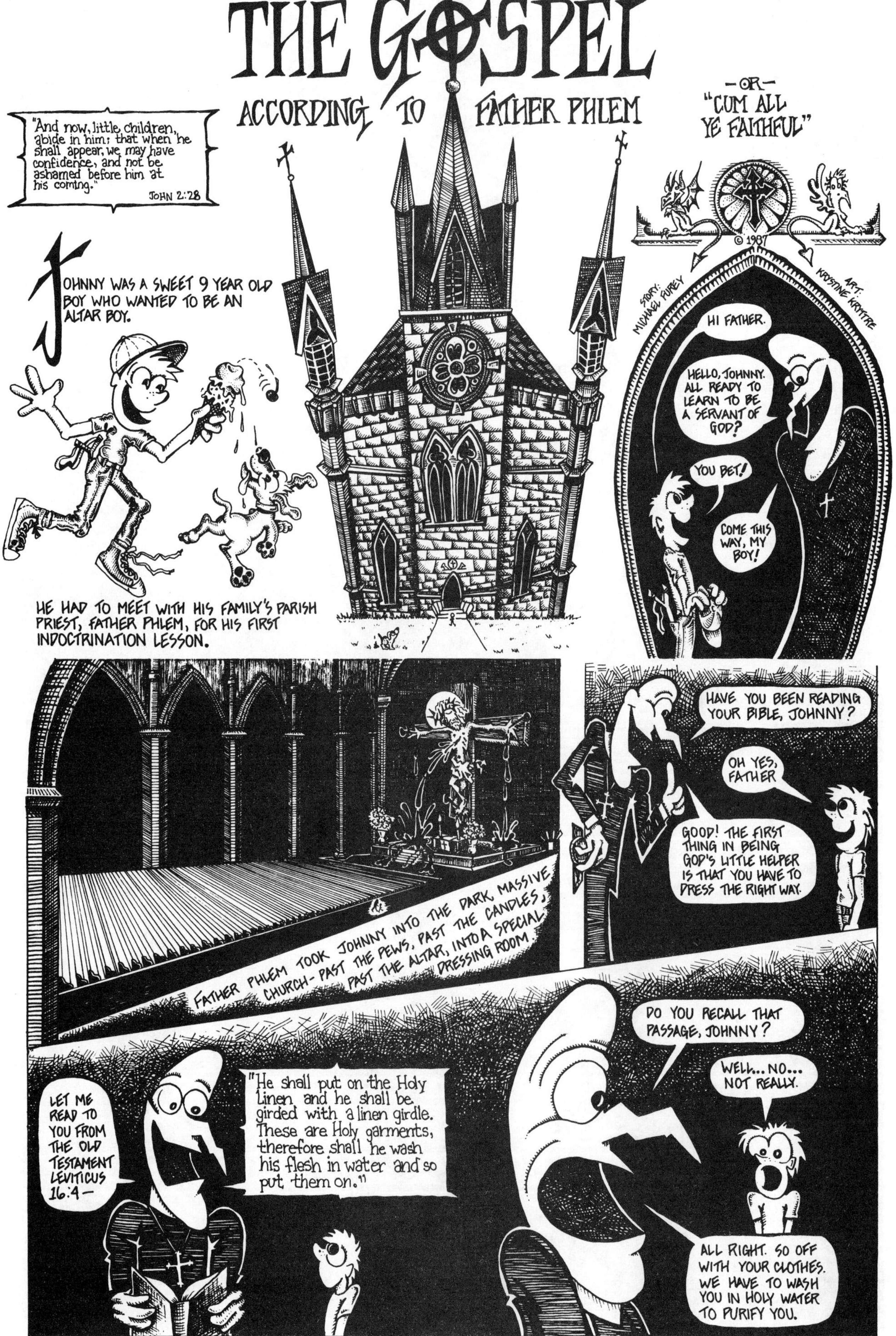
THE GOSPEL
ACCORDING TO FATHER PHLEM
-OR-
"CUM ALL YE FAITHFUL"
"And now, little children, abide in him; that when he shall appear, we may have confidence, and not be ashamed before him at his coming." JOHN 2:28
© 1987
STORY: MICHAEL FUREY
ART: KRYSTINE KRYTTRE
JOHNNY WAS A SWEET 9 YEAR OLD BOY WHO WANTED TO BE AN ALTAR BOY.
HE HAD TO MEET WITH HIS FAMILY'S PARISH PRIEST, FATHER PHLEM, FOR HIS FIRST INDOCTRINATION LESSON.
HI FATHER.
HELLO, JOHNNY. ALL READY TO LEARN TO BE A SERVANT OF GOD?
YOU BET!
COME THIS WAY, MY BOY!
FATHER PHLEM TOOK JOHNNY INTO THE DARK, MASSIVE CHURCH- PAST THE PEWS, PAST THE CANDLES, PAST THE ALTAR, INTO A SPECIAL DRESSING ROOM.
HAVE YOU BEEN READING YOUR BIBLE, JOHNNY?
OH YES, FATHER
GOOD! THE FIRST THING IN BEING GOD'S LITTLE HELPER IS THAT YOU HAVE TO DRESS THE RIGHT WAY.
LET ME READ TO YOU FROM THE OLD TESTAMENT LEVITICUS 16:4—
"He shall put on the Holy Linen and he shall be girded with a linen girdle. These are Holy garments, therefore shall he wash his flesh in water and so put them on."
DO YOU RECALL THAT PASSAGE, JOHNNY?
WELL... NO... NOT REALLY.
ALL RIGHT. SO OFF WITH YOUR CLOTHES. WE HAVE TO WASH YOU IN HOLY WATER TO PURIFY YOU.

JOHNNY, TRUSTING FATHER PHLEM COMPLETELY, TAKES OFF ALL HIS CLOTHES.
FATHER PHLEM QUICKLY UNDRESSES HIMSELF ALSO.
BOTH COMPLETELY NAKED, FATHER PHLEM TAKES JOHNNY TO THE HOLY WATER FOUNTAIN AND STARTS WASHING JOHNNY'S INNOCENT BODY.
AS HE GETS TO JOHNNY'S CROTCH, HE AGAIN QUOTES FROM LEVITICUS 22:11-
"But if the Priest buy of any soul, he shall eat of it. And he that is born in His house, they shall eat of His meat."
FATHER PHLEM WAS NOW WASHING HIS OWN CROTCH AND SHOWED JOHNNY WHAT THE LORD MEANT BY MEAT.
YOU MEAN I HAVE TO EAT THAT?!
NOT "EAT IT" MY YOUNG, NAIIVE LAD... LET ME SHOW YOU... FOR INSTANCE IN NUMBERS 18:10-
"In the most Holy place shalt thou eat it, every male shall eat it. It shall be most Holy unto thee."
YOU SEE JOHNNY, THIS IS WHAT BEING CLOSE TO GOD IS ALL ABOUT!
FATHER PHLEM COULD TELL JOHNNY WAS STILL CONFUSED, SO HE TRIED A DIFFERENT APPROACH.
AGAIN HE QUOTES FROM LEVITICUS 14:15-
"And the Priest shall take some of the log of oil and pour it into the palm of his left hand."

SO HE TOOK JOHNNY'S LEFT HAND AND FILLED IT WITH OIL.
THEN HE FILLED HIS OWN LEFT HAND.
FATHER PHLEM, NOT WANTING TO EMBARRASS THE BOY, STARTED JERKING OFF AND TOLD JOHNNY TO DO THE SAME.
HE COULD TELL JOHNNY LIKED WHAT HE FELT.
THE BIBLE IS ALWAYS RIGHT.
ALL OF A SUDDEN...
FATHER PHLEM! I'VE GOT TO SEE YOU!
KNOCK! KNOCK! KNOCK!
IT WAS BROTHER BOYLE, THE BENEDICTINE MONK.
WHAT'S WRONG, BROTHER?
FATHER, I'VE GOT THESE BOILS ALL OVER MY BODY!
FATHER PHLEM HAD BROTHER BOYLE LAY DOWN ON THE FLOOR.
YOUR LUCKY DAY! YOU ARE GOING TO LEARN A LOT ON YOUR FIRST DAY. SEE THE BROTHER'S BOILS. YOU'VE ALREADY LEARNED ONE WAY TO EAT OF THE FLESH, AND THIS IS ANOTHER WAY.
HE QUOTED FROM LEVITICUS—
"And in the place of the boil there be a white rising or a bright spot, white and somewhat reddish, and it be shewed to the Priest."
WITH THAT, HE KNELT DOWN, PICKED OUT A BIG, JUICY BOIL...
CHEWED BIT AND SUCKED AND CHEWED
UNTIL IT BROKE, AND HE SUCKED IT UP!

TRY IT, JOHNNY.. FOR EACH BOIL WE POP WE'LL DO A STATION OF THE CROSS TO EASE THE PAIN OF THIS LIFE!
JOHNNY LIKED PLAYING WITH HIMSELF, BUT THOUGHT FATHER PHLEM WAS OFF HIS ROCKER!
SO AS FATHER PHLEM WAS BUSY SUCKING PUS FROM BOILS, JOHNNY GOT HIS CLOTHES AND GOT THE HELL OUT!
HE WENT HOME AND TOLD HIS MOTHER
?!
HIS MOTHER TOLD HIS FATHER
HIS FATHER TOLD THE POLICE
FATHER PHLEM IS NOW SERVING TIME IN A STATE MENTAL FACILITY FOR WAYWARD PRIESTS.
QUAAACK!!
JOHNNY STILL REMEMBERS HIS TEACHINGS.
YOU BET!
END

NIHILIST ROMANCE

KRYSTINE KRYTTRE
© 1986

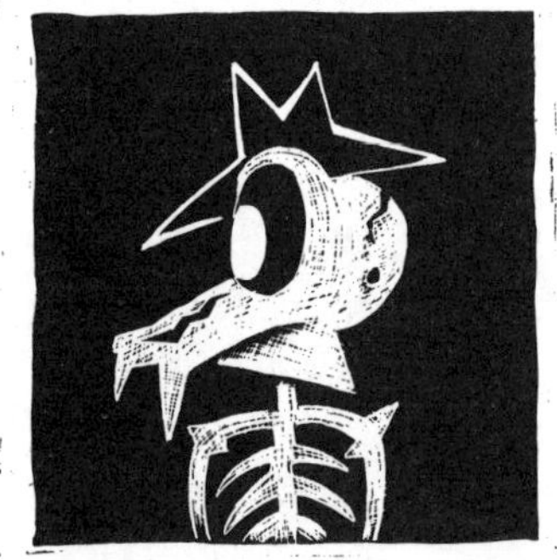

YOU'LL NEVER KNOW THAT I LOVE YOU

...CAUSE I'LL NEVER SAY IT–

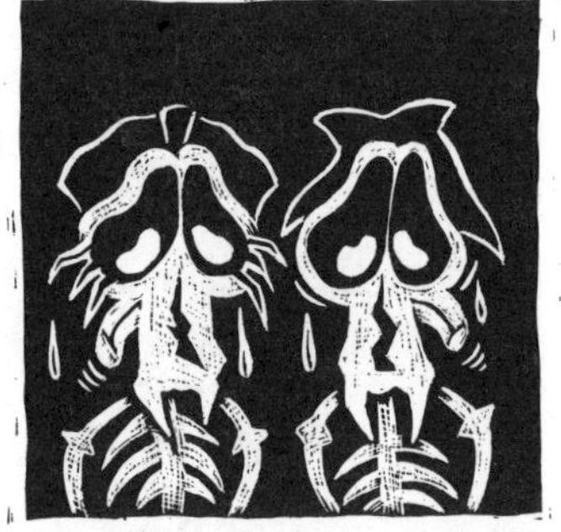

BUT THAT DOESN'T MEAN I DON'T

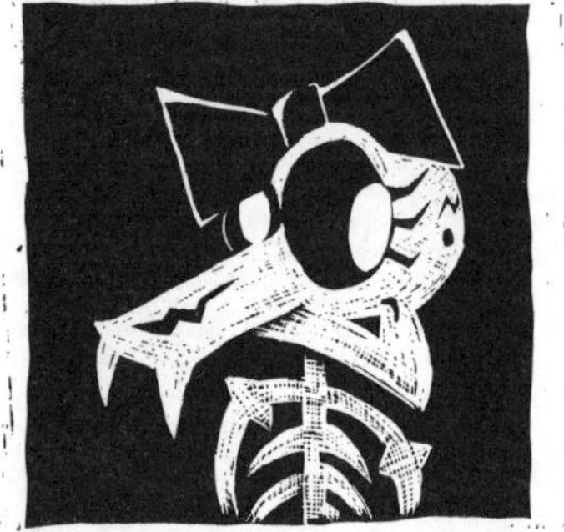

THINK ABOUT IT A LOT.

KRYSTINE
KRYTTRE '88

NEXT 5
MILES

M. K. BROWN

I was born in Connecticut where, at age eight, on Christmas Eve I saw Santa Claus in the sky from the window of the upstairs bedroom. At first I thought I was imagining things. Then the silhouette passed across the moon and I could clearly see the eight galloping reindeer, the sleigh full of presents and Santa, in the sleigh, leaning forward with one arm raised. The question occurs to me now: was he flogging the reindeer? I prefer to think that he was pointing the way to deserving children like me (this was before my bout with kleptomania).

After attending several art schools, I moved to the West Coast, married, gave birth to a daughter who has a good sense of humor, divorced, and am currently living in Northern California. There are fifty-four stairs to my house, thus I have strong legs and receive a certain satisfaction from observing people much younger than I am (especially those who run regularly), gasping for breath and leaning on the railings when they reach the porch. Not many salespeople come up to my door, which is good because I am very busy with metaphysical matters.

Over the years I have studied and fooled around with all forms of art, music, dance, sports, crafts, sewing, cooking, sandal-making, yogurt-making, bread-making, jewelry, knitting, horseback-riding. I have jumped and fallen off horses and had my arm in a cast so that I couldn't draw or wash my own hair and had to go to local beauty salons for six weeks until the cast came off, during which time I was given a new style every five days. The best was "Southern Belle." I am now considering a blue streak (ultramarine).

I wish to extend warm greetings to fellow cartoonists in this book and to readers. My hope is that, in the face of the world's great travails, we can continue to express and enjoy the human condition in all its glory. Over and out.

I Can't Work Today
A STUPID POEM by M·K·BROWN ©1987
I can't work today,
All the old ghosts are
Hanging around.
Everything
Looks Stupid!
My clothes
Are uncomfortable
in fact, NOTHING works today;
Even the dog
Watching me
Rankles.
And the SKY,
A "funny" blue now,
Keeps Changing Color!
I see a bowl of fruit on the table.
There are faces in it.
I wonder how Liz Taylor is doing.
The end

 M·K·BROWN

COPING WITH CHAIN-SAW MASSACRES

ODD MOON RISING

CONDENSED THWARTED HORROR

© '87 M·K·BROWN

THE MOON TONIGHT LOOKS ODD, ANNETTE. IT GIVES ME RATHER A QUEER FEELING, IF YOU KNOW WHAT I MEAN.

JULES, WHAT DO YOU MEAN?

OH, YOU KNOW, LIKE THE LAST TIME!

REMEMBER?

JULES, NO.

REMEMBER THE NIGHT I TURNED INTO A DOG?

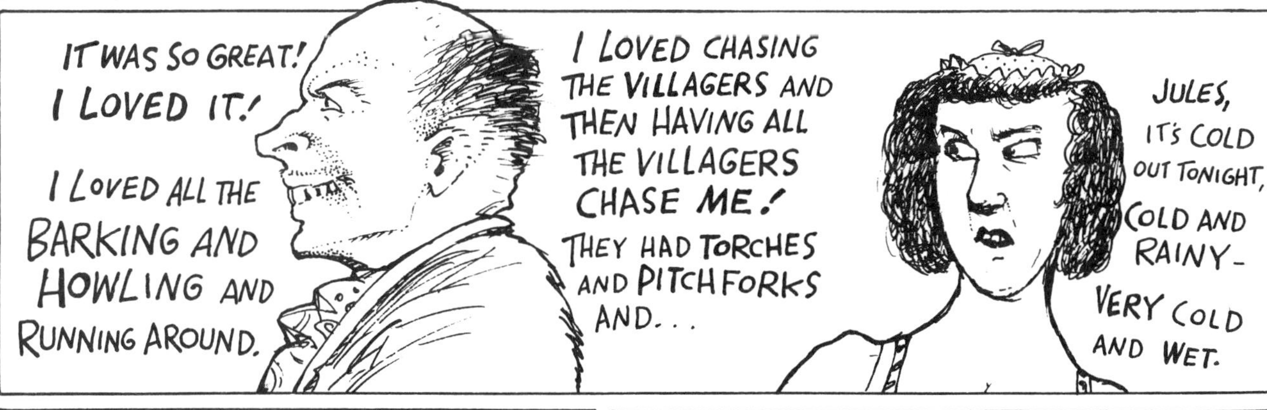

WHITE GIRL SINGS THE BLUES
(GET DOWN)

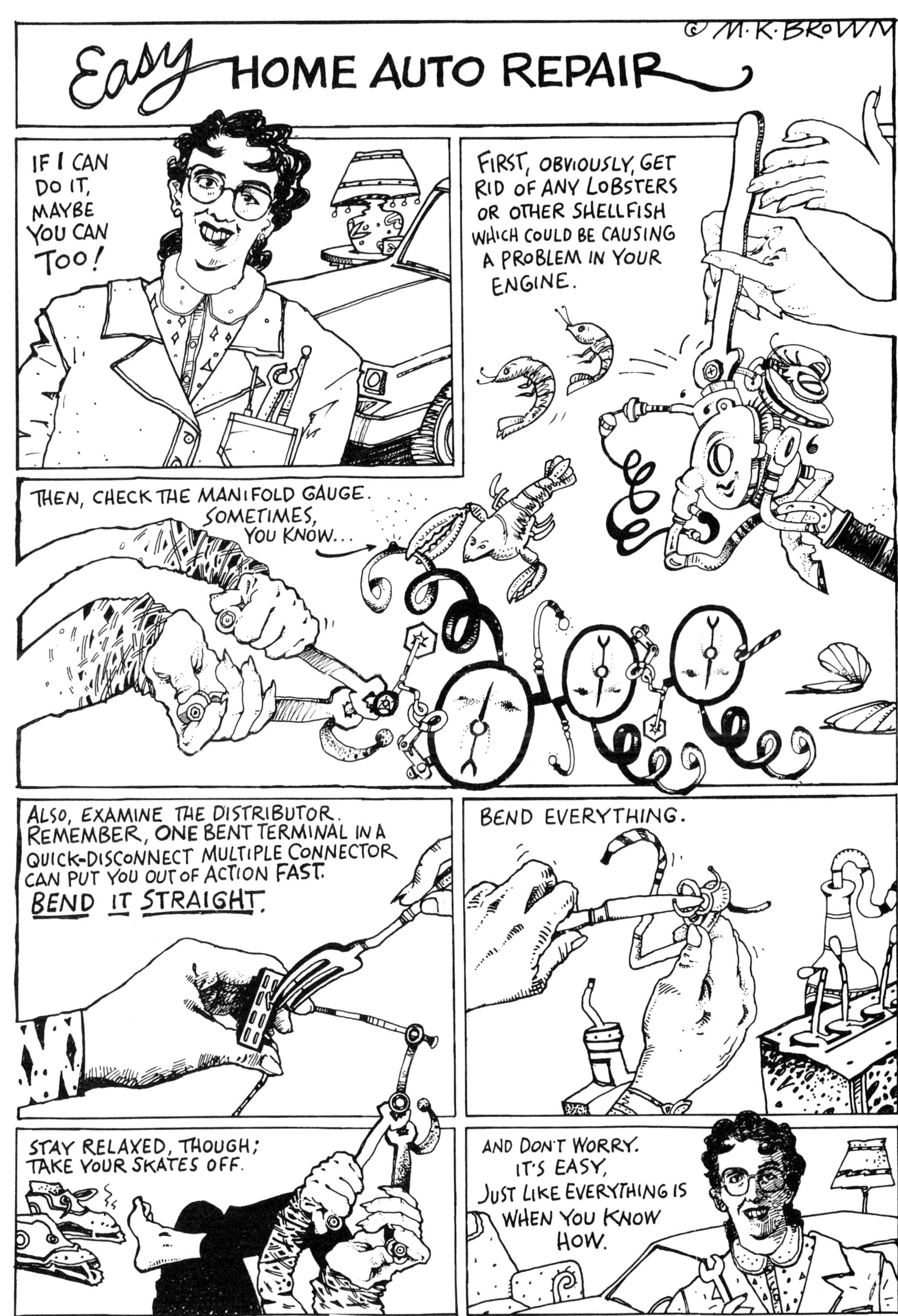
© M·K·BROWN
Easy HOME AUTO REPAIR
IF I CAN DO IT, MAYBE YOU CAN TOO!
FIRST, OBVIOUSLY, GET RID OF ANY LOBSTERS OR OTHER SHELLFISH WHICH COULD BE CAUSING A PROBLEM IN YOUR ENGINE.
THEN, CHECK THE MANIFOLD GAUGE. SOMETIMES, YOU KNOW...
ALSO, EXAMINE THE DISTRIBUTOR. REMEMBER, ONE BENT TERMINAL IN A QUICK-DISCONNECT MULTIPLE CONNECTOR CAN PUT YOU OUT OF ACTION FAST. BEND IT STRAIGHT.
BEND EVERYTHING.
STAY RELAXED, THOUGH; TAKE YOUR SKATES OFF.
AND DON'T WORRY. IT'S EASY, JUST LIKE EVERYTHING IS WHEN YOU KNOW HOW.

THEY CAME FROM SPACE
A TRUE-LIFE Sci-Fi SOCIAL DRAMA By MARY K. BROWN
Salt Lake City, Utah 1984
RAFAEL
SEARS
SALT LAKE MEDICAL·DE
B STREET
A QUIET DAY LIKE ANY OTHER
MORNIN' BILL
MORNIN' SAM
MORNIN' DOROTHY
GOOD MORNING, BILL - ITS A WARM DAY
...ANYWAY, MY MOTHER SAID IT WAS 110° IN THE SHADE OR SOMETHING TODAY
WELL, ITS TOO HOT IF YOU ASK ME
REALLY
WELL, GOOD-BY MARION, I MUST BE GETTING BACK TO THE OFFICE!
NOW REMEMBER WHAT I TOLD YOU!
I WILL, DR. WOO - NO MORE CHOCOLATES OR NUTS

MORNIN' LOU
MORNIN' BILL
MORNIN' MAE
MORNIN' BILL
MORNIN' NELLIE
MORNIN' BILL
MORNIN' BILL
MORNIN' BILL
A QUIET DAY. . . . BUT NOT LIKE ANY OTHER
ALT LAKE CITY
EDICAL · DENTAL
GOOD MORNING, DR. WOO HOT ENOUGH FOR YOU?
GOOD MORNING WILLIE
GOOD MORNING DR. WOO
GOOD MORNING LEONA
LEONA WILL YOU PLEASE SEND IN MR. BURNS
OK
HERE PUT THIS ON
TELL ME, MR. BURNS, HOW LONG HAVE YOU HAD THIS AWFUL TROUBLE?
UM,
SINCE I WAS A CHILD

SINCE YOU WERE A CHILD, HUH?
WELL, LET'S SEE WHAT WE CAN DO ABOUT THAT RIGHT NOW HOLD STILL
NOW, MR. BURNS, I WANT YOU TO COUNT FROM TEN TO ZERO! GOT IT?
OK.... HERE GOES!
TEN
ZIT ZIT
ZIT
ZIT
ZIT
ZIT ZIT
HEY
WHAT THE HECK'S GOING ON HERE?!
I'M PARALYZED!
I CAN'T TALK
THE MARTIANS HAVE GOT ME
THEY'RE TAKING ME AWAY
INTO SPACE
THIS ISN'T HAPPENING

HELP
HELP
HELP
SPSS
BZT,
?
MM
MN
BZZZ
ZZ
BZZ
MMMM
BZZZZ
ZZZT
PFFT
PFFT
M
SPSS
SST
SPSST
SPSST
MSPST
BZZST
SPZZST
I DON'T
BELIEVE
THIS
OH!
ZIT
ZIT ZIT
ZIT
ZIT
DR. WOO!...
I HAD AN
AWFUL
DREAM!
THAT WAS
NO DREAM,
MR. BURNS
THAT WAS
NO DREAM
END

GUIDE DOGS

©'87 M·K·BROWN
Frank, watch out!
For Pete's Sake.
Whoops!
I wouldn't if I were you, Marion,
I just wouldn't.
Say, Anthony, don't you think you should eat something before you have another beer? You still have to drive the Indy 500, remember.
Let's get out of here, Phil. This place is a dump.
Just look at what you're doing! First you dropped your car keys into that bag of spinach, and now you're putting the whole thing into the vegetable bin. You'll never find your car keys there, Kristine.
Stan, if you want my opinion, I'd sell Nat. Res. and I'd hold off on the Con. Cap. for two weeks, or at least until we see the prospectus.
My bowl is empty, Stan.
Isn't this nice? Sure beats doing taxes, doesn't it, Neil?
Sure does, Sparky, thanks a lot.

©1986 M·K·BROWN
THE RIGHT BRAIN AND THE WRONG BRAIN
RIGHT
January 2, 1987
Dear Louise,
Harry and I were overjoyed
with the exquisite coffee mak-
er, which now holds a pro-
minent place in our kitchen.
I have always war
WRONG
enjoyed
now holds a
I have
always wanted a
RIGHT
Macy's
WRONG
Macy's
RIGHT
WRONG
RIGHT
RIGHT
WRONG
WRONG

©1986 M·K·BROWN

LET'S DO THE WHITE GIRL TWIST (LIKE WE DID LAST SUMMER)

MARRIAGE MIRAGE

FREE GLUE SAMPLE!
© '87 M·K· BROWN
OH MY GOD!
I've just received a free glue sample!
FREE GLUE
Maybe I should glue something!
I could glue all my shoes together!
ha ha ha
I could glue these drapes together.
I could glue the lamp to the telephone,
Or, the telephone to the table.
But why would I do that?
That's stupid.
Why should I have to glue everything just because it comes in the mail?
Well,
maybe just this one little item.

©1986 M·K·BROWN
ESPEAKINK SPANICH en MACY'S
JHAU DO JOU DO?
I BEG YOUR PARDON?
SQUEEZE ME, DO JOU ESPEAK ENGLAISH?
OH!
SÍ, SÍ, SEÑOR.
¡ES POSIBLE HABLO INGLÉS CON TODOS LOS VECES!
¿QUÉ?
I SAID YES, I SPEAK ENGLÉS WHAT DO YOU WANT?
WELL,
I WOULD LIKE UN BRASSIÉR; 36D, POR MI AMIGA, CON RED LACE CERCA DE THE CENTRO Y CON SOME TASSELS POR LAS OTRAS COSAS.
OH,
QUÉ VERY TRISTE,
NO, I'M SORRY, WE . . .
ONLY HAVE WHAT'S THERE.
ADIÓS!
ADIÓS. Y GRACIAS POR NADA.
YOU ARE QUITE WELCOME, AND GRACIAS TO YOU POR SHOPPING MACY'S

SINGLES BAR
M.K.BROWN ©1979

HI THERE MY NAME IS ANDREW MY FRIENDS CALL ME ANDREW WHAT'S YOUR NAME?

CAROL

WELL, CAROL! WHAT DO YOU THINK ABOUT THE WAY I'M SITTING?

WHAT DO YOU MEAN?

I MEAN REALLY- DO YOU LIKE MY ELBOW RESTING ON MY KNEE THIS WAY?

TOO COCKY? TOO STRANGE?
I BEG YOUR PARDON?

ARE YOU DEAF?
WHAT?

HOW ABOUT THIS!

OR THIS?

CAROL! DON'T GO AWAY! I WAS JUST KIDDING AROUND HA HA HA HA

SAY!

WHAT DO YOU THINK ABOUT THIS?

HUH?

SERIOUSLY CAROL! EVER SEE ANYBODY DO THIS?

WELL, GOODBY CAROL! IT WAS NICE MEETING YOU!

JULIE DOUCET

Born December 31, 1965, at Montreal, Quebec Province, Canada. . . . I'm French. Childhood without problems. Then adolescence: I went to a convent with nuns and Jesus. Girls only (except Jesus). We were wearing a green polyester costume . . . GRWXZT! After, the university: fine arts. But I left after three years to do comics. I went on welfare and began to publish my own mini comic, *Dirty Plotte,* both in French and English. At the same time I discovered the wonderful world of American comics and started to send my cartoons to some magazines. . . . My first appearance is in *Heck! Comic Art of the Late 1980s.* Then in *Weirdo, Wimmen's Comix, Buzzard, Rip-Off, Drawn & Quarterly.* In two years I've published fourteen mini comics. Then, recently, *Dirty Plotte* became a real regular comic book(!) published by *Drawn & Quarterly.* Uh well, that's it for the moment, I think. . . .

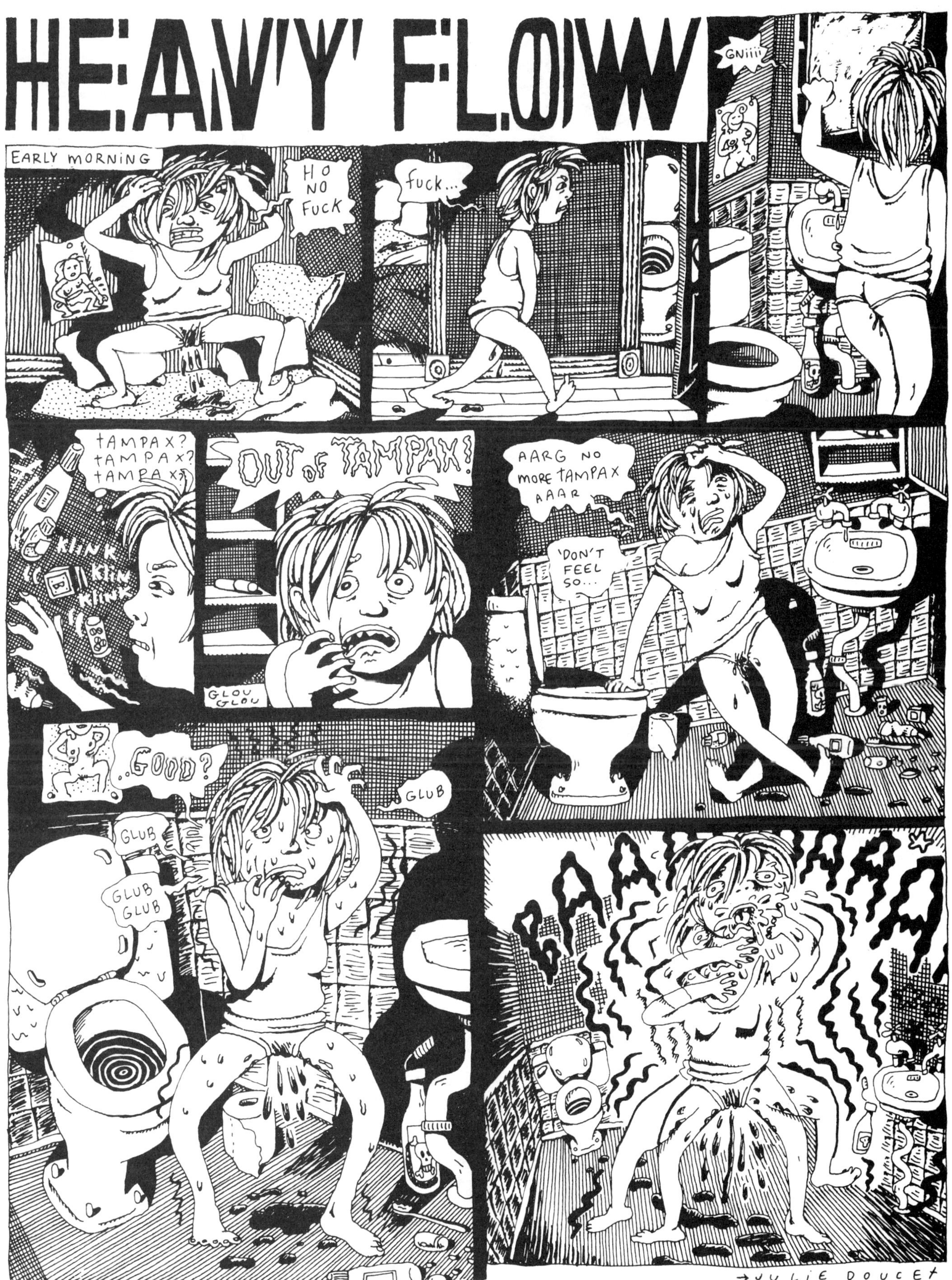
HEAVY FLOW
EARLY MORNING
HO NO FUCK
fuck...
GNiiii
TAMPAX? TAMPAX? TAMPAX?
KLINK
KLIN
KLINK
OUT OF TAMPAX!
GLOU GLOU
AARG NO MORE TAMPAX AAAR
'DON'T FEEL SO...
...GOOD?
GLUB
GLUB
GLUB GLUB
→JULIE DOUCET

URRRRGL
CRR
CRAC
CRR
CRR
CRR
URRRR
BANG BANG BANG
CRASH
416
BING BANG SMASH'EM UP...
CRASH
A FEW FEET LATER...
SPICE
22
J. DOUCET

FUCK!
HUR
UUR
KORTEX
?!
B-2
MM! SMELLS FISHY!
SNIF?
julie doucet

HU?
DRUGSTORE
RUMMAGE
RUMMAGE
TAMPAX
TAMPAX
END
julie doucet

THE MAGIC NECKLACE
BY JULIE DOUCET 88
TRANSLATED BY MICHAEL WILL
"MY MOTHER GAVE IT TO ME"
I DUN NO!
HONEY, WHAT A PECULIAR NECKLACE!
YES, IT'S MADE OF TEETH. IT'S VERY, VERY ANCIENT...
JULIE WHERE THE HELL IS THAT NECKLACE OF TEETH?
"AND IT WAS HER MOTHER WHO GAVE IT TO HER."
YOO HOO MOTHER? ARE YOU ASLEEP?
"WHEN I WAS LITTLE, MY GRANDMA SPOKE OF THE NECKLACE..."
GOT YOUR EYE ON THIS, DON'TCHA? WELL, WHEN I WAS A WEE SMALL GIRL...
AAH!
MY OWN SAINTLY MOTHER GAVE IT TO ME
WILL YOU TAKE THIS AND GO AWAY? I'M TRYING TO WORK!
MERCI MMAN
AND DOWN THROUGH THE AGES...
MY CHILD, YOU ARE OFF TO THE NEW WORLD. GO WITH GOD AND TAKE THIS...
YES YES YES
THIS IS YOURS NOW. WEAR IT ALWAYS - IT WILL BRING YOU WEALTH AND BEAUTY
J.D. 88

A NOBLE WOMAN GAVE IT TO ME...
RÉVOLUTION LIBERTE! YEAH!
A MORT A MORT
MY, WHAT A LOVELY HEAD
....ON HER DEATH BED.
TCHAC
CAUGHT-CHA!
WITH MAGIC...
...I DIVINED ITS UNIQUE HISTORY!
WHY, IT'S AN INFUSION OF HORSE TEETH... A PANACEA! NEVER MUST I PART WITH IT
MM
WHAT'S GOING ON?!
THIS, CHILD, WILL CURE ALL OUR PAIN!...
HA!
COUIC
HA LAA SERVOISE QUE J'AI BUUUE HIER SOUERR
TCHING TCHING
PINK PINK PINK
TING TING
ALMS FOR THE POOR!
REPEAT AFTER ME, I, III, IIII, IV, ...
I
II
V
IIII
I III UM
GRAT
I'VE GOT SOMETHING FOR YOU!
OOH IT'S GORGEOUS!
OOOH
JD 88

WHERE DID YOU FIND IT?
WELL, YESTERDAY WE WERE CRUCIFYING THIS GUY...
YESTERDAY
GET UP!!
PAW!
CNI!
SHLOK
SHLAC
SIDDOWN!
BUMP
CAN YOU HANG AROUND FOR A SEC? I GOTTA TAKE A LEAK
M...
BOUUH
BOUUH
HAAA
SUDDENLY
POC
POC
POC
?!
HO
A TOOTH!?
ROTTEN
PTUI
OH... I GET IT.
KOF
SAY, THEY'RE KINDA PRETTY
EASY TO POKE A HOLE...
CROUII
CROUII
CROUII
CROUII
CROUIII
CROUII
CROUII
CRR
END
j.d. 88

"MY CONSCIENCE IS BUGGING ME"
BY JULIE DOUCET 1989

SO, WHERE TO NOW?
WE GO HOME.
PTOUI

AS USUAL!..
URGL

HEY! CALM DOWN!
JEALOUS! JEALOUS!
HA HA

HE! HO! STOP!
mm?
?

YEAH!
OH BOY
FFART!

WOW! WHAT A HUNK!
?
ENOUGH!!

HO NO! I KNOW HIM!
OOOH DARLING WHAT'S YOUR PLEA-SURE? OOUH
HELLO JULIE ...EUH
YEEEAHH HI! HI!

HE HE HE HEY GOOD LOOKIN'
BYE
BYE!

HEY THAT'S ENOUGH! GET OFF THAT CAR!
C'MON RELAX!

HUMPF! RELAX YOURSELF!
SLURP
OH YOU DON'T DESERVE TO HAVE ME FOR YOUR CONSCIENCE
YOURE SO A FUCKING DEADBEAT!

YOU! YOU'RE KILLING ME!
HEY! i'M REALLY GETTING TO YOU!

OH YEAH SHE'S REALLY GETTING TO ME!!!
BITCH!

I DON'T KNOW WHERE I'M AT ANYMORE...

MY BRAINS ARE SCRAMBLED!

...I'M ALWAYS UNSHAKEABLE... COOL AS A CUCUMBER!
PEE PEE 2E SAILOR

ONE DAY IT'S GONNA BE TOO MUCH!

!!!
OH... IT'S YOU....

KISS
...

END
JD 89

VIVE LA DIFFÉRENCE!

(HURRAY FOR THE DIFFERENCE!)

SHE EATS FROZEN MEALS AND SHE SLEEPS ON A BLOCK OF ICE!
miom miom
So i LAY ON TOP OF HER FOR WARMTH
PSSCH
PSSCH
PSSH
PSSCH
i'M HER BOY FRIEND!
mm
mmm
PSSCH
AFTER...
YOUR BED IS FULL OF FROZEN DiRT!
YES, TiME TO CHANGE iT THEN
READY?
GO!
BRRR!
PAGE 2 J.D. 89

WE'LL FILL IT UP.
O.K
HEY LOOK AT ALL THESE NIFTY THINGS
...HAIR, BLOOD, SPERM, BOOGERS, KLEENEX ....
IT'S LIKE A PAINTING
A PAINTING? WHY YES!
THE DAY AFTER
MODERN ART MUSEUM
HERE IS YOUR $5000.00 THAT PAINTING IS ASTOUNDING!
THA THANK YOU VERY MUCH!
YOU'RE WELCOME
PIT
COME ON WERE GONNA BUY A FUR COAT FOR YOU!
HA YOU!
END PAGE 3 J.D. '89

PROLOGUE
JULIE! YOU'RE 14 NOW, YOU SHOULD WEAR A BRA! YOU'RE A WOMAN
YES MOM
MATH
GEO

GO TO HELL MOM!!! NEVER! i'LL NEVER WEAR THAT THiNG!!
OKAY i'M GOING TO SEE MY ESTHETICIAN... SEE YOU LATER!
YEAH MOM BYE mom!

AND i STILL DONT WEAR A BRA!
MY BREAST iS SMALL AND SOLiD ANYWAY...
BEEP BEEP!
1990

"BUT NOT SMALL ENOUGH TO BE UNSEEN!..."
HEY LOOK AT THESE SUGAR TITS!
UMPF!.. PIGS!

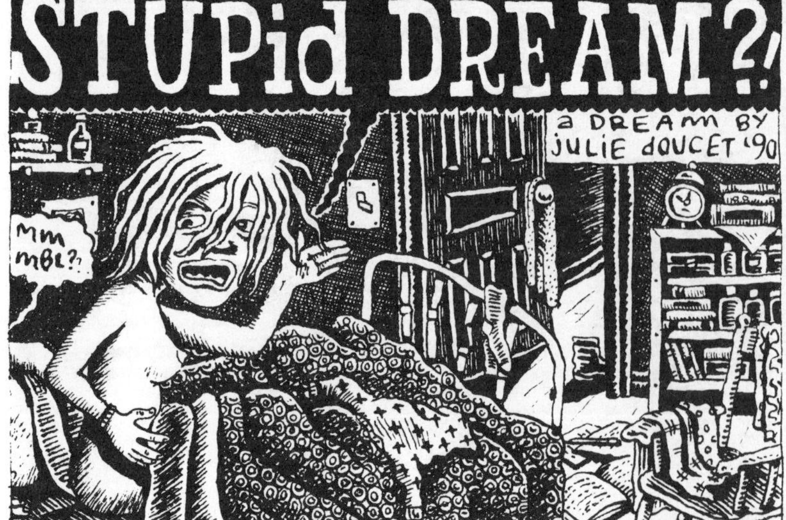
SO Why i had that STUPid DREAM?!
a DREAM BY julie doucet '90
mm mBL?!

i'M SO HAPPY i'M GONNA BUY MYSELF A BRA!
MAX
ONE

3RD FLOOR LADIES
BRAS
SALE
CASH
WOW... LOTS OF PEOPLE HERE!
SECURITY BRA
UH NO NO NOT THAT ONE...
SPORT STYLE $15.99
HO! THAT'S FOR ME!
MODERN BRAS NEW
YEEAH NICE MODEL!
OOPS IT'S NOT MY SIZE
BRA NEW
TWO

OH SHiiiiT!!!?
BRA NEW
Hu! UNBELIE-VABLE!
FUCK!!! THAT MODEL WAS REALLY JUST MADE FOR ME WHAT i'M GONNA DO NOW !!?? IT'S NOT FAIR!
2ND FLO TOYS
MY GOD!! WHAT HAPPENED HERE!!?
COUGH IT... IT'S HA NU-CLEAR BOMB MISSSS...
CRR...
IT... COUGH
A NU-CLEAR BOMB!?
ALL RIGHT!! SO EVERYBODY MUST BE DEAD TOO AT THE LADIES SECTION!
UP STAIRS
THE... THE PLACE IS EMPTY!
3RD FLOOR LADIES
WHAT THE HELL DOES IT MEAN!??
THREE J.D.'90 END

ALINE KOMINSKY-CRUMB

I was born in Long Beach, Long Island, in 1948. My mother went into labor on a yacht. I spent my first seventeen years in an upper middle class ghetto, surrounded by ostentatious materialism and rabid upward striving. My parents fluctuated between tenuous prosperity and abject poverty. They fought constantly. This was a fertile breeding ground for "The Young Bunch," a comic persona I developed in my early twenties. To say that I never fit into this world of "post-war jerks" is an understatement (I can perversely brag that no boy in high school ever asked me out), but such intense alienation has provided me with years of comic-tragic material. Even now, a short visit home to Long Island or North Miami Beach keeps me going for months.

I graduated from Lawrence High School in 1966, became wild and promiscuous, took any drug offered to me, attended S.U.N.Y. New Paltz (ran away pregnant), went to Cooper Union for one semester and finally managed to earn a BFA in painting from the University of Arizona, a swell, fun school. During this period I started writing and illustrating stories about my life to "crack up" my pals.

At age twenty-two I moved to San Francisco and started drawing comics "for real." I was influenced by cartoonists Justin Green, Kim Deitch, and R. Crumb as well as George Grosz, Freida Kahlo, and Matisse. I published my first story in 1971 in *Wimmen's Comix #1*. Since then I have had a checkered career. I edited a benefit book, *El Perfecto*, for Tim Leary (I later found out his girlfriend bought a stereo with the money). I did stories for later issues of *Wimmen's Comix*, *Lemme Outta Here*, *Arcade*, *Manhunt*, and others. I had two solo books come out in the mid-late seventies, *Power Pak#1* and *#2*, as well as a first *Twisted Sisters* with Diane Noomin and two issues of *Dirty Laundry* with my husband, Robert Crumb (we each drew ourselves in the same panel). I finally became editor of *Weirdo* magazine in 1987. I put out ten issues of that great publication and have just laid it to rest, not without some sadness.

Right now I'm working on more autobiographical stories and painting some deeply disturbing oil portraits. I'm about to pack up and move to France with my husband and daughter.

I'm very excited and deeply satisfied that this version of *Twisted Sisters* exists!

A SCAM A DAY
by Aline Ricky Goldsmith Kominsky-Crumb
© 1989
NEVER NEEDS PAINTING
QUALITY SIDING
thriving neurosis
STUDEBAKERS
DIAMONDS
stoopid values
LOSER SCHEMES
OPEN SESAME GARAGE DOOR OPENERS
Bad Taste
GROWING UP AS
ARNIE'S GIRL
FUCKIN' JERKS
YOU SAID THE "F" WORD... DADDY!
AWRIGHT AWRIGHT!! GIVE 'EM BACK THEIR GODDAMN MONEY! SCHMUCKS!
I STARTED OUT AS THE LITTLE PRINCESS..... THE FIRST PRECIOUS GRANDCHILD!
YA GONNA MARRY A DOCTAH!
OH MY GHOD SHE LOOKS LIKE RITA HAYWORTH! GAWGEOUS!!
OBJECT OF FASCINATION TO NEW POP ARNIE!
I'M SO FUCKIN' BAD... HOW'D I MAKE THIS PERFECT CREATURE??
I PERFORMED LIKE A TRAINED CHIMP...
SHIRLEY TEMPLE
TAKE ME BACK TO MY LITTLE GRASS SHACK IN HILO...
THE FIRST FEW YEARS WERE GOOD... I DIDN'T NOTICE THE PSYCHOTIC EDGE YET!
BUNCH WUVS HUHR BAYBEE!

AT AGE 4½ MY BROTHER WAS BORN & MY PARENTS MOVED US TO THEIR POST WAR JERK DREAM HOME.
WHAT'S WRONG WITH AKKIE?
YEAH, WHAT'S THAT BABY GOT TO BE MISRAHBLE ABOUT?
LOOK AT THIS GAWGEOUS HOUSE HE'S BAWN IN!!
WAH! WAH!
I'LL TAKE HIM TO THE DOCTAH.
THINGS GOT WORSE... MY BROTHER WAS DIFFERENT...
FAGGOT!
THAT STOOPID THING IS NOT ALIVE!
POOR TEDDY... HE'S SO SAD
HE WANTS TO DIE.
CUT THAT SNIVELING!
GIMME THAT!
WE'RE GONNA PLAY FOOTBALL!
NO LEAVE US ALONE I DON' WANNA!
DON'T BE SO MEAN T'HIM DADDY!
HEY BUD OUT BIG MOUTH!
SO YA WANNA STICK YA BIG FAT NOSE IN EVERYBODY'S BIZNISS HUH??
HE'S RIGHT I DON'T KNOW ANYTHING!
JUST LIKE HUHR MUTHAH!
I WAS ONLY TRYING TO PROTECT AKKIE!
YOU DON' KNOW NUTHIN' YUR A STOOPID GIRL... GIRLS DON' KNOW SHIT!!
YA GOT THAT!
WHY DON'T YA LEAVE HER ALONE?!
ARE YOUEW TELLIN' ME HOW TA' HANDLE THESE MONSTAHS?!
YEAH, I AM! I GOT SOME RIGHTS AROUND HERE!
SHIT YOU DO. I DON' SEE YOU PAYIN' THE BILLS!
WELL WE WOULDN'T EVEN HAVE THIS GAWGEOUS HOUSE IF MY FATHER HADN'T PAID FOR IT!
I MADE THEM FIGHT.
I COME FROM A HI-CLASS FAMILY.. NOT SCUM LIKE YOURS!
GIRLS HAFTO BE GOOD OR ELSE MEN GO WILD!
YA SPOILED PIECE O' SHIT... FAT ASS CUNT!
GOOD... GO SNIVEL TO YOUR MOMMY ......
TEDDY WANTS TO DIE
I HATE YOU... I'M GONNA CALL MY MOTHER!
BAD SEED COMPLEX

BIZNIZZ WAS BAD...
GAWD-DAM CHEAP JEWS 6 ORDAHS CANCELLED TODAY.. I GOTTA COME UP WITH SOME NEW HYPE FOR THESE SCHMUCKS!
HEY EVERYONE, I'M HOME!
SPOILED BRATS!
WHERE'S YA MUTHAH?
SHE'S NEXT DOOR HAVIN' CAWFEE!
LAZY SLOB
I'M YUR FATHAH... DON' I GET A HULLO OR NUTHIN' HUH??
OH HI DADDY... HOW WAS YUR DAY??
ROTTEN!
WHAT'D YOUSE KIDS DO TAHDAY?
HI DA DA!
OH.. WE PLAYED, I HAD A BALLET LESSON AN' AKKIE WENT TO HIS PSYCHIATRIST
MOMMY HAD A BAD HEADACHE!
SEE YA LATER WE'RE GONNA WATCH CAPTAIN VIDEO NOW.
GIN
FULL GROWN BY AGE 9!
MY GHOD LOOK AT THAT ASS! ITS FABULOUS.. SHE'S GONNA TURN INTO A SLUT NOW!
STILL AN INNOCENT KID.
MUCH TO MY HORROR...
GOTTA PINCH THAT THING!
THIS FINE ASS IS GONNA GET YOU BY HONEY!
SHUD UP DADDY YUR GROSS.. YUCK DON'T SAY THAT STUFF.
BEDDER GET USE TO IT
I HATE IT.. DON'T PAY ATTENTION TO IT!
ITS SO BIG + OUT THERE..
THIS IS FUN.. I GOT HUHR ALL IN A CONIPTION!
EVEN WORSE...
I WONDER IF I CAN PLUCK THESE HAIRS OUT?!
I DON' WANNA GROW UP... EVEN THO I HATE BEING A KID LIVING WITH MY PARENTS!
BUDDING BREASTS!*
HIPS STARTING TO BLOSSOM.
ALL THE GROWN UPS I KNOW ARE VERY YUCKY... ESPECIALLY THE MEN... I HATE THEM!
*THEY'VE NEVER GOTTEN BIGGER!
I OVERHEARD ARNIE + HIS PAL PUNCHIE..
YEAH PUNCH YA GOTTA SEE THAT KID'S ASS! SHIT ITS MAGNIFICENT!
OH YEAH... I'LL HAFTO CHECK IT OUT! BEDDAH WATCH HUHR LIKE A HAWK SHE'LL WANNA SCHTUP BEFORE YA KNOW IT!
OVAH MY DEAD BODY... I'LL KILL ANY ONE THAT I CATCH WITH HUHR!
YEAH THAT'S RIGHT ARNIE.
GIN

I TRIED TO KEEP A LOW PROFILE, BUT.....
PERVERT NEIGHBOR...
LEONARD, JUST LEAVE ME ALONE!
HEY C'MERE BUNCHIE, I GOT SOMETHIN' TO SHOW YOU!
LOOSE MAN'S SHIRT TRYIN' TO HIDE BODY
C'MON DON'T YOU TRUST ME?!
NO LEONARD I DON'T... YOU'VE SQUIRTED ME ALREADY!
MEANWHILE MY MOTHER GOT BIGGER & NASTIER...
GET AWAY ARNIE, YUR SUCH AN ANIMAL!
C'MON SWEETS AREN'T YA GONNA LET ME??
I HATE MYSELF.
I HAVE THE CURSE!
MONEY GOT TIGHTER... ARNIE WAS A DESPERATE LOSER... I WAS PAINFULLY AWARE...
LOOK DADDY I GOT ALL A'S
GREAT...I'LL PAY YA $10 FOR EVERY A!
WHY DAD?
'CAUSE.. I'M GONNA MAKE NIGGERS* BUY EXPENSIVE ENCYCLOPEDIAS YOU DUMB LITTLE SHIT!
REPORT CARD
THAT'S NOT RIGHT DAD!
WHAT, WHAT YA SAY YA LITTLE BITCH?? YEW LIKE LIVIN' IN LUXURY HUH? HUH?? WELL HOW DO YOU THINK I GET MONEY??
I DUNNO, BUT I DON'T CARE IF WE LIVE IN A BIG HOUSE WITH A MAID!
I'D BE HAPPY IN AN APARTMENT... ALL THIS STUFF DOESN'T MATTER!
YEW.. WAN' THE WHOLE FUCKIN' WORLD TO THINK I'M A FAILURE?!
DESTINED TO BE A REBELLIOUS BOHEMIAN!!
ARNIE HAS A BREAKDOWN...
WHAT A MOUTH ON YEW.. I'M GONNA SHUT IT UP!!
NO.. LEAVE ME ALONE DADDY!
HELP STOP GLUG GLUG
BIRTH OF SEXUAL MASOCHISM
LATER HE'S CONTRITE....
JEEZ..HE'S SO GROSS WHEN HE'S BEING PATHETIC!
I'M SORRY KID... I DUNNO WHAT CAME OVER ME!
I GOT A LOT O' PRESSURE ON ME.. YUR MOTHER'S NOT NICE TO ME!
I UNDERSTAND DADDY.. I'M NOT MAD IT WAS MY FAULT FOR MAKING YOU SO ANGRY!
* SORRY..HE USED HORRIBLE WORDS!

HE BOUGHT ME EXPENSIVE UNWANTED GIFTS... I HAD TO ACT EXTREMELY APPRECIATIVE!
OH WOW! HOW TERRIFIC! I'VE ALWAYS WANTED TO BE LIKE LLOYD BRIDGES ON SEA HUNT!
I FEEL SO DUMB..
YEAH + I'M GONNA PAY FOR THE BEST LESSONS MONEY CAN BUY!
THANKS DADDY I'M VERY EXCITED... I CAN'T WAIT!
YA LOOK LIKE A REAL PRO IN THAT OUTFIT!
MY MOTHER SCREAMED AT HIM FOR SPENDING MONEY ON ME..
YOU'RE AN IGNORAMOUS.. WE GOT PILES O'BILLS + NO FOOD IN THE FRIDGE + YOU BUY HUHR THIS EXPENSIVE CRAP... YA JERK!
YOU'RE TAKIN' IT ALL BACK!
DON'T TELL ME WHAT TO DO WITH MY DOUGH!!!
WHY AM I SO BAD + UGLY TOO?
WITH THAT FACE SHE NEEDS MORE THAN THAT STUFF!
I WANNA FIND HUHR SOME RICH SCHLUB HUS-BAND... SHE NEEDS FANCY LESSONS!
I TRIED TO COVER UP MY ZITS + DISGUISE MY FLAWS...
I NEED MORE PANCAKE!
HEY HURRY UP IN THERE GAWGEOUS...
YA CAN'T SHINE SHIT!
YEARS LATER: I WENT TO COLLEGE, TOOK DRUGS GOT DRUNK, PREGNANT, RAN AWAY + WAS HAVING A WILD TIME.
HEY YOU BEAUTIFUL SEXY TOTALLY RIPE WOMAN!
I WANNA MAKE LOVE TO YOU!
LET'S GET HIGH!
SLUM GODDESS
MAKE LOVE NOT WAR
ARNIE FOUND OUT ALL ABOUT MY SINS + HE WAS STRANGELY AWED BY MY FEARLESSNESS... THEN HE DIED OF CANCER..
YA KNOW I GIVE YA CREDIT FOR HAVIN' THAT BABY + GETTIN' IT ADOPTED + NOT TELLIN YUR MOTHER.
YOU DO? I THOUGHT YOU'D SAY I SHOULD'A' TOLD ER!
NAH SHE'D'VE NEVAH LET YOU FAHGET IT.. SHE'D DRIVE US BOTH NUTS!*
YA GOT GUTS!
ARNIE'S BEEN DEAD FOR YEARS NOW... BUT I SOME-TIMES IMAGINE WHAT HE'D BE UP TO NOW??
SPAS
INFLAT-ABLE
FAULTY GYM EQUIPMENT
$1.99 PER MONTH
SOLAR POWERED
HOME TANNING BOOTHS
HYDROPONICS
QUICK-WEIGHT LOSS SCHEMES
FAT BUSTERS
STARCH BLOCKER
HIGH COLONIC
FACE LIFT IN A JAR
secret EGYPTIAN FORM-ULA
CRYSTAL HAIR GROW CAP
I'M SURE GLAD THE HUBBY IS NICE TO OUR DAUGHTER!
YEAH... MY FATHER WAS A CHARACTER.. AND ITS EASIER TO THINK KINDLY OF HIM WHEN HE'S NOT AROUND TO TORTURE ME!
IS THIS THE END?
* SHE STILL DOESN'T KNOW + WON'T UNLESS SHE READS THIS... OR YOU TELL HER!

WON TONS...
LET'S HAVE TAKE-OUT TONITE
HOT N' GREASY
By Aline (ALWAYS ON A DIET) KOMINSKY CRUMBOWITZ
MOO GOO GAIPAN
THURSDAY SPECIAL
CHINA-JADE
FREE DELIVERY
CAN USE CHOP STICKS
LUCSHIOUS NOODLES
US JEWS LOVE CHINESE FOOD

THE WOMEN IN MY FAMILY REALLY KNOW HOW TO EAT.
MMM.. THESE RIBS ARE SOO JUICY..
EGG ROLLS NOT GREASY
WANT ONE?
YEA SHURE PASS 'EM.
I ♥ FRIED RICE

BUT THEY HATE TO COOK...
CALL VINNIE'S WILL YA PLEASE?!
THERE'S NOTHING TO EAT HERE!!
I DUNNO WHAT TO MAKE!
FRIGIDAIRE
YEA GOOD IDEA BERNIE... I'LL ORDAH AN X-LARGE GARBAGE PIZZA & 2 SIDES OF GARLIC BREAD... AWRIGHT!?
YEA SHURE TAHRIFFIC

BUT ALAS.. POOR ME STRANDED OUT HERE IN CALIFORNIA, EPICENTER OF BLAND FOOD,... THIS FRESH AIR MAKES ME HUNGRY...
IT'S SO SWEET & HEALTHY HERE.. I GUESS I'M LUCKY.
I CAN HAVE FRESH HOME GROWN FOOD.
BUT I'D KILL FOR A HOT PASTRAMI ON RYE WITH RUSSIAN DRESSING, COLESLAW & AN EGG CREAM TO GO!

OH IF I COULD JUST SPEND AN HOUR AT WOLFIE COHEN'S RASCAL HOUSE IN N. MIAMI BEACH..
WHAT'LL IT BE HONEY?
FREE KOSHER PICKLES
FREE PICKLED BEETS
FREE COLESLAW
FREE SOUR TOMATOES
CHARMING WAITPERSONS MEMORIZE YOUR ORDER
FREE ROLLS & BAGELS
rumble
FOOD ON THE BRAIN

OF COURSE, THE MOST FUN IS TAKING THIS FAB-FARE HOME TO ENJOY IN PRIVATE WITH INTIMATE FRIENDS AND FAMILY...
AWRIGHT, WHO HAD THE CHEESE BLINTZES?
BRISKET
FLANKEN WITH NOODLES
SMOKED WHITEFISH
WHERE'S MY LATKES?
The Original Wolfie's
MIAMI BEACH
NOTHING MORE REASSURING... WITTY REPARTEE... FALCONCREST IN THE BACKGROUND....
SO YOU THINK I'M GONNA GET HEARTBURN!
PASS THE BAGELS.
I NEVAH SAID THAT!
YOU GIVE ME INDIGESTION!
MMMM
OH MY GAWD!
PEPSI
THEN EVERYONE CAN FLOP ON A CHAISE LOUNGE
NICE PIECE O CHAWCLATE?
CAWFEE ANYONE?
JUST BLEW MY DIET!
I'LL GO VOMIT
WILL YA LISTEN TO ALL THOSE RESCUE SQUAD SIRENS... THEY'RE DROPPING LIKE FLIES OVAH HERE!! OI!! SIGH!
YEA.. SO HOWSE THE NEW MALL GOING ACROSS THE CANAL WHEN'R THEY GONNA FINISH IT AWREDDY...??
BUT NOW BACK TO MY PRESENT PREDICAMENT.. WHAT DOES OUR LITTLE RURAL TOWN HAVE TO OFFER WHEN I HAVE THOSE DESPARATE CRAVINGS?
WE HAVE OUR OWN LITTLE CHINESE RESTAURANT WITH TAKE-OUT.
EGG ROLL - TOMATO BEEF CHOW MEIN, MU SHU PORK, CHICKEN + BROCOLLI
SMELLS GOOD!
OH MY GHOD.. THEY GAVE ME MUSTARD, KETCHUP + TACO SAUCE... NO DUCK SAUCE...!!
WRAWNG KIND OF NOODLES!
KETCHUP
MUSTARD
TACO SAUCE
CHINA CORRAL
STYROFOAM CONTAINERS.
WHAD DO I CARE?! I WASH IT DOWN WITH SOME CALIFORNIA WINE!
AFTER EATING I HAVE A THROBBING MSG HEADACHE......
BES' LIL' PIZZA IN TOWN!
PIZZA PATIO
JES' LIKE HOMEADE!
FLATTENED WHITE BREAD WITH AMERICAN CHEESE... CAMPBELLS TOMATO SOUP... SLICED HOT DOGS + CANNED PINEAPPLE!!!....
MY NEIGHBOR WHO RAISES HORSES RECOMMENDED THIS!
L-LEWS LIL' CHEF..
UNKOSHER DOG NO ONIONS NO FRESH TOMATOES GOYISH MUSTARD
EVERYTHING'S CALLED LIL'.. AIN'T THAT CUTE?
HOWSE IT GOIN' ARLEEN?
OH FINE LEW... NICE DAY!
ITS BIG
ITS CHEAP
I EAT IT... BUT ITS ONLY A SAD REMINDER OF A JUICY KOSHER HEBREW NATIONAL ON A STEAMED BUN WITH A REAL PICKLE.
ASTROTURF FLOOR

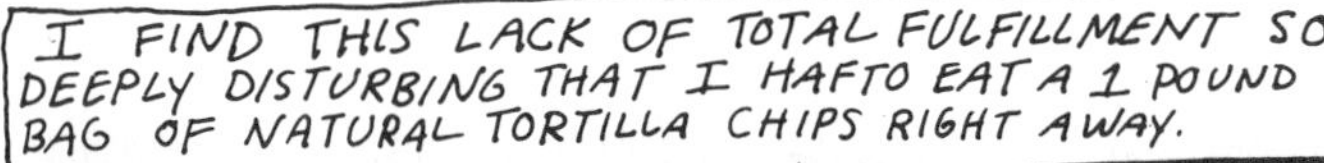
I FIND THIS LACK OF TOTAL FULFILLMENT SO DEEPLY DISTURBING THAT I HAFTO EAT A 1 POUND BAG OF NATURAL TORTILLA CHIPS RIGHT AWAY.

NOW I'M A BLOATED FEEDBAG FROM ALL THIS SALT + GREASE...

SO DO YOU FIND YURSELF ASKING... IF SHE'S SO MISERABLE WHY DOES SHE STAY IN SUCH A CULTURAL DESERT?? SHE'S AN AHTIST SHE COULD LIVE IN PARIS FOR GOD SAKE!!
MAYBE I'M JUST COMFORTABLE WITH MY ALIENATION
PERHAPS I JUST LOVE TO COMPLAIN?!
VERY NEGATIVE BEHAVIOR PATTERN... BUT IF IT WORKS??
MAYBE I SHOULD LEAVE FOR AWHIE.. A TRIP EAST BACK TO MY ETHNIC ROOTS!

SO INSTEAD OF FRUITLESS FANTASIES I GO DIRECTLY TO LONG ISLAND AND END UP AT MY COUSIN IRENE'S HOUSE..
SO HOWSE THE HICKS OUT THERE IN CALIFAWNYA? WHADD'YA THINK OF MY NEW KITCHEN?
WHAD'RE WE GONNA DO FUR DINNER
WE'LL ORDAH TAKE-OUT HOW 'BOUT SUSHI?
IT LOOKS GREAT.. THE FRIDGE IS YUGE...
NAH, ITS NOT FILLING.. I LIKE THAT NEW ETHIOPIAN THEY GIVE YA ALOT!
HOW ABOUT DELI?

OI, WE'RE SICK O' DELI... WE HAD IT 4 TIMES LAST WEEK!
HOW 'BOUT THAT WESTUHN BAR-B-QUE THEY GOT STEAK 'N CHILI, RIBS + MISQUITE GRILLES!! ITS THE LATEST THING!!
THEY GIVE YA ALOT TA' EAT... GOOD VALUE.. VERY FILLING!
YOU'LL LIKE IT.. YA LOVE THAT WESTUHN LIFE DONCHA?!
ITS SOMETHING DIFFERENT FOR A CHANGE.

THEY IGNORE ME... THEY'RE TOO USED TO OUT-ARGUEING EACH OTHER!
WELL I WOULDN'T MIND CHINESE OR EQUADORIAN OR ARMENIAN
AWRIGHT... QUIET AWREDDY.. I'M CALLING BUCKAROO BAR-B-QUE....

SO I HAVE A CHILI DOG THAT TASTES ALL WRONG BUT FOR TOTALLY DIFFERENT REASONS. IT TASTES TOO JEWISH!
THE DOG IS HIGH QUALITY KOSHER BUT THE CHILI IS TASTELESS LIKE MY GRANDMOTHER'S ITALIAN FOOD.. THIS IS KINDA LIKE KETCHUP + OVERCOOKED MEATLOAF WITH A FEW BAKED BEANS THROWNIN!
THIS HOT DOG GIVES ME DEEP INSIGHT.......

FOOD & EMOTIONS.. I FONDLY THINK OF PAST NURTURING... MY GRANDMA FANNY'S HOUSE
HERE'S SOME MONEY MY SWEET LOVE... GET SOME BAGELS + LOX AT SCHILOWITZ'S & GET A TREAT FOR YA-SELF... I'LL FINISH MY CLEANING + THEN WE'LL EAT!!
OK NANNY I'LL BE BACK IN 15 MINITS
I'D LIKE A BLACK + WHITE COOKIE PLEASE..
HERE YA GO DEAH.- AN' SAY HULLO TO YUR GRANDMA FOR ME!
THANK YOU MRS. SCHILOWITZ... I WILL.........
I CRINGE WHEN I RECALL OTHER TIMES...
YA GAWD DAM ASSHOLE.. YA STOOPID MONSTAH!
SHUDDUP IN FRONT OF THE KID!
SCHMUCK!
GO GET YA-SELF A SAND-WICH AT HERB'S. GET OUTA HERE!
I'D LIKE TA KILL YOU
FOOD IS SO POWERFUL... ITS ALMOST PSYCH-EDELIC... A KALEIDASCOPE OF EATING + FEELING
VIN ROUGE
SUCH MEMORIES
BACK TO COUSIN IRENE'S.
OI MY ULCER IS ACTING UP AGAIN. IRENE.. GET THE MALOX... WIL YA PLEASE?
AWRIGHT.. I'M GOIN TA GET IT... I'M EXHAUSTED... I HAVE NO ENAHGEE.
HOW COME YOU LOOK SO HEALTHY?
YOU DON'T LOOK YUR AGE!
I DON'T FEEL TOO GREAT RIGHT NOW...
ONLY 39 YRS. OLD.. SAME AGE AS ME!
AHH! YOU LOOK FABULOUS!
SO SEVERAL DAYS LATER:
MMM.. I HEARD THAT DANDE-LIONS TASTE GOOD!
I HAFTO ADMIT I MISSED THIS SPARTAN LIFESTYLE!
SO I DON'T FIT IN.... I'M NOT A WHITE PERSON!!
BUT I HAVE LESS CELLULITE THAN MY COUSIN!
AND MY CHILD HAS BLONDE HAIR + LONG LEGS....
MAYBE I'M PART OF SOME... EVOLUTIONARY PROCESS!!
...END..

Le Bunché de Paree Turns 40

Glamor + Champagne

Romance Art

GET BACK I'M NOT READY!

STILL JUTS OUT.

NEEDS MORE SEX!

CUTE NEW FRENCH OUTFIT!

CAN STILL STAY UP 'TIL 5 AM 3 NIGHTS IN A ROW WITHOUT DRUGS!!

MOTHER

RESPONSIBILITY

KIDS

HOME IMPROVEMENTS

Time Lurches on... Especially when Your Having Fun!

YOU'D THINK IT WOULD ALL BE ANTI CLIMACTIC... AFTERALL, I'VE BEEN CALLING MYSELF "THE 40 YR. OLD HOUSEWIFE" FOR YEARS!!

WELL I'M REALLY 37½ BUT I'M SAYING I'M A 40 YR OLD HOUSEWIFE SO IT WON'T BE SUCH A SHOCK WHEN IT ACTUALLY HAPPENS!

OH I CAN'T BELIEVE YOU'RE 40... YOU DON'T LOOK THAT OLD!

WELL WORKING OUT HELPS!

I HOPE I LOOK THAT GOOD WHEN I'M OLD!

22 YR. OLD IN AEROBICS CLASS.

ON THE ACTUAL DAY OF MY 40th BIRTHDAY I WAS IN A CHATEAU* ON AN ISLAND IN THE MEDITERRANEAN...

WE KILLED THIS COCHÓN FOR YOUR BON ANIVERSAIR MADAM!!

YOU ARE THE MOST BEYUTEEFUL GUEST IN OUR PETIT VILLAGE MADAM CRUMB.... WE ARE HONORED TO HAVE YOU!!

I'M OVERWHELMED I DON'T KNOW WHAT TO SAY...

WELL LET'S EAT + DRINK!

GEE AT HOME IN CALIFAWNYER I'M AN OLD HAG AWREDDY... I HAFTO LEARN FRENCH!!

* BET YOU CAN GET A LOT OF SYMPATHY UP FOR ME!

I'M EATIN', DRINKIN' & SMOKIN' & I FEEL SO GREAT!!
I THINK I LOVE PATE' MORE THAN ANYTHING IN THE WORLD!
EVERY THING'S A STILL LIFE!
MORE THAN RED WINE?
THAT'S A HARD ONE.

IS THIS A CUBIST BUNCH FANTASY??
MAYBE I WENT TO TOO MANY MUSEUMS AT A FORMATIVE AGE!!
IF I CAN FIGURE THIS OUT I CAN ESCAPE FROM LONG ISLAND!!
I'LL JUST READ SOME BOOKS ABOUT AHT & POETRY & OTHER CULTURED STUFF... I'M GONNA REALLY STUDY THIS!

SOME O' THESE AHTISTS DIED REAL YOUNG BUT THEIR LIVES WERE SO INTENSE!
NOT LIKE MY FAMILY... THEY LIVE LONG & DULL LIVES..
Lust For Life
BRASAI
BRASAI
MOVEABLE FEAST

EVEN ARNIE PASSED ON SOME MYTHOLOGY
YEA... 1945 WAS THE BEST YEAR O' MY LOUSY LIFE!
WHY DADDY?
'CAUSE I WAS WITH MY BUDDIES IN PAREE & THERE WERE LOTS O' SWELL FRENCH BABES
WHAT'S PAREEE?
AHH ITS JUST THE BEST BURG IN THE WHOLE DAM WORLD...- THATS ALL YOU NEED TO KNOW!!
C'N I GO THERE?
NAH... NOT NOW... GO T' BED.. WIL YA PLEEZE!
S
P

ITS NO WONDER I HAVE A ROMANTIC OBSESSION ABOUT A PLACE!
THE MIND IS READY TO COME TO LIFE AFTER YEARS OF AESTHETIC DEPRIVATION!
L.I.

SOME PLACES REALLY DO LIVE UP TO OUR WILDEST EXPECTATIONS!!
OVERWHELMED BY FLOOD OF EMOTION

AND YET CERTAIN PERSISTANT REALITIES HAVE A WAY OF INTRUDING.
WHY DO THEY ALL HAVE RED GERANIUMS?
A WARM DAY IN PARIS... NOTHING I HAFTO DO!
RING RING
I MUST'VE DIED! & WENT TO HEAVEN!
ST. EMILION
AAAAA*..? I CAWLED TO WISH YOU A VERY WUNDAHFUL 40th BIRTHDAY DEAH!!
HOW'SE YUR HUSBAND ROHBIT... ALL BY HIMSELF THERE IN CALIFAWNYER?!
THANKS
YEAH, YEAH... SO I HOPE NOW THAT YUR 40 YOU'LL GROW UP AWREDDY.
FINE
YEA SURE!
HOT POINT
SHE'S RIGHT, I STILL THINK OF MYSELF AS A BAD TEENAGER MOST O' THE TIME.
I WEIGH 125 POUNDS C'N YOU BELIEVE IT? I'M IN THE INNAH CIRCLE OF WEIGHT WATCHERS!! I WEAH A SIZE 6 DRESS... MY OLD CLOTHES ARE HANGING OFF MY BODY AWREDDY!! AND I'M USING THAT RETIN-A-CREAM & MY SKIN LOOKS SO TAHRIFFIC!! EVERYBODY SEZ I LOOK GAWGEOUS & YOUTHFUL... THEY CAN'T BELIEVE IT... I'M TELLIN' YOU!
HOW COME I HAFTO WORRY ABOUT LOOKING OLD & BEING IMMATURE AT THE SAME TIME?
MY MOTHER'S VOICE IS WAFTING OUT ONTO THIS BEAUTIFUL STREET.
BUT WHO CARES?! SHE'S ON THE OTHER SIDE OF THE OCEAN!!...
SHE CAN'T RUIN THIS SUMMER EVEN THO SHE'D LOVE TO... THIS IS THE BEST SUMMER I'VE HAD SINCE 1959....
FLASHBACK 29 YEARS AGO:
MOMMY CAN'T I PLEASE GO TO ART CAMP WITH MY BEST FRIEND STEPHANIE KARASICK??
NO DAHLING!! FOR YOUR OWN GOOD I'M SENDING YOU TO SLIM-FAST REDUCING CAMP.
YOU'LL THANK ME FOR THIS LATER!
NOT AT ALL OVERWEIGHT
BUT MOMMY... I WANNA BE AN AHTIST LIKE MATISSE!
YEA BUT YOU DON'T WANT TO BE A FAT, UNPOPULAR AHTIST, DO YOU??
NO?!
YOU C'N DO AHT IN YOUR FREE TIME AT CAMP... IT'S A GOOD HOBBY FOR YOU DEAH!
BUT YOU'RE GONNA LEARN ABOUT CALORIES! THE IMPORTANT STUFF!!
*MY MOTHER NEVER CALLS ME BY MY NAME... INSTEAD ITS THIS LONG DRAWN OUT "A" SOUND WITH A SLIGHT QUESTION.

I GOT TO MEET A LOT OF FAT NEUROTIC GIRLS.
HI I'M IN THE BLUEBIRDS.
YEA.. I'LL SHOW YA 'ROUND I'VE BEEN COMIN' HERE FOR 6 YEARS.
WHAT ARE YOU DOIN' HERE, ANYWAY?
I DUNNO
I'M FAT BECAUSE I HAVE INNAH FRUSTRATIONS.. I GO TO A PSYCHIATRIST.
WOW!
CAMP SLIM FAST

I LEARNED SOME INTERESTING STUFF.
ITS KIND OF RELAXING BEING AROUND THESE FATSOS!! THEY LIKE TO LAY AROUND.
WE'LL TELL YA WHERE WE KEEP THE SECRET FOOD STASH!
AM I ONE O' THEM?!?
WOW THANKS.. I'M FLATTERED!
TOMORROW AFTER WEIGH-IN... WE'LL SNEAK TO THE GENERAL STORE DOWN THE ROAD + GET SOME SUPPLIES!!
YEAH.... I'M OUTA M+M'S!!

I DEVELOPED A DEEP LUST FOR FOOD....
YOU'RE RIGHT DIANNE... THIS PAY DAY IS TOPS... SO CHEWY + YET CRUNCHY!!
NO WAY... PAY DAY DOESN'T TOUCH REESE'S PEANUT BUTTER CUPS!
I GO FOR THESE WISE POTATO CHIPS I JUST CAN'T STOP EATIN' 'EM.
CAMP SLIM FAST

AND AN UNHEALTHY FEAR OF THE SCALE.
PAY DAY M+M'S ICE CREAM
YOUR UP 3 LBS.. WE'LL HAFTO INCREASE YOUR EXERCISE + DECREASE YOUR CALORIES!
THINK THIN
DETECTO
I DUNNO HOW I GAINED!?

AND THEN DEFIANCE OF ITS TYRANNY.... WE'RE SUPPOSED TO BE ON A VIGOROUS HIKE BUT INSTEAD WE'RE AT THE CANDY COUNTER!
I'M STAHRVING
I'M ALWAYS FAMISHED!
I'M SO SICK OF SALADS.... YUK + COTTAGE CHEESE!!
THEY'RE TRYING TO STAHRVE US TO DEATH!
YEA THIS IS LIKE A CONCENTRATION CAMP THAT OUR PARENTS PUT US IN!
OREO
WISE

IN THE END I GAINED 10 LBS. + A SECRET SATISFACTION.
I CANNOT BELIEVE YOU DID THIS TO ME... I SPENT $1,000. + LOOK AT YOU...
YOU DID THIS, TO HURT ME.
I DUNNO HOW IT HAPPENED MOMMY... MAYBE THIS COUNTRY AIR MADE ME HUNGRY!
NO I DIDN'T DO IT ON PURPOSE!
WE'LL TALK ABOUT THIS LATER YOUNG LADY!!
FIRST LET'S HAVE LUNCH.. I COULD EAT A HAWSE!
CAMP SLIM FAST

* YEA.. SO HOW MANY TIMES HAVE YOU HEARD ME SAY THIS BEFORE??? WELL I'M STILL NEUROTIC + A "BAD" GIRL TOO!!

Just Think... I could've ended up looking like Marlo Thomas instead of Danny!
if only I'd had a
NOSE JOB
© 1989 by Aline Kominsky-Crumb
I DREAMT ABOUT THIS SONG LAST NITE... IT CAME INSIDE A MAD MAGAZINE... REMEMBER IT???
"She had a nose job, she had a nose job, now her nose turns up instead of hangin' down.... She had a nose job, she had a nose job and now she's the prettiest girl in town! She used to be a freak, 'til they overhauled her beak, She had a Nose Job!!"
Rhino plasty
Reshaping the Nose
In nose surgery, the incision is usually made in the lining, to avoid an external scar. Skin is then lifted to give access to the bones and cartilage that determine the shape of the nose
Nasal bone
Cartilage
Fibrous tissue
Cartilage
Dense resilient tissue
To remove a bump, some cartilage is shaved away. This may widen the nose so that bones must be broken and reset to narrow it. To soften the tip for sculpturing, cartilage at the end can be trimmed. To build up a nose, bone or cartilage can be moved from elsewhere in the body
Source: "Plastic Surgery for Men," Reardon and McMahon, Everest House
The surgery typically takes an hour to an hour and a half. Afterward, the nostrils are usually packed with gauze to support the nasal passages as they heal.
The nose is also fitted with an external splint or cast that is removed after about a week. Swelling and discoloration of the tissues around the eyes and nose typically persist for weeks. It may be six to nine months before the finished product can be fully assessed.
The procedure: Once accepted for surgery, the patient's face will be photographed from many different angles, assessing the size and shape of the nose in relation to the rest of the face. The doctor and patient then arrive at a probable surgical plan.
GROWING UP WITH COSMETIC SURGERY ALL AROUND ME... AT 40 I CAN'T HELP DREAMING ABOUT SURGICAL POSSIBILITIES.
OTHER WOMEN HAND ME THEIR PLASTIC SURGEON'S CARD WITHOUT ME ASKING...
YEARS OF AEROBICS HAVEN'T DONE MUCH FOR THESE SADDLE BAGS!
HOW PERFECT DO I HAVE TO BE??
JUST A LITTLE LIPOSUCTION COULD SUCK THAT UGLY SCHMALTZ RIGHT OUTA THERE!
BUT I COULD GO FOR THAT SLEAK, STREAMLINED MODEL!
TOO BAD I'M NOT THE BAGGY PANTS TYPE!
I'M PROBABLY TOO OLD FOR THIS DRESS ANYWAY... IF I WAS SENSIBLE I WOULD PACK IT AWAY FOR THE SOF... IT'LL BE A COLLECTOR'S ITEM ONE DAY!
SKIN TITE STRETCH ITALIAN KNIT.
MUST HAVE FLAWLESS BOD TO LOOK GOOD IN THIS GARMENT

I MIGHT BE KINDER + GENTLER IF I WASN'T LUGGING AROUND THIS EXCESS BAGGAGE!
ALWAYS AFRAID I'LL KNOCK OVER SOME KNICK-KNACK
I'M NOT IN A GOOD MOOD!
10 lbs. 100% FAT
10 lbs 100% FAT
ONE TIME MY BUTT KNOCKED OVER A PEWTER CANDELABRA IN A FANCY STORE + I HAD TO PAY FOR IT. (WHOLESALE OF COURSE)
UH OH WE DID SOMETHING NAUGHTY!!
YOU CLUMSY.....!!
I'M SORRY IT WAS AN ACCIDENT!
BUT ENUFF... I REALLY SHOULD BE WORRYING ABOUT MY FACE...
WHAD D'YA THINK?
A LIFT?
WOULD IT MAKE MY HAIRLINE RECEDE?
WHAT IF THEY MADE IT TOO TIGHT
MAYBE AN EYELID JOB?!
ITS HARD TO PUT MAKE UP ON THESE WRINKLES!
BUT I KNOW A WOMAN WHO HAD HER EYELIDS LIFTED TOO MUCH + NOW SHE CAN'T CLOSE THEM!
HOW ABOUT THESE DULAPS?*
I'VE HAD THESE SINCE I WAS 19.
LAVENDAR CONTACT LENSES??
*DULAPS ARE DOG JOWLS
BUT SERIOUSLY.. I'M NOT (PROBABLY) READY TO DO ANY O' THIS 'CAUSE I REMBER... LONG ISLAND, 1962...
ME 'N MY PALS IN JR. HI
PROMINENT NOSES, OILY SKIN + FRIZZY HAIR WERE THE NORM... (NO, WE JEWS ARE NOT A CUTE RACE!)
ANY GIRL WITH A SMALL NOSE, NO ZITS + STRAIGHT HAIR WAS AUTOMATICALLY POPULAR...
YUCH... I CAN'T STAND PEGGY LIPTON* SHE'S SO SHALLOW + STUPID!!
SHE'S REALLY MISERABLE DEEP DOWN.
YEAH. THAT'S RIGHT.
*SHE LATER MOVED TO HOLLYWOOD, STARRED IN MOD SQUAD + MARRIED QUINCY JONES.
BUT THAT YEAR AFTER CHRISTMAS, ALONG WITH THE MIAMI TANS...
A STRANGE NEW PHENOMENON..
PUG NOSES + LOTS OF EYE MAKE-UP + COVER UP UNDER THE EYES..... A DISTURBING EPIDEMIC!
ME 'N MY PALS DEVELOPED A "BIG NOSE PRIDE" PLUS WE GOT TO WHERE WE COULD TELL WHICH DR. DID EACH NOSE!
I COULD NOT STAND TO LOOK LIKE A CARBON COPY!
DR DIAMOND
CREEPY
DR SILVER
THEN ONE DAY AFTER SUMMER 63... I WAS SITTING IN THE LIBRARY....
HIYA BUNCH.. HOW WAS YA SUMMAH?? WAS CAMP KEE WAH AS FAB AS EVER??
WHO IS THAT BUTTON-NOSED BEAST? SOUNDS LIKE MY FRIEND STEPHANIE KARASICK, BUT IT DOESNT LOOK LIKE 'ER!!
UH... DO I KNOW YOU?
ITS ME DOODY HEAD! I JUST HAD MY NOSE + CHIN DONE, MY HAIR STRAIGHTENED.. I GOT BLUE CONTACTS + I LOST 20 POUNDS!!
ITS LIKE SHE HAD A HEAD TRANSPLANT... I DON'T KNOW IF I CAN LIKE HER ANYMORE?!
HOW COME BOYS GET TO KEEP THEIR NOSES?
WOW.. YOU LOOK TOTALLY DIFFERENT!
DO YOU STILL LIKE ME??
SURE!
SEVERAL MONTHS LATER: I DISCOVERED MARIJUANA + THE "VILLAGE."
EVERYBODY LOOKS DIFFERENT HERE!
HEY.. WAN' YUR PORTRAIT DONE GIRLIE?
I THINK I LIKE IT!
I THINK I'M A AHTIST...

MY GHOD THIS IS WHAT I LOOK LIKE TO OTHER PEOPLE!!
MY NOSE IS YUGE + MY MOUTH IS SMALL..
SO I CLOSED MY SHEITEL* AND DEDICATED MYSELF TO AHT.
THIS GREASY MOP COVERED UP + FED MY PIMPLES!
I TRIED TO COVER THEM UP WITH THICK ORANGE MAKE UP..
I FELT HIDEOUSLY REPULSIVE BUT I WAS BECOMING A BEATNIK + CONSOLING MYSELF WITH IDEAS ABOUT SPIRITUAL DEVELOPMENT + ESCAPE FANTASIES.
MY SENSITIVE FOLKS KICKED THIS ALREADY BEATEN DOG!!
GET OUTA THAT BATHROOM ALREADY...
YOU CAN'T SHINE SHIT!!
AN' GET THAT HAIR OUTA YUR FACE!
AN THEY WERE COOKIN' UP A SCHEME..
ARNIE WE GOTTA DO SOMETHING WITH THAT DAWDER OF OURS! FOR STARTERS A NOSE JOB!!
WHAD'AM I MADE OUTA MONEY?
YA WAN HUHR TO GET A DECENT HUSBAND??!
EH.. SHE'S NO DUMMY, SHE'LL SNAG SOME SCHMUCK.
I WANT A DOCTOR OR A LAWYER... WE PAID FOR ALL THOSE LESSONS.. THIS FAMILY HAS TO MOVE UP!
THAT NITE:
WE'RE GETTING YUR NOSE DONE THIS EASTER...ISN'T THAT GREAT?!
B..BUT..BUT I'M USED TO MY FACE THE WAY IT IS..
THAT'S NO REASON.... YOU'LL BE POPULAR... YOU'LL BE HAPPY DON' WORRY!
NOW SHOULD I CAWL DR. DIAMOND OR DR. SILVER??
LATER WE'LL GET YUR FACE SANDED + YOU'LL GO TO WEIGHT WATCHER CAMP NEXT SUMMER!!
YOU'LL START COLLIDGE BEEYUDIFUL!
TWO WEEKS LATER AT DR. DIAMOND'S OFFICE
NOW MRS. GOLDSMITH.. LET'S TAKE A LOOK AT THESE BEFORE + AFTER SHOTS.
OH THEY'RE GAWGEOUS!
I THINK WE'LL TAKE THIS ONE!
LET'S HAVE A LOOK NOW..
OH YES WE'LL NARROW + SHORTEN + DO SOME SCULPTING. IT WILL BE A DRAMATIC IMPROVEMENT IN THIS CASE!!
HERE'S AN IDEA OF WHAT IT'LL LOOK LIKE AFTER SURGERY.
GAWGEOUS MAGNIFICENT!!
DR. CAN YOU RECOMMEND A GOOD DERMATOLOGIST?
SO I RAN AWAY... TRIED TO GET TO MIAMI..... BUT...
WASHINGTON D.C.
AWRIGHT MISS... YOU'LL HAFTO COME WITH ME!
SHIT!
YOUR PARENTS ARE VERY CONCERNED ABOUT YOU YOUNG LADY!
GR
YOUR FATHER + I HAVE DECIDED WE'LL WAIT UNTIL SUMMER TO HAVE YOUR OPERATION
OK
YEAH + IF YA RUN AWAY AGAIN I'LL BEAT THE SHIT OUTA YA... YA HEAR!?
IF I MAKE IT TO 18 THEY CAN'T CONTROL ME!
UNGRATEFUL MONSTER
SO I MANAGED TO MAKE IT THRU HIGH SCHOOL WITH MY NOSE!!
STOPPED WEARING MAKE UP
ALSO STOPPED SETTING MY HAIR ON FROZEN ORANGE JUICE CANS! NATURAL LOOK!
I WAS THE ONLY ONE O' MY FRIENDS WITH THEIR "ORIGINAL" FACE!
6 MONTHS LATER STYLES HAD CHANGED
IS THAT BUFFIE ST. MARIE?
GHOD SHE'S SO SEXY. SHE LOOKS LIKE JOAN BAEZ!
THIS IS CORNY... BUT WHAT THE HELL?!
-END-
* CURTAIN

Merci Areevwahr Ameriker
by
Love it or Leave it
Benedict Arnold Bunch
pathetic romantic?
4 by 4's
49'ER Fever
nintendo
NINJA TURTLES
SHIT HAPPENS!
WEAPONS
Drugs
RAINBOW SPONGGY BREAD
COTE DU RHONE
Lycra
Rouches
sport shoes
main architectural feature garage
CAN I REALLY DESERT A SINKING SHIP??
I'LL ALWAYS TAWK WITH A GRATING NEW YORK ACCENT!
I DON'T KNOW IF I CAN STAND ANOTHER DAY IN SCHLUBURBIA? GET ME TO A QUAINT MEDIEVAL VILLAGE!
A FANTASY?? PERHAPS... YES I'M A HOPELESSLY ROMANTIC FRANCOPHILE (SORT OF) & ESCAPIST.. STILL I HAVE SOME NOTEWORTHY INSIGHTS ABOUT MY HOMELAND!
CHARADE IS MY FAVORITE MOVIE!!
DEUX GOTS
CAFE AU D
LIVE QUAINT ACCORDEON MUSIC
PARIS
JUST THINK OF ALL THE FAMOUS ARTISTS + WRITERS WHO'VE SAT RIGHT HERE!
SPOT FOR FUTURE SMALL DOG
NOBODY THINKS I'M AMERICAN... AS LONG AS I KEEP MY MOUTH SHUT!
AND MAYBE YOU BETTER LISTEN.... I'M TIRED OF WEARING "SCHLOCK ABSORBERS"* JUST TO STAND LIVING HERE!!
I HOPE THESE PRETTY FLOWERS WILL BLOCK OUR VIEW OF THESE HIDEOUS "LIFESTYLES."
MOMMY WHY DOES THE NEIGHBOR'S HOUSE LOOK LIKE A POLICE STATION?
I THOUGHT I WAS ESCAPING THE SUBURBS WHEN I FLED LONG ISLAND.
* NOT DRINKING HAS REMOVED MY MOST POWERFUL SCHLOCK ABSORBER ...YES I'M AWFULLY HIGH STRUNG!!

DON'T GAG ME!
YOU GUYS ARE SO BITCHIN'
HAS NORMAL REFINED FAIRLY INTELLIGENT PARENTS
HEY CRUMBS... KEEP ON TRUCKIN'!
BOSS TRUCKING
WHAT WE NEED IS MORE FREEWAY ACCESS!
BUT I'M JUST AN ELITIST SPOILED BRAT.... ALL THESE SWELL REGULAH FOLKS JUST LOVE US... YEA WE'RE JUST A COUPLE O' LOVEABLE ECCENTRICS!
OH EARLINE & BOB... YUR PLACE IS AS CUTE AS A BUG'S EAR!
CHAIN LINK FENCES!
I BETTER GO TO A HYPER-AEROBICS CLASS IMMEDIATELY. I NEED MORE ENDORPHINS!
WELL I MEAN I HAVE NOTED A FEW REPULSIVE BEHAVIOR TRAITS & CULTURAL ARTIFACTS!!
I HAF TO RANT & RAVE TO YOU. EVERYONE AROUND ME IS TIRED OF LISTENING AWREDDY!
JEEZIZ I'M GONNA HAFTO PACK UP ALL THOSE OLD RECORDS I LOVE SO MUCH!
CRAZY JEWISH WOMAN.
EARTHMOVING EQUIPMENT ON THE BRAIN
I LIKE THOSE PATE SCRAPS?!
MOMMY I DON'WANNA LEARN FRENCH!
WHEN I WAS A KID I READ A BOOK CALLED "THE LITTLE HOUSE". IT MADE A DEEP IMPRESSION ON ME.
BIRDS SANG IN THE TREES.
WHEN I GROW UP I'M GONNA LIVE IN A CUTE LITTLE HOUSE IN THE COUNTRY.
NOW HORDES OF BOTTOM FEEDERS & NEUROSURGEONS ARE MOVING IN ALL AROUND ME & I'M NOT GRACIOUSLY WELCOMING THEM.
I WAS HERE FIRST BOO-HOO-SNIVEL... YOUR RUINING MY PRETTY VIEW
I'M A SENSITIVE AHTIST... I NEED UNDISTURBED BEAUTY ALL AROUND ME TO FEEL CREATIVE!!
GET ME TO A DECAYING FRENCH CHATEAU FAST!!
MY HOUSE IS CUTE & HUMBLE. YUR ALL A BUNCH O' SWEAT HOGS!
SLIGHT DIVERSION: A CUTE YOUNG CARTOONIST CAME TO VISIT ME RECENTLY & HE SUGGESTED THAT I DRAW A BEAUTIFUL ME. SO HERE IT IS.. THIS IS SUPPOSED TO MAKE ME FEEL MORE POSITIVE ABOUT MYSELF!? HMM!
BOYS & MEN. THIS IS WHAT I REALLY LOOK LIKE!
THAT OTHER HIDEOUS ME IS JUST HOW I FEEL ABOUT MYSELF!
OOPS! SORRY. SOPHIE ORDERED ME TO STOP TALKING ABOUT MY FEELINGS!
P.S. LOOK FOWARD TO MORE OF THIS AS I LEARN TO LOVE MYSELF!

STILL RANTING!!... THIS UNSTABLE SUBURBAN ATMOSPHERE CAUSES IRRATIONAL BEHAVIOR (ESPECIALLY IN AN UNUSUALLY SENSITIVE SOUL LIKE ME.).....
I MUST GO TO OAK-WOOD-POINT-GLEN MALL IMMEDIATELY... I NEED AN APPLIANCE + SOMETHING LYCRA... MAYBE MORE HOLES IN MY EARS...
UPSCALE NEW HOME WITH NUMEROUS, MEANINGLESS ROOF ANGLES
ON THEIR WAY FOR A SATURATED FAT BREAK.
QUICK... INTO MY ALWAYS RELIABLE TOYOTA STATIONWAGON!
DOUGHY BODIES IN GENERIC SPORTS CLOTHES
CLOSE UP HAIR DOS
TOILET PAPER ROLL FRONT.. POODLE PERM GROWN OUT IN BACK.
FRANKENSTEIN LOOK ALIKE
I HAFTO LIVE WITH THESE!
I FORGOT I'M AGORAPHOBIC... I CAN'T BREATH... MY ARMS ARE NUMB, I'M GONNA FAINT OR THROW UP OR BOTH... I DON'T KNOW HOW TO GET OUT!!
SPENDING IS SATISFYING.
VOICE ACTIVATED FLOWER
GREATLY REDUCED DESIGNER EVENING GOWN
MACY'S
MAYBE I HAVE LOW BLOOD SUGAR?!?*
EARTH CRAFT
ACRAME
TIE-DYE
I'LL SEE IF I CAN FIND SOMETHING TO EAT IN THE MALL!
Tastes Like The Real Thing!
STUFFERY
CHIC-A-FIL
FRIED CHICKEN PRODUCT
I SMELL GREASE I'M STARVING NOW!
99 FILLINGS
COME STUFF ME N' YOU!
TEE CO TACO?
TCBY FROZEN YOGURT?
NACHO ITALIAN BROCULLI CHILI SWEET N' SOUR TOFU THAI PEANUT YOGURT BACO BIT AVOCADO SUNFLOWER SEEDS... DELI HOT N' SPICY
99¢
Mr. Tato
MACY'S
BUK! BUK! GREAT! BUK!
* Many YUPPIE women I know blame all types of rotten behavior on this condition!
I'M MOMENTARILY SATIATED... AFTER ALL I WAS RAISED TO RESPOND POSITIVELY TO THE AMERICAN WAY!
BUT WAIT A MINIT! I'M NOT IN GREAT NECK... I'M NOT MARRIED TO THAT MILD MANNERED DENTIST....
POST ADOLESCENT.
WHO ARE THESE PEOPLE I WALK AMONG?
THE DOG CAN TELL I'M A JEW!
PINK, OVERWEIGHT CHRISTIAN ANIMAL & BUSH LOVING, RACIST NON-THINKING GUN OWNING-HOME OWNING SPORTSFANS!
PRAISE THE LORD!
DOWN BOY
TYPICAL WESTERNERS
JUST TAKE A LOOK AT OUR FOOTWEAR!! SHOES REALLY MEAN A LOT TO ME.. I CAN'T TAKE IT... AWRIGHT.. SO EVERYBODY ISN'T ABLE TO BUY THEIR FOOTSY WEAR IN EUROPE BUT STILL...
AM I AN ELITIST SNOB YET?
FINALLY FOUND THESE IN A SMALL SHOP IN MARSEILLES.
POORLY MADE
GARRISH COLORS
SPENT 3 YEARS LOOKING FOR THE PERFECT SHOE!
CHEAP SPORTS LOOK
FINE ITALIAN LEATHER
BLACK OF COURSE
RIPPLED GUMMY SOLES

AND WHAT AM I PASSING ON TO MY YOUNG CHILD, SOPHIE ??
SHE'S LOADED WITH NATURAL ABILITY IN MUSIC + OF COURSE IN ART.... BUT LOOK!!
TEENAGE MUTANT NINJA TURTLES.. TEENAGE MUTANT NINJA TURTLES.....*
SOF... WHERE'D THAT SONG COME FROM?
OH I HEARD IT ON SAT. MORNING TV AT MANDY'S... THEN WE WENT TO WATCH RACHAEL GET BAPTIZED IN THE JACUZZI AT THE NEW CHURCH!
RAD RAD YUCK!
DRUG FREE
C'N I HAVE SOME FRUIT WRINKLES?
* ITS AN INSIDIOUSLY CATCHY TUNE... I CAN'T GET RID OF IT!
BUT LET'S GET REAL! THIS CRAPPY MONOCULTURE IS EVERYWHERE... RIGHT? MAIS OUI!
THERE ARE PROBLY CONDOS ON THE DRAWING BOARD THIS VERY MINUTE THAT WILL HAVE A GREAT VIEW OF MY PERFECT MEDIEVAL VILLAGE!
MOST LIKELY OWNED BY THE SAME MALAYSIAN CONSORTIUM THAT JUST BOUGHT 8,700 ACRES NEAR ME IN CALIFORNIA.
MACDONALD HAMBURGER
THIS COULD PUSH ME TOWARDS TERRORISM!
PLUS THERE ARE PLENTY OF THINGS, TOTALLY AMERICAN THINGS THAT I'M TOTALLY HOOKED ON!!
HI I'M DR. EDELL
TALK RADO
Crystal 2% LOW-FAT MILK
NON FAT FROZEN YOGURT
PAINLESS DENTISTRY
MY OWN PERSONAL GHETTO BLASTER
BON JOUR SA VA?? OUI, OUI!
MEAT LOAF
CHEAP LONG DISTANCE PHONE RATES!
6-PACKS OF DIET COKE
DIET COKE
DIET COKE
DIET COKE
MEXICAN FOOD
HOT SAUCE
DIET
AND THE BATHROOMS HERE ARE SO LOVELY, CLEAN + CONSISTENT!!
FLUSHER IS USUALLY IN THE SAME SPOT + PRETTY OBVIOUS HOW TO USE IT!
IN FRANCE YOU MIGHT FIND A HOLE OR ANY OTHER VARIATION!
MERDE
OH MY GHOD HOW CAN I MAKE IN THAT?!
BUT I HAFTO!
I'M SO SECURE + COMFY ON MY THRONE!
UP TIGHT ANAL RETENTIVE
ALSO I HAFTO ASK MYSELF IF MY ALIENATION FROM MY OWN CULTURE ISN'T THE MAIN SOURCE OF MY ARTISTIC INSPIRATION ?!?
SO WHAT'S WRAWNG WITH PAINTING LOVELY PICTURES THAT PEOPLE ACTUALLY LIKE?
WOW! I CAN LIVE RIGHT NEAR MATISSE'S VILLAGE!
COULD I POSSIBLY STAND LIVING IN A PLACE I FEEL COMFORTABLE IN??
I DUNNO... I NEVER KNOW WHAT TO DO... THAT'S THE SWELL PART OF BEING A TRUE NEUROTIC! I NEVER HAVE THE PERFECT PUNCH LINE...
RATATATATAT
FWEE OOOOO
BOIYOIYOING
BUT MEANWHILE MY FRIENDS DIANE + BILL GAVE ME MY VERY OWN STRESS REDUCING NOISE-BOX FOR CHRISTMAS!
SO AT LEAST I CAN ADD TO THE OBNOXIOUSNESS WHILE I'M HERE!
HERES TO YA ASSWIPES!
FIN.

MARY FLEENER

Los Angeles is where I was born, September 14, 1951, and I spent most of my childhood in suburban sprawl, mainly West Covina, California. My mother was an artist and as soon as I realized all the paintings in the house were hers, I was motivated to try and do the same. By the fourth grade, I had decided school had nothing to offer me and I was quite content to draw pictures during lessons. This, along with my natural sarcastic sense of humor, did not endear me to my teachers. Fortunately, our family moved to Vancouver, Canada. My art talents were encouraged in school and I received a far better education. We moved back to California by the time I was in high school, and I was totally involved in the art curriculum and fully expected to attend art college, but my parents were against it. In fact, when I won the 1969 National Union Carbide High School Art Contest in New York, my teachers were more impressed than they were, so I went to a local junior college that was okay. I took LSD practically every day for two years and kept a B-plus average. I was a printmaking major at a university, but by senior year was bored and burnt out on art so I dropped out and became a rock musician. I got a job in a music store, got a bass guitar, and two years later was working in bars. This got real old and was a hard life-style. I met my husband (a guitar player, surfer, computer programmer) in 1977. We lived in Redondo Beach and I got a job in an art store which got me *back* into the art scene and from 1978 to 1981 I was doing shows and selling my stuff. All this time, since 1969, I had secretly harbored a desire to do underground comics. In 1984, a friend of mine sent me an article that Matt Groening wrote about the "New Comics" and something in me snapped. From this article I obtained the address of *Weirdo* and it went from there. Comics are an exhilarating form of expression even though many long and lonely hours are spent at the drawing board. It is time well spent. My work has been in *Weirdo, Rip Off Comics, Snarf, Prime Cuts, Drawn & Quarterly, Wimmen's Comix, Tits 'n' Clits, L.A. Weekly* and the *Village Voice*. My two solo books are *Hoodoo* (adaptations of Zora Neale Hurston stories) and *Slutburger Stories* (true tales about my life). I've done illustration work for *Entertainment Weekly* and for a James Brown CD from Polygram records.

My hobbies are: (still) playing bass, gardening, water gardens (ponds, koi, goldfish) and surfing (body boarding). I have three cats and one dog.

OH MARY, I LOVE YOUR CACTUS GARDEN. DID YOU MAKE THAT CERAMIC HEAD OVER THERE?
YES, AND THERE'S QUITE A STORY BEHIND IT, TOO. LEMME TELL YA 'BOUT...

SKULLS n' STIFFS
I NEEDED TO GET AWAY! WE'LL HAVE FUN AT MY DAD'S HOUSE. JUST US GIRLS!
YEAH! WHO NEEDS GUYS TO HAVE A GOOD TIME!
PALM SPRINGS 15M
DESERT HOT SPRINGS 2MI
MARY FLEENER©1988

WE CAN GO TO TH' SPAS AND THE THRIFT STORES AND DO AN ART PROJECT...
HEEYYY... LET'S MAKE A PLASTER CAST OF YOUR FACE AND USE IT IN CERAMIC CLASS!

WHY MY FACE?
BECAUSE, SOMEONE TRIED TO CAST MINE ONCE AND THAT PLASTER ON MY FACE MADE ME FEEL LIKE I WAS BEING BURIED ALIVE!

DESERT HOT SPRINGS
Mortuary
WE'RE HERE! IT'S THE HOUSE BEHIND THE... UH... UM...
LOVELY

DAD'LL BE HOME LATER SO LET'S PUT OUR STUFF INSIDE THE PATIO AND GO SHOPPING FOR TONIGHT'S DINNER.
AND PLASTER

WHATEVER POSSESSED YOUR DAD TO BECOME A MORTICIAN FER CHRISSAKE?!!
I GUESS HE WANTED STEADY WORK. YOU KNOW, YOU HAVE TO GO TO COLLEGE AND TAKE CLASSES. YA JUST DON'T FALL INTO IT.

NOW GO GET SOME VASELINE. WE NEED IT FOR THE CASTING SO THE PLASTER DOESN'T STICK TO YOUR FACE. I'LL RUN NEXT DOOR AND GET A BAG... MEET YOU AT THE CAR, OK?
OK

VASELINE carbolated
VASELINE carbolated
VASELINE carbolated
↑ 1/2 OFF Sale ↑
VASELINE Regular
VASELINE Regular
LOTION
GREASE
GOOP
I GUESS THEY'RE ALL THE SAME. OH GOOD! THIS ONE'S ON SALE...

SO WHAT'S YOUR DAD LIKE?
HE'S OK-NOW. HE USED TO BE PRETTY WILD. ALL HIS PALS IN KENTUCKY WERE. THEY'D GET JACKED UP ON PILLS, MOSTLY SPEED.
WOW!
YEP! THEY'D GET DRUNK AND CARRY ON FOR 3 OR 4 DAYS; PLAY CARDS, GET IN FIGHTS...

AS A KID I REMEMBER HIM GOING TO THE MEDICINE CABINET AND GETTING HIS PILLS. HE'D SAY: "THINK I'LL TAKE A BLUE ONE ANNA RED ONE ANNA YELLOW ONE..." ... MY POOR MOTHER...

WELL... THIS IS IT.
LOOKIT THAT BIG POOL TABLE! Oboy! OOOOH... I LUV Thee Décor!
THIS IS WHAT HE GOT IN MEXICO? A BLACK VELVET PAINTING AND A WROUGHT-IRON LAMP! OHMIGOD...!

AS YOU CAN SEE, HE'S BEEN A "BACHELOR" FOR A LONG TIME NOW
HE'LL LIKE THIS CHICKEN CURRY, I'LL BET!
HOWDY GURLS!

WHATCHOO COOKIN'?
SHOOOORE SMELLS GOOD!

DAMN! THAT CURRY WAS FIT T'EAT! SO WHAT'S THE PROGRAM TONIGHT, GURLS?
OH, JUST SOME ART PROJECT OR SUMTHIN'
WELL! ME N'MAH LADY FRIEND ARE A-GONNA RAISE HELL! heh...heh...heh... AW, WE GONNA JUST DRINK A BIT...heh...

YOU GURLS HAVE SOME FUN NOW!
'BYE DAD

OBOY! NOW WE CAN GET STONED!
SPRONG!
GAWD, WILLYA AT LEAST WAIT 'TILL HE DRIVES AWAY?

LET THE CASTING BEGIN!!

I'VE ALWAYS WANTED TO DO THIS...
ALL RIGHTY... DID YOU SMEAR VASELINE ON YOUR FACE? I'M ALL DONE MIXING
THIS STUFF IS SORTA TINGLY.

ALL DONE!!
MMMM...
MMMMM
GEE, I HOPE THOSE STRAWS ARE OK- YOU CAN BREATH CAN'T YOU? IT'LL BE HARD IN 10 MINUTES. YOU SURE YOU'RE OK? YOU SURE?

MMMM!!
?
!
VASELINE CARBOLATED PETROLEUM JELLY

MM!!!!!
YOU DIDN'T USE THIS VASELINE, DID YOU?
YOU GOTTA BE BURNING UP! IT'S JUST LIKE MENTHOLATUM!

WE'RE GETTIN' THIS OFF NOW! WOW! IT'S HARD ALREADY AND WARM...OK... HERE GOES... IT'S LOOSE...
UMMMM!!

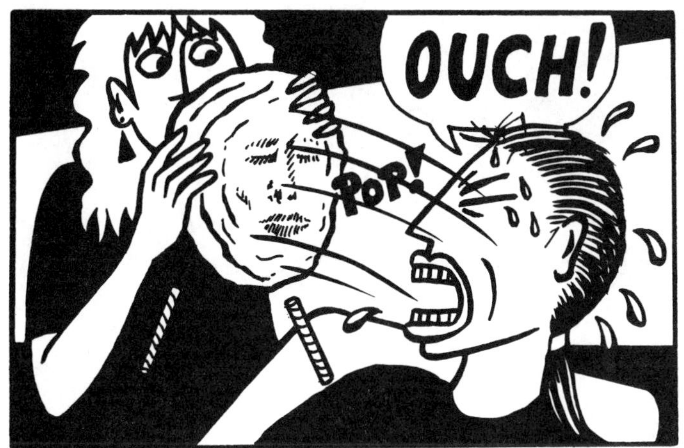
OUCH!
POP!

MY FACE LOOKS SUNBURNED!
YOU LOST SOME EYELASHES TOO.
PICK PICK
HIYA GURLS! AH'M BACK! WHATCHOO ALL DOIN'?

WE MADE A FACE CAST BUT THE FEATURES ARE KINDA FLAT...
HMMM... THAT'S 'CUZ TH' FLESH IS SOFT AN' KIN MOVE AROUND...

!!!
YOU NEED SUMTHIN' FIRM. SAY, I GOTTA GUY NEXT DOOR IN TH' WORK-ROOM. YOU KIN CAST HIM BEFORE I PUT ON HIS MAKE-UP!
YOU MEAN A DEAD GUY? WHY NOT? LET'S DO IT!

WE GOTTA USE A FLASH-LIGHT SO TH' NEIGHBORS DON'T THINK WE'RE OUT HERE FOOLIN' AROUND...
WHY?
SSSHH!

HEY! HERE'S MY LATEST JOB! COME TAKE A LOOK.

YEP! NICE OL' GENT. FUNERAL'S FRIDAY, ACTUALLY, TWO OF 'EM... ONE AN EVENIN' SERVICE
EWUUU! TODAY'S SATURDAY. THIS GUY'S GOTTA SIT HERE A WHOLE WEEK?!!
NOW LET'S GET TO THE WORKROOM

YOU USE ALL THIS NORMAL MAKE-UP!
LIQUID FOUNDATION PALE
MASCARA
Mabelline WHITE
EYE SHADOW MIXED
LIP COLOR
Max Factor base
BLUSH LIGHT
BLUSH DARK
BLUE
WE HADDA TAKE CLASSES IN IT AT TH' COLLEGE. YOU START GETTIN' THAT PLASTER MIXED!
ARE YOU SURE THIS IS... UH... OK?

SURE IT'S OK?!? HE'S DAID, HE DON'T CARE! C'MON OVER HERE MARE-REE!
...GET THIS PLASTIC OUT O'TH' WAY...
PLASTE
A-1
10lb
SO THIS IS "THE COOLIN' BOARD".

LET'S COMB HIS HAIR BACK... HADDA HEART ATTACK ON TH' FREEWAY. HMM... ONLY 48, TOO. SHOOT! HE WUZ JUST A KID. THERE, HE'S ALL TIDY NOW...

ULP.
SEE HOW FIRM HIS FACE IS?
POKE! POKE!

UH... WHAT'S THIS STUFF ON HIM?

JUST VASELINE! KEEPS 'EM MOIST.
GROSS!! HE PUT THAT COMB BACK IN HIS POCKET! YUCK!

Y'KNOW, SUDDENLY I FEEL LIKE I'M INVADING HIS PRIVACY EVEN IF HE IS DEAD.
THAT'S THE FIRST SMART THING YOU'VE SAID ALL EVENING!

"CAN YOU IMAGINE IF HIS WIDOW RECOGNIZED HIS FACE ON YOUR CERAMIC PIECE AT AN ART GALLERY SHOW?"
EEEEE!!! IT'S GEORGE!

GURLS, I UNDERSTAND YER APPREHENSION! SAY, MARE-REE, YOU'VE TAKEN ANATOMY RIGHT? HOW'D YEW LIKE A HUMAN SKULL?
OOOOOH... A REAL HUMAN SKULL?

NOW DAD, I DON'T THINK...
OH... tsk! IT'S JUST A SKULL...!
SHADDUP!
IT'S AN INTERESTIN' STORY, HONEY.

"THEY FOUND THIS YOUNG GIRL IN THE DESERT, BADLY DECOMPOSED, AN' SENT THE HAID DOWN TO L.A. FOR DENTAL I.D. NATURALLY, IT WUZ A CLOSED CASKET CEREMONY AN' SHE WUZ BURIED, AN' THAT WUZ THAT."

"THEN, SIX MONTHS LATER, AH GIT TH' HAID BACK IN THE DAMN MAIL! NOW WHAT AM I GONNA DO? TELL HER MAMA AND DADDY AND THE PASTOR, THAT WE BURIED HER WITHOUT NO HAID?!? SO I KEPT IT AN' MY MOUTH SHUT."
FRAGILE
DO NOT BEND
WELCOME

"...I CLEANED IT WITH SOME ACID AND... IT'S YER'S IF YOU WANT IT, MARE-REE"
OH, IT'LL LOOK GREAT ON MY DRAWING TABLE. I'LL PUT A CANDLE ON IT. A BLACK CANDLE!
NO!

THAT DOES IT! I WON'T DRIVE BACK TO L.A. WITH A CURSED SKULL IN MY CAR!! THEY'RE ILLEGAL, TOO, AREN'T THEY, DAD?
UH...YEP, BUT OL' MARE-REE HERE IS SMART!
NO WAY!!

TWO MONTHS LATER
HAPPY BIRTHDAY I MADE THIS! IT'S A COOKIE JAR!
I THOUGHT I'D GIVE YOU THE LID NOW. COOL, HUH?
I WANTED A SKULL...
SHE NEVER DID FINISH THE REST OF THE COOKIE JAR!

SO!...HA! HA! THAT'S THE STORY ON HOW I GOT THIS! HA! HA! HA! WOTTA WEEKEND! HAHAHA!

HM... I THINK I'LL GO GET SOME MORE WINE AND SEE HOW TH' GUYS ARE DOING WITH TH' BARBEQUE.
HEY WAIT!! LEMME TELLYA ABOUT MY GAY GHOST STORY IT'S REALLY FUNNY! IT'S TRUE, TOO. HEH... HEH..! OH WELL.

THE END

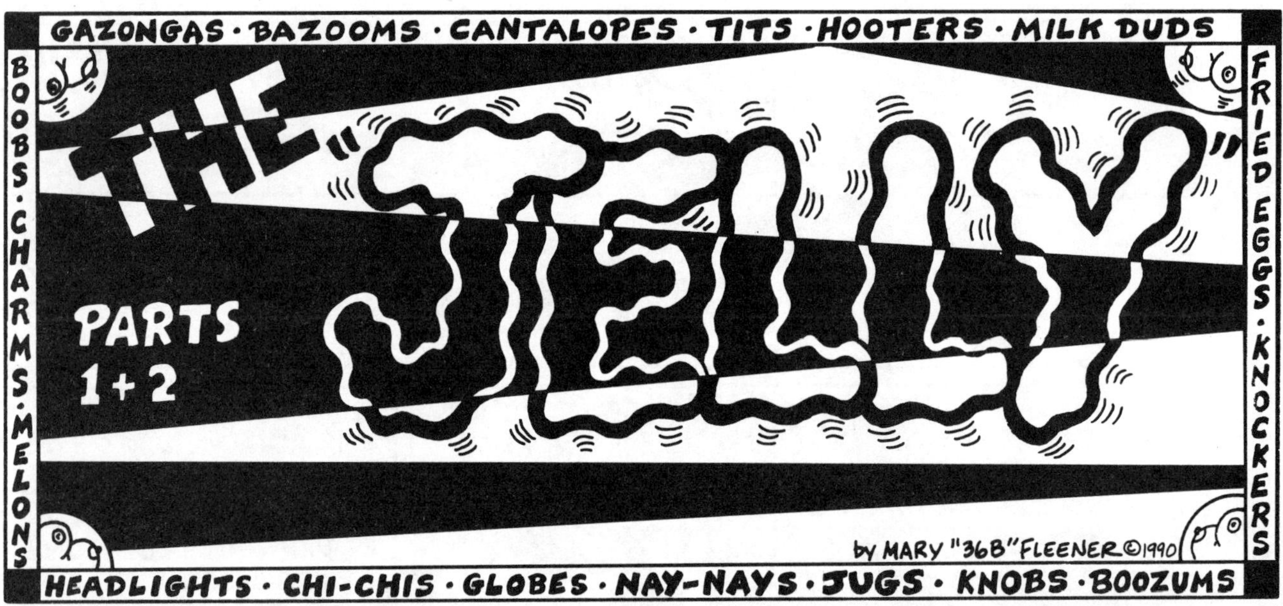
GAZONGAS · BAZOOMS · CANTALOPES · TITS · HOOTERS · MILK DUDS
BOOBS · CHARMMS · MELONS
FRIED EGGS · KNOCKERS
THE "JELLY"
PARTS 1+2
by MARY "36B" FLEENER ©1990
HEADLIGHTS · CHI-CHIS · GLOBES · NAY-NAYS · JUGS · KNOBS · BOOZUMS

THIS IS A REAL STORY ABOUT A GIRLFRIEND OF MINE WHO HAD HUGE BREASTS. WE BECAME PALS IN COLLEGE...
PART 1
"GETTING TO KNOW YOU"...
giggle
LEGALIZE IT
BLACK POWER
STOP THE WAR
ERA
Fleetwood Mac
STEAL THIS BOOK
MY MAJOR MY JOB MY LIFE MY LIKES MY DISLIKES MY DEGREE MY SAT SCORES MY BIG PLANS.......
SHE'S FALLING IN LOVE, AND ALL HE CAN DO IS STARE AT HER CHEST!

SOMEONE THOUGHT OF A NICKNAME THAT WAS LOW CONSCIOUS, RUDE AND KINDA GROSS. NATURALLY, IT CAUGHT ON!
I HEARD YOU GUYS WANT TO TALK TO ME ABOUT YOUR PARTY TONIGHT.
YEAH! BRING YER GIRLFRIEND
Y'KNOW! TORPEDO TITS!!
WELL, UH... SHE'S A... ...UH...UH...
YEAH!
SHE'S A VERY INTELLIGENT PERSON!!

WE BECAME ROOMMATES AND ONCE I SAW HER NAKED FROM THE WAIST UP. IT WASN'T A PRETTY SIGHT.
MARY! DO YOU (brush, brush, brush) HAVE ANY SHAMPOO I (brush) CAN (brush, brush) BORROW?
YEAH, SURE...
DALI
DADA
POSADA
SURREALISM
ARTSPEAK
PRINTS
STOOP SHOULDERS FROM ALL THAT WEIGHT
STRETCH MARKS
SCRATCH SCRATCH

I THINK SHE WAS UNCOMFORTABLE BECAUSE, FOR "THE TIMES", HER DRESS WAS SUBDUED, EVEN A BIT CONSERVATIVE ESPECIALLY WHEN WE'D GO OUT IN PUBLIC
DO I LOOK OK?!?
HA! HA! WE'RE JUST GOIN' TO A MOVIE! NOBODY'S GONNA BE LOOKIN' AT YOU IN A DARK THEATRE!
ANTIQUE CLOTHING
BUT SOMETIMES THEY DID LOOK, LIKE THIS ONE NIGHT WE WENT TO SEE "FELLINI'S SATYRICON" FOR THE 5th OR 6th TIME...

WE WEREN'T EVEN **IN** THE THEATRE WHEN TWO GUYS WE VAGUELY KNEW FROM SCHOOL CAME OVER AND STARTED **TALKIN' TRASH.**

AFTER THE FILM, THEY CAME OVER TO OUR APARTMENT. **MY** PRESENCE WAS CERTAINLY **NOT** REQUIRED

AND, AS ALWAYS, SHE'D HAVE A BRIEF FLING AND GET DUMPED AFTER A WEEK OR SO. SHE NEVER REFUSED A **"SUITOR"**.

I REMEMBER ONE DAY I MET THIS CUTIE WHILE BICYCLING. HE SEEMED LIKE SUCH A **NICE** BOY...

WELL, ALL IT TOOK WAS **ONE LOOK** WHEN I INTRODUCED HIM TO MY ROOMMATE. SUDDENLY, HE DIDN'T LOOK SO GOOD ANYMORE.

JUST TO CONVINCE YOU READERS HOW **BAD** IT WAS... WE DECIDED TO GO TO A *Renaissance Faire* AND MADE DRESSES JUST FOR **THEE** OCCASION.

I HAD TO USE MY MOTHER'S SEWING MACHINE AND SINCE SHE LIVED ACROSS TOWN, WE MADE PLANS TO MEET AND LEAVE FROM MY PARENTS' HOUSE.

IT WAS **WEIRD** SEEING YOUR **DAD** ACT LIKE A SLOBBERING **SEX FIEND!**

AT *Thee Faire*, IT WAS HIDEOUSLY **HOT**, EVERYTHING WAS **OVERPRICED** AND **I HATED EVERY MINUTE OF IT**. THE PURPLE DRESS, HOWEVER, WAS A BIG HIT.

A WEEK LATER I SAW THE PHOTOS. THEY WERE AMAZINGLY... **CONSISTENT.**

THERE WAS LOTS OF GOOD **LSD** GOING AROUND THAT YEAR, SO OUR LI'L GANG GOT TOGETHER **MANY** WEEKENDS FOR ALL-NITE PARTYING AND ONE NIGHT **THE VIBES** GOT **HEAVY**...

WHEN WE ALL BEDDED DOWN, STILL BUZZED BUT DETERMINED TO GET SOME REST, ONE OF THE GUYS GOT **FRISKY...**

IN THE MORNING (ABOUT **NOON**, ACTUALLY) I TALKED TO THE GUY WHO WAS GRABBING HER ALL NIGHT

AS A ROOMMATE **"THE JELLY"** WAS OFTEN BURDENSOME. **ALL** THE GUYS **SHE** LIKED WEREN'T INTERESTED (AS I OFTEN FOUND OUT)...LIKE THIS ONE WINNER FROM BERKELEY.

BOY! DID SHE HAVE PROBLEMS. I WAS BEGINNING TO FEEL LUCKY TO HAVE **NOT** INHERITED MY MOTHER'S **D-CUPS.**

JUST ABOUT A MONTH BEFORE WE GOT SEPARATE PLACES, MY ROOMMATE AND I WENT OUT FOR THE VERY LAST TIME.

"THE JELLY" WAS **REALLY** STARTING TO GET ON MY **NERVES!**

HER NEW COAT WAS ONE OF THOSE STINKY-AFGHANI-INSIDE-OUT-SHEEP-SKIN THINGS. REMEMBER THOSE?
DEFINITELY A CANDIDATE FOR THE FASHION HALL of SHAME
FUR YELLOWED WITH AGE
STIFF
CRUDE EMBROIDERY
SUSPICIOUS BROWN SPOTS ON FUR (BLOOD?)
WAY OVERPRICED
AND TO THINK SOME POOR MOUNTAIN SHEEP DIED... FOR THIS?

I WANT SOME JACK DANIELS n' APRICOT BRANDY!
NO! YOU GET DRUNK TOO FAST... AND IN THAT DRESS...!
I WANT JACK DANIEL'S, I WANT BRANDY!
FINE, BUT, YOU'RE NOT DRIVING! WE'LL TAKE MY CAR!

WE GET TO THE PARTY, LUCK OUT AND FIND A PARKING PLACE RIGHT ACROSS THE STREET
I HOPE THESE PEOPLE HAVE GOOD HOMEOWNER'S INSURANCE!

IT WAS FESTIVE! PEOPLE WERE PASSING OUT HANDFULS OF PILLS, DRINKING, SMOKIN' n' SNORTIN' and PROPOSING MARRIAGE!
HAHA HAHAHAHA HAHAHAHA HAHAHAHA
I'M BORED ALREADY
HEY, I LOVE YEW...
GO DIE.

I DECIDED TO CHECK OUT ANOTHER PARTY AND LEFT "THE JELLY". SHE'D ALREADY MADE SOME "FRIENDS".
WANNA SNORT SOME?
WANNA DANCE?
NEED A LIGHT?
LISSEN, I'M GOING DOWN THE STREET, OK? YOU WANT TO COME?
WANNA BEER?
HARDLY. I'M HAVING FUN...
BITCH!

THE OTHER PARTY WAS WORSE AND EVEN MORE PATHETIC... WHEN I RETURNED THERE WAS NO "JELLY" AND NO BOOZE!
SHE DRANK ALL THIS!? I HOPE SHE ENJOYS HER HANGOVER TOMORROW...
yew dance so good
HEY MAR-EE!
C'MERE!
APRICOT BRANDY IMPORTED ROTGÜTTEN

WELL, WELL, WELL... I WONDERED IF YOU MANIACS WOULD BE HERE! WHAT'S UP?
WE SAW YER DOG IN YER CAR!
A PINK ONE, eh? hahaha...
A DOG?
YEAH! YOUR POODLE! AWW... SHE'S LONLEY IN THERE! LET HER OUT!!!
AWWW...

MY PARENTS HAVE A POODLE, NOT ME! PLUS, SHE'S A TINY LI'L THING! BOY, ARE YOU GUYS WASTED!
SHE FOLLOWED YOU, THEN! HA! HA! HA!
HA!
FREE TH' (hic) POODLES!
FTW
GO CHECK IT OUT!

?

THE "POODLE" WAS NONE OTHER THAN "THE JELLY" FUCKING SOME GUY! THEY HAD THE FUR COAT OVER THEM. IT DIDN'T HIDE MUCH.

UH! UH! UH! OH! OH! OH! OH!
WHAT SHOULD WE DO?!
I DUNNO..!
I HOPE SHE'S ON TH' PILL!
YES, FORTUNATELY. I KNEW THIS WOULD HAPPEN IF SHE WORE THAT STOOPID PURPLE DRESS...

NOTHING COULD REMOVE THE SPOT AND IT STAYED THERE FOR THE LIFE OF THE CAR

WE PARTED ON BITTER TERMS. I GOT A BOYFRIEND AND SINCE I WAS HAPPY and SHE WASN'T, ALL OF A SUDDEN I'M THE Whore of Babylon!

THE END?

SLUG FEST!
by MARY FLEENER ©1989

SEX
VIOLENCE
GORE
TABOOS
MAGICK
VOODOO SLAVE
BLOOD N' GUTZ

BIRDS!! THAT'S WHAT I NEED! THE BEAUTY OF NATURE n' ALL THAT...

I SPENT TOO MUCH MONEY AND BOUGHT A BIRD FEEDER AND A Charming MEXICAN CLAY BIRDBATH.
COME n' GET IT, GUYS!!

1 WEEK LATER ~
WHAT'S WRONG WITH THESE STOOPID BIRDS!!?!

THEY'RE CHECKING IT OUT- DON'T WORRY, THEY'LL COME.
DUMB BIRDS..! THIS IS RIDICULOUS... UNGRATEFUL LI'L CREEPS...

LOOK!

SQUAWK!
SQUAWK!

AFTER A FEW WEEKS OF OBSERVATION, WE NAME THE BIRDS ACCORDING TO THEIR **DEFORMITIES.** (*)**PESTICIDE USE? THE WATER? THE AIR?**

(*) ENCINITAS HAS **LOTS** OF GREEN HOUSES & FLOWER FIELDS

ONE THING I **DIDN'T** PLAN ON ATTRACTING WERE **BIRDS** THAT **EAT** OTHER BIRDS!

ABOUT THIS TIME I BEGIN TO SEE **SLIMY SLUG TRACKS** EVERY MORNING IN THE KITCHEN AREA.

ALSO **MICE!** THE BIRDSEED IS NOW **EVERYWHERE**, SO THE RODENTS JOIN IN THE **FEAST** AND **MOVE RIGHT IN!**

THE CAT IS AN EFFICIENT **NIGHT STALKER.**

THE **NEXT** NIGHT, I GOT UP TO CHECK ON KITTY'S **KILL** WHEN I DISCOVER **THREE GIANT** SLUGS CRUISING AROUND THE KITCHEN FLOOR. I INSTANTLY KILL A **FOURTH** ONE.

AND THAT **SLUG MUCUS** IS ALMOST **IMPOSSIBLE** TO GET OFF YOUR SKIN!! I **EVEN** USED THAT GRITTY CLEANSER AND IT WAS **STILL** SLIMY! **DIS-GUSTIN'!**

THIS SUDDEN INVASION DIDN'T **JIVE** WITH MY **ECOLOGICIAL** CONCERNS.

I ACTUALLY SPEND SEVERAL DAYS (shudder) CLEANING THE KITCHEN
THEY'VE BEEN HERE FOR WEEKS! WHAT ARE THEY EATING? SEEDS? NAAAH...

BEER
HOOTCH
LAGER
BREW SKY
ALE
SUDS
HOPS
AMAZING!! HOW COULD HE (OR SHE!) CLIMB UP 12 BEER CANS WITHOUT KNOCKIN' 'EM DOWN?
I GUESS THEY DO LIKE BREW!
BEER CANS INTENDED FOR RE-CYCLING ALL TOO OFTEN END UP AS THESE "SCULPTURES" or "TOWERS"

THEN! ONE NIGHT, I WAKE UP TO GET SOME WATER
HI, KITTY... CATCH ANY MORE..? GASP!!
CLICK!
EEEUUUW!

TWO GIANT SLUGS WERE EATING THE CARCASS OF A FRESHLY KILLED MOUSE!!
I THOUGHT SLUGS ONLY ATE GREEN STUFF! LOOK AT 'EM PEEL THAT FLESH... NOISY EATERS, TOO! I YAM DISGUSTED.
SLURP SLURP SLUUUURP!
SLURP SLURP SLURP SLURP SLURP
DID YOU KNOW?
INSIDE A SLUG'S MOUTH, THE "TONGUE" OR RADULA IS COVERED WITH ROWS OF TINY SHARP TEETH - IT MOVES BACK AND FORTH LIKE A LITTLE FILE!
FROM: "SNAILS" A LERNER NATURAL SCIENCE BOOK
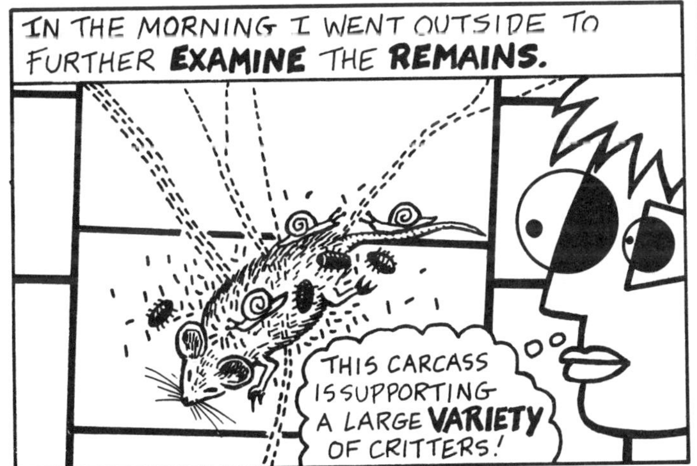
IN THE MORNING I WENT OUTSIDE TO FURTHER EXAMINE THE REMAINS.
THIS CARCASS IS SUPPORTING A LARGE VARIETY OF CRITTERS!

THE BIRD FEEDER GETS TOSSED AFTER I FIND A SPARROW TRAPPED INSIDE BECAUSE I LEFT THE LID OFF.
THIS IS WHAT YOU GET FOR BEIN' SUCHA GREEDY LI'L F'CK'ER! OK NOW... RELAX... ...sheesh..!
PEEP!
PEEP!
PEEP!
PEEP!
THE BIRD GOT OUT & WAS O.K.

EVEN THE BIRDBATH FAILS TO PROVIDE THE ambiance I SEEK...
HEY MARY-COME LOOK! THERE'S SOMETHING IN THE BIRDBATH WE'VE NEVER SEEN BEFORE!
OH REALLY?
ETERNALLY SMART-ASS HUBBY

HA HA HA HA HA HA HA HA
GET OUTTA THERE YA DUMB CAT!!!
AND YOU- SHUT UP!!

EPILOG...

EVERYTIME THE CAT DRANK FROM THE BATH HE KNOCKED THE **"BOWL"** OFF THE **PEDESTAL,** SO I HAD TO MOVE IT TO SOME **OTHER** PLACE.

EVEN SO, I **WASN'T** SURPRISED TO FIND IT **TOPPLED OVER** THE **NEXT** DAY. WHEN I LIFTED IT, **WAS I SURPRISED** TO FIND A **FAMILY OF POSSUMS** UNDERNEATH!

AS SHE LUMBERED OFF WITH HER **KITS,** I SAW THE SMALL STILL FIGURE IN THE GRASSES. AFTER CALLING SOME **WILDLIFE** PEOPLE I REALIZED IT WAS HOPELESS.

THE **MOTHER** CIRCLED THE YARD FOR **HOURS** AND WHEN SHE FINALLY LEFT I KNEW I HAD TO HAVE A LITTLE **FUNERAL**.

SO, DID I **UPSET** THE **BALANCE of NATURE** OR **WOT?** THIS LI'L *Comedy of Errors* DEMONSTRATES WHAT **MAY** HAPPEN WHEN SUDDEN **CHANGES** ARE INTRODUCED INTO AN ENVIRONMENT–LIKE MY BACK YARD.

AND I'M **STILL** PAYING FOR MY **MISTAKE!**

The End

LESLIE STERNBERGH

I was born in 1960—the year of the rat. Growing up ten miles from Three Mile Island, mutation was inevitable. I have a lot of really red hair and more thoughts in my head than the legal speed limit allows. I left York, Pa., on my twenty-first birthday, shooting into the festering swill-pit of New York City like a constipated turd from a clenched sphincter. I never looked back

When I was four, I discovered my grandpa Don's *Playboy* magazines. I was a Little Annie Fanny Fan. A lot of my first published stuff was soft-core for *Screw* and other nifty pornotronic venues. I did the DC Comics Workshop in '82. It disinclined me toward mainstream comics, even as I found gnarlier places to publish.

At the 1983 San Diego Comics Convention, I met Dori Seda. She urged me to do something for *Wimmen's Comix*, which officially kicked off my underground comix career. Playing a hunch regarding my pre-Raphaelite appearance, I art-modelled to survive. It worked so well that since then I've modelled for some fashion layouts, and suffered from bouts of high self-esteem. I stopped sitting still for money when I met and married Adam Alexander: inventor, mathematician, life-long Manhattanite.

Now I live in New York City with Adam and Gotto and a trillion weird cultural artifacts. I will live here forever. I'm currently cartoon editor for *Stop* magazine, and work with the Psychedelic Solution Gallery.

JOYCE BRABNER

I started out in comics by appearing as a character in my husband Harvey J. Pekar's autobiographical series, *American Splendor.* A recent article announced that most of our personality has "set" by age 11. At that age I was busy organizing, dressing, and undressing all the little "Girls, Girls, Girls!" I played with. Not surprisingly, I was later active in the women's health rights movement, directing a women's counseling center, while supplementing my income working both as a costumer, and with people in prison.

In comics, my work as editor and co-author of nonfiction "comics-as-journalism" keeps me in trouble. The first book in my on-going series *Real War Stories* (Eclipse) was pulled into court by the U.S. Department of Defense. That $2.00 threat to national security can now be read legally in public high schools—the boys lost. I published *Brought to Light* (Eclipse) in partnership with the Christic Institute, and am working on *Not Someone I Knew*, a comic book about date rape, which will be published later this year.

NOT AN *OBSESSION*; NOT A *COMPULSION*; A *DESIRE*, PERHAPS CULTURALLY INCULCATED, CONSUMERISTIC IN A CONSUMING SOCIETY, TO ATTAIN THE **PLATONIC IDEAL WARDROBE** IN THE BELIEF THAT IT WILL IMPART *MYSTICAL POWERS!!* (IE., THE POWER TO CLOUD MEN'S MINDS, TO GET A BETTER JOB, TO BE MISTAKEN FOR AN ACTRESS FROM "*ALL MY CHILDREN*") WITH THIS IN MIND I ETERNALLY SEEK THAT *ULTIMATE ACCESSORY*-- THE SECOND THING WE CRUISE BELOW THE NECK-**GREAT SHOES.**

I HAD SEEN THEM ON EIGHTH STREET A YEAR AGO FOR $108.00 AND NOW, HERE THEY WERE FOR ≡GASP≡ FIFTEEN BUCKS-
SALE
8
7
LUMPEN ASSHOLETTES
LOOK-MOOD SHOES!
HAHA
'MOOD SHOES' INDEED- THESE BABIES ARE IRIDESCENT LENTICULATED PLASTIC SPIKES-SHOES LIKE THESE BEG ANYONE TO REFUTE THEIR GREATNESS-PFAH!!
...IS IT-IT'S-HOLY SHIT, A PERFECT FIT!! THE UNIVERSE LOVES ME! IT'S MY LUCKY DAY!!
REMINDER TAKE YOUR PROZAC
SECRETARIAL HEEL-SKEW
ON A ROLL, I ALSO PICKED UP SOME NIFTY TEN-DOLLAR TRANSPARENT LUCITE WEDGIES...
WHY NOT? I'M CELEBRATIN' NOW! WHOOPEE!
CAN I HAVE THE OTHER ONE OF THESE, TOO?
RUBBER TUBING BRACELET
DING! DING! DING!
SHOP-ALERT! OKAY! STOP! YA CAN'T TOP THESE!!
THE VOICE OF REASON
I WENT OUT AND TRIED ON EXPENSIVE IRIDESCENT OUTFITS, KNOWING I WOULDN'T BUY THEM, ALL TO MATCH THOSE AMAZING SHOES. I WAS HIGH-ON SHOE ENERGY!!
THOSE SHOES... THOSE SHOES... LOOK AT 'EM THEY'RE CHANGING COLORS...
EET LOOKS NISE ON-
YEAH, LIKE, UH, JOAN CRAWFORD
LOOKS LIKE TWO MIDGETS HIDING ON THOSE SHOULDERS-1986 FASHION DIDOES
SAY, WHERE JOO GET THOS' CHOOZ?
OH, LEMME TELL YA ALL ABOUT IT-
WHEN I ARRIVED HOME...
LOOK! I PRIED UP THE SOLES OF THESE PLASTIC SHOES AN' PUT CIGARETTE BUTTS IN 'EM!!
CRAZY HUBBO
GREAT! AN' YOU LIKE THESE, TOO!
OH, YEAH -THEY'RE GREAT!
ALL AGLOW
HEE HEE HEE
"GOTTO"
TERMINAL CLUTTER
YES, I'D FOUND SHOES TO DIE FOR, SHOES OF MY DREAMS, I WAS AFLOAT ON SPIKE-HEELED WINGS OF FOOTWEAR FULFILLMENT...
ADAM'S RATTY OL' LOAFERS
THAT NIGHT WE WENT TO THE SAINT* FOR A PARTY. THAT SHOE ENERGY WAS WITH ME.
*FORMERLY THE FILLMORE EAST, HIPPIE-TYPES...
WHILE THERE, WEARING THOSE MAGICAL ITEMS, RIDING HIGH ON THE CREST OF MY OWN FASHION WAVELET, I WAS INTRODUCED TO PETER MAX, THEN TIM LEARY!!!
LESLIE DOES COMIX!
COMIX? COMIX?!
BEAUTIFUL!
WITH THE RIGHT SHOES, ANYTHING IS POSSIBLE!!

The Avenue B~Girls Present:
"REHASHION FASHION" with carmina piranha
THOSE OF US WHO SPEND OUR DAYS IN THE TURGID URBAN NON-RENEWAL ZONES OF DOWNTOWN MANHATTAN ARE ALL-TOO-AWARE OF THE FRIGHTENING FACT THAT THERE SEEMS TO BE NOTHING NEW - YOU KNOW, REALLY NEW - UNDER THE CULTURE-SHOCKED SUN. SO LET'S CELEBRATE ANYWAY..! NOSTALGIA HAS CAUGHT UP WITH ITSELF. REMEMBER LOOKING FORWARD TO THE 90'S? GO AHEAD AND PRETEND YOU STILL DO. IT'S OKAY...
DON'T CUT UP THIS MAGAZINE - JUST XEROX ME ON CARDSTOCK, THE CLOTHES ON PAPER!
HAIR NOW! WHY SEW Extensions TO YOUR HEAD WHEN YOU CAN SEW 'EM TO A HAT INSTEAD!! Braids/Hair from 14th Street - "Wig Heaven"
cut only the white dotted line, OK?
-BRAID YOUR OWN! -USE LOTS OF COLORS!
You'll stand out from the crowd in this Adorably Adulterated Adolfo Suit~ and those skirt-blazer sleeve-pockets! Très deep! The midriff skirt-top is cool, too - HOW did I ever wear this any other way?!? Get sewing, ladies!!
"Fun Über Alles"
FOR THE SURREALISTS
GO AHEAD! TRY IT! SEE ALL OF THE 225 LOOKS POSSIBLE (AND THAT'S NOT COUNTING THE HYDRANT!)
YEE-HA!
LOOK! THERE'S LOTS MORE!
git Along, Gal In these Nifty, thrifty ol' COWBOY BOOTS $25 & up at Metropolis Apparel Co.
WORDS 'N' PICTURES © 1990 BY LESLIE ("L.S. ALEXANDER") STERNBERGH - "YEAH, SO?"

cut a slit on the dotted line
HEY ROCKY! Watch me pull a rabbit outta muh HAT!!
Real Leather, of course
IT'S A TEA TRAY! -IT'S A BAT! NO! IT'S a pneumatic INFLATO-HAT! $8.98
cut dotted line
If you're gonna wear a pound of Major Earrings... ...then do your holes a favor~design your own! "Notions" District, 37th & 6th has it all!
Getcher old cowhands on this hand-tooled bag for $90!
Hats & Bag are from Little Rickie
"I DREAM OF JUGHEAD" in this swell "SPIKE" hat, $30 by John & Wendy.
MASONIC AND ASTROLOGICAL SYMBOLS, HANDPAINTED ON A GINCHY VINTAGE BOLERO FROM METROPOLIS APPAREL CO. MAKE THIS THE WILD LOOK FOR MY DINNER DATE AT JERRY'S 103 WITH LEE, THE COOL PROSECUTING ATTORNEY FROM THAT RITUAL ABUSE CASE IN MOUNT ME, NEW JERSEY...
LIKE, CAN YOU BELIEVE THAT THIS SEXY Black SHEER Silk TURTLENECK IS FROM L.L. Bean?
YOU'LL BE SURE TO HIT A HOMER IN THIS LOVELY MARGE SIMPSON WIG!!!
Bra-cuda Attack! This hand-painted Bustier is based on bras by TANIA FERRIER, at ENELRA.
(We do hope these are made available soon! In BLUE!)
Also from Little Rickie: Van Gogh Tie worn as a sash belt, $20
cut only so far
SPECIAL THANKS TO MATT GROENING FOR CONVINCING MARGE SIMPSON TO POSE FOR THIS DRAWING!
CUT ME.
FISHNET FINGERS
"HIP"
WORD BUCKLES are still a valid Fashion Statement! "READ MY LIIIPS"
FAKE FUR, OF COURSE
DRESS HOT FOR SUMMER! SSSSSSS!
sigh Remember those salacious suede HOT PANTS of the early 70's, that came in Lurid colors like Royal purple, Mustard Yellow, and Rust? Life was simpler then... SEARCH THE THRIFT STORES-OR PAY MODERN PRICES (TRY CLEVELAND...)
Nail Extensions by Axel, the master of surreo-sauvage chic
"Fur mini-need I say more?
FUNKY
Like stretchy lycra stockings with SPIKE HEELS~
FAT THIGHS? GARTERS!
"Have All Your Friends Sign a pair of tights!! Collect 'em on the run!"
Be real extravagant and make CUT-OFFS from Tripp's Iridescent Jeans~$68 at Trash & Vaudeville ~or be real PRACTICAL an' just buy the HOT PANTS for $54-Shineon!
"ROLL-ON" BOOTS! The kind preferred by SUPERHEROES!!! Available in Midnight Black and SCARLET, $85 at Patricia Field~also in ankle-high versions. Check out the mythical footwear at Joseph's Shoe Imports, too. OOH, LA-LA!
carmina sez: "One is NEVER TOO OLD for White cotton ANKLETS"
"DEATH BEFORE ENNUI"
PLATFORM SHOES are GREAT for self-defense AND seeing in CROWDS!! THESE little cuties are from MUDHONEY.
GO AHEAD, BUCKLE US! YEAH! AGAIN! -TIGHTER!
WORN UNDER MULTI-STRAP SUEDE PUMPS FROM BAKER'S

WATCH THIS MAN
SIGH
I'M SO TIRED... THINK I'LL HAVE SOME PIZZA AND GO HOME TO BED.
DINNER at BEN'S
Sternbergh ©'89

DO YOU HAVE THE TIME? DON'T I KNOW YOU? — ISN'T YOUR NAME YARROW OR —
FOLK CITY
TWELVE-ISH.. NO, I DON'T KNOW YOU.
IT'S THAT FROOT LOOP I SAW IN THE McDONALD'S

LOOK/HERE'S A CLOCK. 12:30, SEE?
DON'T I KNOW YOU??
NOT UNLESS YER, UH, INTO COMIX OR ART.. UH, I'M ON MY WAY HOME NOW....
I USETA READ COMIX WHEN I WUZ A KID...

SO LISTEN, LESLIE, WANT SOME UPS? I'LL GIVE 'EM TO YA FREE. WILL YOU BUY ME A SLICE? I'M OUTA WORK, Y'KNOW...
I KNOW THE FEELING-ONE SLICE OF SICILIAN AN' A COKE, LARGE.
SHIT! I DON'T BELIEVE THIS-HE GOT MY NAME OFFA THIS PACKAGE I'M CARRYING.. OH, HELL...

YEAH, I'M BROKE-EVEN THO' PEOPLE SAY I'M WELL-DRESSED
...UH... BEATS DRESSING BADLY.
RIGHT! RIGHT! SO, YOU LIVE IN THE VILLAGE?
SHK SHK SHK SHK
LOWER EAST SIDE. LISSEN, ARE YOU TRYING TO, UM, ATTACH YER-SELF TO ME? I MEAN, I MAY SEEM FRIENDLY, BUT——
NO! NO, I UNDERSTAND! OF COURSE NOT!

SO YOU REALLY CAN'T SPARE ANY CHANGE, HUH?
NO.

DID HE GO? DON'T TURN AROUND - I'M GLAD I'M TOO TIRED TO CARE ABOUT THIS...
WOW, I THINK HE'S-- YEAH, HE'S GONE
MUNCH MUNCH MUNCH

SO LESLIE, WHY DON'T YOU GIVE ME YOUR TELEPHONE NUMBER??
AW GEEZE...WELL, HE'S NOT VIOLENT; HE'S NOT SOMEONE WHO KNOWS WHERE I LIVE; HE'S NOT PACKIN' A GUN; HE'S NOT A GANG MEMBER *SIGH* HERE GOES-
SO WHY DON'T YOU TAKE A HIKE?
OKAY, YOU-YOU SLAG!!!

MUNCH MUNCH
SLAG?! -SLAG?? SLAG??!
June 26 '84

©1984 BY LESLIE "BORN TO RAISE EYEBROWS" STERNBERGH • NOO YAWK! • Sternbergh '84

I WAS OFF TO A KIND OF **SLOW** START...

HI THERE! I'M DOING A *SURVEY* FOR *BUSINESS WEEK* MAGAZINE! SO WHAT'S *YOUR* FAVORITE DRINK?

GET LOST.

I DECIDED TO TRY IT **WITHOUT** MY *GLASSES*.

SOMEHOW TOO, I FAILED TO MASTER THE FROSTED GLASS "CHASER" TRICK--

ULP -OH WELL... WHY WASTE CHAMPAGNE...

C'MON, RED! I'M A **REGULAR** HERE! YA GOTTA *DRINK* WHAT I *BUY* YA!

WHY INDEED...

HI.

EVERYONE KEPT ASKING ME TO DANCE TOPLESS. I REFUSED.

COME ON IN! STEP RIGHT UP- PARTY GIRLS!! PARTY GIRLS INSIDE!

BUY ME A DRINK?

BUY ME A DRINK?

BUY ME A DRINK?

YOU DANCIN?

YOU GONNA DANCE?

HEY BABE- GONNA *DANCE*?

ARF!

YOW!

SHAKE IT, BABY!!

YOU DANCE?

YOU GONNA DANCE?

I WAS MISTAKEN FOR SOMEONE BY TWO STRANGE MEN.

SHEEIT! *YOU* AIN'T BUTCH'S OL' LADY! LOOKADAT!!

MAH GOD!!! BABE, YOU GOTS A *TWIN*! HOOO-*EEE*!

GEE...

THAT NIGHT I GOT PAWED BY MEN FROM ALL OVER THE WORLD...
'AT'S RIGHT LUV-OI'M F'M LAWND'N!!
GEE, UH, THAT'S JUST, ...DUCKY.... NOW WILLYA MOVE YER HAND?
FINALLY, JOHN ARRIVED AS CLOSING TIME DRAGGED NEAR. BOY, WAS I MESSED UP!
ARGH-
$4 BEER
DEAR GOD- THEY'RE PLAYING A SONG OFF ONE O' MY SPARKS RECORDS!!
I STAGGERED HOME HAPPY...
SONY
Coca-Cola
Castro
BOY, AM I -hic- CROCKED! BUT LOOKAT DISH CASH! WOW!
PUT THAT AWAY! WE'RE IN TIMES SQUARE!
BUT THE NEXT DAY -- WHAT A HANGOVER! THAT STUFF MUST'VE BEEN IMPORTED FROM HELL- OR MAYBE ARKANSAS. ($9.00 A GLASS) AT ANY RATE IT WAS THE PITS. I WOKE UP AT SEVEN-THIRTY- AND COULDN'T WALK STRAIGHT 'TIL WELL AFTER NOON....
TURN OFF THAT LIGHT!!!
THAT'S THE SUN!!
STAR TREK
SO, THAT'S IT. YEAH, I WENT BACK- ONCE. THE NEXT DAY. HAD TO-- I'D GOTTEN SO DRUNK I LEFT MY GLASSES THERE. NAH, NEVER AGAIN... HUH? WHADAYA MEAN, NOT SO SLEAZY? WHAT'S THE SLEAZIEST YOU EVER DID,- MASTURBATE WITH A MANHOLE COVER? NO, OF COURSE I MADE IT UP. NO, THE TEXTURED KIND.
BESIDES- I NEEDED SOME GOOD STORY MATERIAL! I HAVE A REP- UTATION TO BUILD!!!
THANX, CARYN.
THERE IS NO END

GIRLS! GIRLS! GIRLS!
STORY: JOYCE BRABNER ©1987 ART: LESLIE STERNBERGH
Our Family moved around a lot. My parents never wanted to live around other people. They said our family had their own way of doing things.
We had to play by ourselves and were encouraged to make up our own games.
GO OUTSIDE AND USE YOUR IMAGINATION!
CAN I HAVE YOUR SCARF, SO I CAN BE CARMEN?
L'AMOUR! L'AMOUR! L'AMOUR!!!

But, when you're the oldest, kid sisters have limited entertainment value.
FIRST, YOU TIE ME UP, THEN I'LL TIE YOU UP, LIKE COWBOYS

The Secret of the Old Clock
A NANCY DREW MYSTERY
Carolyn Keene

When I was 10, I got to live in my first Real Suburban Neighborhood, where there were lots of kids, and some of them were even my age. I had great expectations.
WHERE'S SPOT? WHERE'S DICK AND JANE?

I hadn't much experience playing kid games with other kids, unless you count School gym.
I try not to think about those days.

I had read a lot of books and sometimes watched movies that showed kids playing. This was before social realism made it big in kids literature. No JUDY BLUME. My first attempts to make friends my own age were a little Shaky.
WHY DON'T WE PUT ON A SHOW? WE COULD FIND SOME MEAN OLD MISER AND CHEER HIM UP AND THEN HE COULD TURN HIS HOUSE INTO AN ORPHANAGE!

I persisted.
NOK NOK
KEEP LOOKING FOR A SECRET PANEL. THERE'S GOT TO BE A MYSTERY AROUND HERE SOMEPLACE.

I learned a good deal.
WHAT'S F·U·C·K?
FUCK
OH! SEXUABLE INTERCOURSE! THEY TOLD ME THAT BECAUSE MY MOM IS PREGNANT.
YOU KNOW ABOUT PERIODS YET?

I tried to identify popular themes and relevant topics. Being a good reader helped.
DAD'S GOT ANOTHER ONE LIKE THIS ABOUT "TROPIC OF CANCER." HERE'S LESBIANS. THEY HAVE THESE CONTESTS IN BOARDING SCHOOLS TO PEE IN BOTTLES.*
Havelock Ellis
The Psychology of Sex
*Really. Ellis was big on women urinating.

An older sister would have been OK with me then, if I could have still had my own room.
FIRST YOU WEAR AAA. SHE'S ALL THE WAY UP TO AA. THESE ARE TEENFORMS.
MOM'S JUST SNAP DOWN, SO SHE CAN FEED THE BABY.

Around 1963, the neighborhood movie house became an "art theater." Kids suddenly couldn't go to the show down the street. Mark O'Donnell's mother said he couldn't even walk past there to school because it was a mortal sin. We had art in school. What was going on?
It was about some guy with x-ray vision so he could see through ladies' clothes. (the first Russ Meyer skin flick)

A couple of days later, we pooled our research.
THE PAPER SAYS THEY GOT "NAUGHTY NUDIES." THE NEW ONE COMING IS CALLED "NUDES AROUND THE WORLD"
A STRIPPER IS WHEN SHE'S GOT ALL THESE BALLOONS ON HER LIKE GRAPES, AND SHE DANCES AROUND AND THE MEN POP THEM WITH THEIR CIGARS, AND SHOW SHE'S JUST WEARING A BIKINI—!!
POP!
♫AN ITSY BITSY, TEENY WEENY, YELLOW POLKA DOT BIKINI...♫

MORE MORE
MORE MORE
THEY LIVE UPSTAIRS FROM THE SALOON ON GUNSMOKE AND THEN SOMETIMES THEY COME DOWN AND DO THE CAN-CAN WITH MISS KITTY
THEY GET MONEY TO TAKE IT OFF, AND THE MEN YELL "MORE! MORE!"
I NEVER SAW THAT
THEY *DID*.

This suggested interesting possibilities. Laura's mom had put a lot of old clothes upstairs in their garage, for playing dress-up. I was getting real tired of "Fashion Model" and "Wedding."
LET'S BE STRIPPERS. WE CAN HAVE A SHOW.

Susan Berman took real dance classes every Wednesday. We had to call her "Miss Susan" during practice.
♫BUFFALO GALS, WON'T YOU COME OUT TONIGHT, COME OUT TONIGHT

Iris sold tickets. When her brother found out, he told lots of his friends. She had to make more

There were costumes to make, and acts to rehearse.
YOU CAN BE THE "MAID OF MONEY," AND PULL THEM OFF, LITTLE BY LITTLE
MONOPOLY
...AFTER YOU CHANGE, YOU CAN BE THE NUDE FROM SCOTLAND. GET KNEE SOCKS FROM HOME.

We looked beyond ourselves for inspiration.
LIFE

Barbara was to be our star attraction.
C'MON, BARBARA! WE'LL GIVE YOU HALF THE MONEY.

This was because when we were "practicing" - we practiced taking our clothes off *a LOT*, dancing around naked every day - we noticed a surprising difference.
OH BABY,* BOOM BOOM BOOM, DO THE STRIP!
*Song we made up.

Barbara's breasts were just starting to stick out, and she had 3 or 4 dark little pubic hairs.

DID YOU SEE HER...YOU KNOWS
HER HILLS.
AND HER, UH, GRASS!
WE BRING HER OUT LAST, AND POINT THE LAMPSHADE TO BE THE SPOTLIGHT.*
(*B.A. in Dramatic Arts, 1973)

Our show was a big success. We even had commercials. Laura's father delivered for Hood Dairy, so we wore his old milkman hats and wrote a song:
♪OH, YOU GOTTA DRINK HOOD, HOOD, HOOD, BECAUSE IT IS ♪ SO GOOD, GOOD, GOOD* ♪♫
Hood DAIRY
*TO THE TUNE OF "BLAME IT ON THE BOSSA NOVA"

We were held over. We collected most of the allowances on the block.
My Dad said when he put on shows as a kid, they only charged two pins for admission, because it was the Depression. I think he really got that from "The Little Rascals."

Laura's brother Stevie finally told on us, and we got raided. Angry mothers, led by Mrs. O'Donnell, crossed down the street to fill my front porch.

When it was all over, it was difficult for my mother to explain to me what I had done wrong.
WE-EL-L, IT'S IMPORTANT TO BE CREATIVE, BUT...
D.H. Lawrence SONS AND LOVERS

CAREL MOISEIWITSCH

I was born and trained in the U.K. and currently live in Vancouver, British Columbia, Canada, where it hardly ever snows or freezes and there are more black leather jackets than mounties. I'm rarely bored or cold in spite of all rumors to the contrary concerning Canadian life, and the only snowshoes I've seen so far are in a museum.

"MORE GUYS THAN GALS ARE FORCED INTO SEX!" STUDY REVEALS
57% OF MEN SAID THEY WERE ENTICED INTO UNWANTED SEX!
WOMEN MADE SEXUAL ADVANCES THAT WERE DIFFICULT TO REFUSE,
THEY TOOK OFF MEN'S CLOTHES.....
MEN REPORTED THEIR PARTNERS WOULDN'T LET GO OF THEIR HANDS,
THEY WERE HELD DOWN......
ANOTHER COMMON REASON FOR UNWANTED SEX WAS A DESIRE FOR MORE EXPERIENCE.....
(BIBLIOGRAPHY - NATIONAL ENQUIRER # 30586-2, MAY 1987)
MOISEIWITSCH © 1989

©1989 MOISEIWITSCH

TAMMY FAYE BAKKER AND HER HOPPIN' SHOPPIN' DEMONS

"LORD HELP ME KEEP THE MALE EGO INTACT"

WONDER CALAVERA AFTER POSADA
WOMAN REVOLUCIONARIA

—TRADITIONAL SINGING GAME—

LITTLE FIGHT IN MEXICO

HAD A LITTLE FIGHT IN MEXICO.
IF IT WASN'T FOR THE GIRLS THE BOYS WOULDN'T GO.

COME TO THE PLACE WHERE THE BLOOD WAS SHED,
THE GIRLS TURNED BACK BUT THE BOYS WENT AHEAD.

WHEN THOSE BOYS AND GIRLS DO MEET
THEY DO HUG AND KISS SO SWEET.

YOU HAD BETTER GET UP, YOU ARE MIGHTY IN THE WAY.
CHOOSE YOU A PARTNER AND COME ALONG AND PLAY!

MEAN WOMAN BLUES

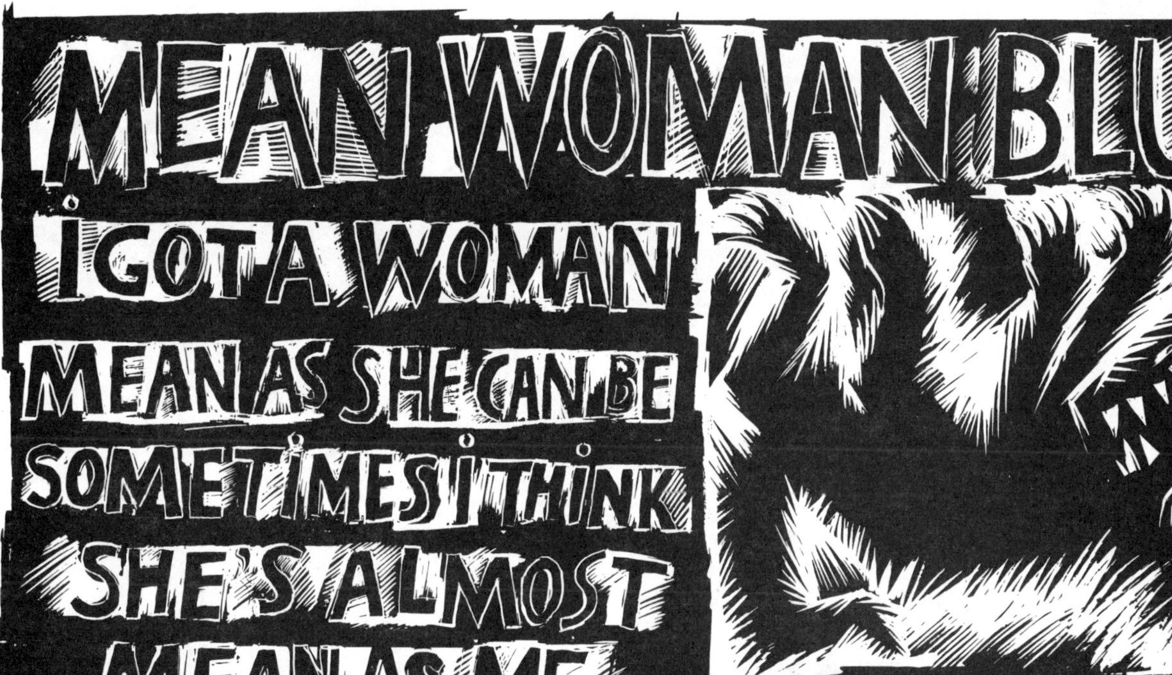

A BLACK CAT UP AND DIED OF FRIGHT.
'CAUSE SHE CROSSED HIS PATH LAST NIGHT.

SHE KISS SO HARD SHE BRUISE MY LIPS.
HURTS SO GOOD MY HEART JUST FLIPS

THE STRANGEST GAL I EVER HAD
NEVER HAPPY 'LESS SHE'S MAD.

SHE MAKES LOVE WITHOUT A SMILE
OOH, HOT DOG, THAT DRIVES ME WILD.

I GOT A WOMAN MEAN AS SHE CAN BE
SOMETIMES I THINK SHE'S ALMOST MEAN AS ME.

PRIAPIC
ALPHABET
MOISEIWITSCH
FEBRUARY 1991
A
ANTI-TANK
MISSILE
LAUNCHER
B
B-52 BOMBER
C
CIVILIAN CASUALTIES
D
DESTROYER
E
EXOCET
AIR TO SURFACE
MISSILE
F
F16 FALCON
JET
G
GAS MASK
H
HIND MI-24
HELICOPTOR
I
INFANTRY
J
JAGUAR
JET

K
KILL RATE
L
LIGHT MACHINE GUN
M
MiG-29 FULCRUM
N
NAPALM
O
OIL SPILL
P
P.O.W.
Q
QUADRIPLEGIC
R
REFUGEES
S
SOVIET SCUD
SURFACE TO SURFACE MISSILE
T
T-55 TANK
U
UNIFORM
US ARMY
V
VICTORY
W
WAR WIDOW
X
EXPLOSION
Y
YOUTH
Z
ZONE

SiREN

FEMME FATALE
MOISEIWITSCH

HIGH ON PMS
I AM VICIOUS
I AM THE NIGHTMARE OF THE CABBAGE PATCH.
I AM A KEWPIE DOLL WITH SUDDENLY WIDE AWAKE EYES AND FANGS AND CLAWS.
I AM THE LIVING DEAD-
SURPRISE,
I WILL SUCK YOUR BRAINS!
CAN YOU DIG THAT, FRED?
MOISEIWITSCH

GUILT WITHOUT SEX

BEASTLEY WOMAN

CAR.WOMAN

THAT THEY ARE ENDOWED BY THEIR CRE-ATOR WITH CERTAIN UNALIENABLE RIGHTS

THAT AMONG THESE ARE LIFE, LIBERTY AND THE PERSUIT OF HAPPINESS

THAT TO SECURE THESE RIGHTS GOVERN-MENTS ARE INSTITUTED AMONG MEN

DERIVING THEIR JUST POWER FROM THE CONSENT OF THE GOVERNED

THAT WHENEVER ANY FORM OF GOVERN-MENT BECOMES DESTRUCTIVE OF THESE ENDS

IT IS THE RIGHT OF THE PEOPLE TO ALTER OR ABOLISH IT.

AND TO INSTITUTE NEW GOVERNMENT, HAVING IT'S FOUNDATION ON SUCH PRINCIPLES AND ORGANISING IT'S POWER IN SUCH FORM AS TO THEM SEEM MOST LIKELY TO EFFECT THEIR SAFETY AND HAPPINESS.” THOMAS JEFFERSON.

CARYN LESCHEN

I wasn't born yesterday, you know. I was born in 1954, the year Matisse died—and I like to think there is some significance to this. Matisse died in Nice, France; I was born in Queens, New York—but I *am* writing this in a French-speaking bar in Montreal. Zut alors!

As a gentler alternative to being "it" in "tag," I spent a lot of time drawing in front of the TV as a child. I drew the inevitable girls in beehive hairdos and strapless, wasp-waisted gowns; I illustrated Beatles' songs and invented my own ads for Maidenform bras. Later I majored in art at Queens College. I lived in the East Village for a while, and then, after spending the first twenty-four years of my life in New York collecting material for my comix, I moved to San Francisco to collect some more.

Aside from television and Matisse, my comix influences include *Mad* Magazine, *Archie* comics, *National Lampoon* from the early seventies and ten years of waitressing. In 1987 I graduated from the California College of Arts and Crafts in Oakland, where I learned to draw hands faster. Since 1983 my work has appeared in *Wimmen's Comix*; I am in *StripAIDS USA* and a few other comic publications. I am also a book and magazine illustrator. I like to make big pastels and little watercolors, both of which are usually somewhat "cartoony"—i.e. intimate group portraits of people hanging out together in a bar or someone's house or outside somewhere having fun.

I don't like to see a big distinction being made between "fine art" and "illustration" and "comics." I make it my political business to blur these lines; my comix are the most "fine art" thing I do. I think of them as cheap little self-made movies where I can control everything. For a while I painted animation cels part time, but all those dancing fruits and vegetables really tired me out.

Though I am no longer a waitress, I continue to increase my exposure to situation comedy—as well as my cool earring collection—by working in a neighborhood artsy-craftsy gift shop. I live with my husband, Jake, a magazine editor who tries to keep me from using too many unnecessary, annoying adjectives. I still draw in the dining room while watching TV.

THE TOILETS OF EUROPE
FUZZY COVER
ROUND
SQUARE
SEE: "TOILETS OF EGYPT"
TRIANGLE
JONNY-PAK
SPACE-AGE
QUAINT
WATCH: "GREAT TOILETS OF THE WORLD" ON YOUR LOCAL PBS STATION
© 1985 Carynlescher
LONDON TOWER OF LONDON
CROWN JEWELS
READS: "BY APPOINTMENT TO HER MAJESTY THE QUEEN"
I've heard of a ROYAL FLUSH but this is RIDICULOUS.
PARIS ALL CAFES
?
Gee, I coulda SWORN this door said, "DAMES"
HOLLAND HOTEL ADOLESCE
like WOW here your shit winds up sitting on a litrel shelf so you can inspect it! of course you'd never have this in the states, like I mean, like at home people are really hung up on their bodily functions, you know, they are so sepressed, really, you cdn understand a whole culture by the way they poop! oh this sure would make a great cartoon! Oh jeez, like, uh, what time is it?
PULL UP
ITALY ROME TRAIN STATION
AT-SA FIVE-HUNDREDA LIRE!
AND-A YOU PASSAPORT!
WILL TWO MARKS COVER IT?
oh god I've been on that train for 16 hours please, God, I hope I have some change...
HOW ABOUT MY FIRST BORN SON?!
extra sox
collection of European crap
cookies
IN GERMANY AUTOBAHN STOP
THE TOILETS ARE VERY CLEAN
Can't you wait until I'm finished?
IN GREECE ALL THE TOURIST GIRLS CARRY AROUND THEIR VERY OWN ROLL OF TOILET PAPER!
GOTTA ROOM?
YA!
YAZOO
YA
Taverna
YOU GOT A ROOM?
Great to be back in the good ol' USA!
hey, honey, bring me another ROLL, willya please?
unread magazines
STUPID
end.

When I was a little girl, I thought I was Betty Cooper, and my mother was Lucille Ball.
WAARAH
AI AI AI AI AI
WAAAH
Betty and Veronica "Identity Crisis"
But Gloria Stavers, editor of 16 Magazine, was always saying.....
Dear Miss Stavers, I'm ugly. What should I do? -Ugly
Dear Ugly, Be Yourself! -G.S.
WIN A DATE WITH FANG
Be Yourself
©1986 Caryn Leschen
To facilitate this, all us girls went to see "Masque of the Red Death", starring Jane Asher, Paul McCartney's girlfriend.
Who dares insult us with this blasphemous mockery?
Then came Jean Shrimpton, who was more accessible, as she appeared on all the commercials during the Monkees. I perfected my English accent and cherished my long, straight hair.
This required years of setting my hair in a Campbell's soup can.
Say, can you directly contact London on that setup?
WAR
MORE WAR EVEN MORE WAR
PROTESTS in central Park, etc.
nightbrace
Who dares insult us with this blasphemous mockery?
slicker, slicker over slicker under slickeraloone!
"Myself", however, sang and played the guitar, so I became Joni Mitchell.
and go round and round and round...
OY SHE SOUNDS JUST LIKE MY NIECE BARBARA
MMM-
Aside from playing at Bell Park Jewish Center sisterhood meetings, one of Joni's pastimes, apparently, was rescuing fellow college students from bad acid trips.
OMIGOD! I can't handle it.
RELAX, sweetie don't be freaked out about sleeping with my boyfriend - it's OK...

One day, I went to see a wild-woman poetess, who crawled around the stage on all fours, in a ripped T-shirt with rags tied around her jeans...
oh god this skirt is so passé
FREE Money
Arista Records
Patti Smith
Under Patti Smith's androgyne gaze, I crawled around the floor of my Chelsea apartment.
one, please
NOW P
I crawled to the movies and saw "Annie Hall"...
Hurrah! Self-depricating intellectual confusion was finally in vogue, and, well, gee, um, oh yeah...
ANNIE HALL
WOODY ALLEN
DIANE KEATON
the one that got away
I thought it was jejune
See: "Holding a Torch" Wimmen's Comix #8 ©1983 (Last Gasp)
CURB YOUR WHEELS
?
In 1981, in San Francisco, I cut off all my hair, and the Dept. of Public Works didn't say rude things to me anymore.
aaaay
how BOUT those 4gers?
aaaY
BUD
I kind of missed it. But I did look a little like Laurie Anderson.
can you say "minimal"?
NO.
Then my apartment was burglarized. In order to keep watch on all the cheap trinkets that remained, I started wearing them - all at once.
NRBQ
B.A.D.
whatsamatter, they didn't like this necklace? I think it's cute.
ARTHUR
Fortunately, Cyndi Lauper arrived on the scene just in time.
WE ARE THE WORLD WE ARE THE CHILDREN
sssh! I can't hear Bruce Springsteen
jingle
jangle jangle
clink clink

Last week, I bought a miniskirt and went to a Monkee concert.
—Peter! I'm all over here! I'm all grown up now!
SPRIT

I don't mind looking like Jean Shrimpton, but I don't think I can take the Joni phase again—I mean, all that angst.
Oy.
Violet! Come watch! David Crosby just got out of jail!

Gloria Stavers has passed on. I wonder, is she "Herself"? Or is she up there trying to look like someone, really?
cloud nine #15
she died of Tragic Hipness
uh oh.
And I created a comic strip character, and call her Violet. I can go on acting like a jerk~ and Violet can ... "Be Herself"
But I look just like Betty!
oh yeah?
Many thanks to Jake.

DISASTROUS RELATIONSHIPSLAND
Hi, Honeeze! Today we will visit madcap "DISASTROUS RELATIONSHIPSLAND" in sunny San José-Steve-Brad, Ca.!
There are many fabulous rides and attractions here in the beautiful Santa Casanova Valley. The Jilt-a-Girl is sure to shake you up - or just TRY a little tenderness on the ... OCTOPUS!
WHEW! That was titti lating! Now why don't we just sit here and wait for the phone to ring at the GIVE-HIM-SOME-SPACE needle?
TOO RELAXED ???? I recommend that you DRIVE YOURSELF CRAZY on the Dump'er Cars!
CAD
CONFUSED? Probably a good time for some BONE-CHILLING REGRESSION on one of the comfy couches here at the (brrrr) HAUNTED HOUSE!
Yikes! It's my PARENTS!
yes, dear.
Golf! When are we going shopping??
SPORTS
In the Original® House of Mirrors, you can meet someone just like you! In fact, exactly like you! Maybe even a bit too much... like... you.
You HATE Billy Joel? Asparagus?? David Letterman?
yuk. ick. blech.
Spandex bicycle shorts?
Oh god those are the worst.

On the Marry-go-Round, grab as many rings as you can ~ and throw them in that clown's face!
Boy, this place sure is in-tense. So why not take a little stroll down International Way? "Get Over" all your Disastrous relationships with a nice SWISS GUY RIDE~ and enjoy a fine birds-and-bees-eye view of a whole League of nation's worth of dating possibilities!
She Matterhorny
AFRICAN RASTA SAFARI
TUNNEL O' LIKE
HASSAN'S HAREM HUT
She Matterhorny
GAY Paree
SPACE CAD
GO. DUTCH
One attraction I found particularly...attractive... was the Tunnel of Luv, where all the blokes are English!
'COR! Fancy all de plonky birds!
I'm a real Jack the lad I am
Bu' I'm ge'-in really pissed... legless..
YEAH BUT WOT'S HE SAYING?
GOD HE'S CUTE
Spare a fag? Oim skint!
"Mick Jagger"
Wotcha, luv! Care to chuck sum arrows?
Now don't get your knickers in a twist...
Yeah-um-there's nothing quite LIKE Disastrous Whateverland. And-uh-there's still-um-time to drag yourself through the MID-WAY LIFE CRISIS!
HAPPILY MARRIED? AND YOU DON'T HAVE ANY KIDS YET???
care to join me, ma'am?
no, thanx. I'm happily married, I think...
you can have it ALL!
End

WIMMEN'S COMIX TAKES A VACATION

Violet in Paris

© 1984 Caryn Leschen

HI, THERE, WANNA GO SIGHTSEE ?

BUT NOBODY WANTED TO HAVE ANYTHING TO DO WITH ME.

SO I TOOK TO THE STREETS OF GAY PAREE, ALONE.

BUT FIRST, WHAT'S THIS - BEHIND THE LOO DOOR ? TWO FOOTPRINTS, AN' A HOLE IN THE FLOOR ?

SO I WENT OFF TO FIND THE COMIC-BOOK STORE, AND A PHONE.

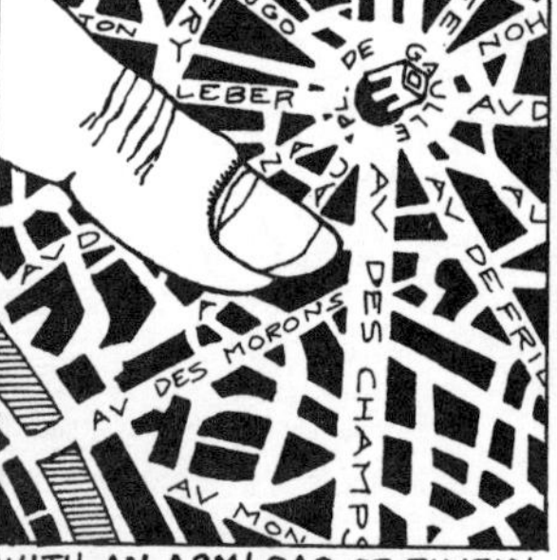

WITH AN ARMLOAD OF TINTIN AND CLARE BRÉTÉCHER I CONSULTED MY MAP FOR THE CHAMPS ELYSÉES.

AND BEHIND ME A VOICE SAID, "I'M CLAUDE DUBUFFET, I'LL SHOW YOU AROUND"

HE TOOK ME TO A SQUAT AT A SLEAZY ADDRESS

"BON MATIN" SAID A WOMAN WITH ONE BARE BREAST

A JUNKIE SNORED ON THE FLOOR - WHAT A MESS !!

NEEDLES ON THE DININGROOM TABLE, DRIED BLOOD

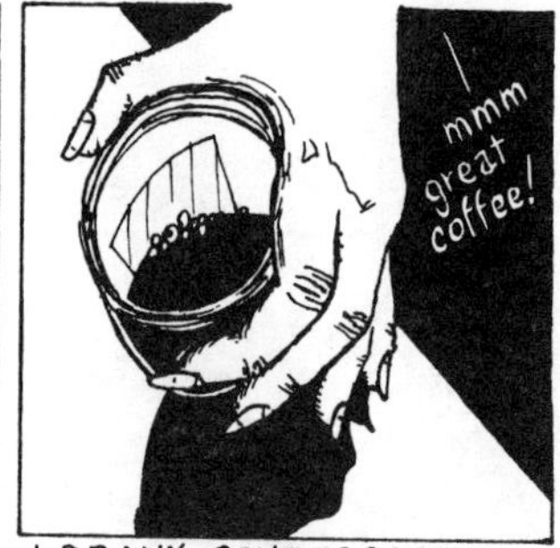

I DRANK SOME ESPRESSO THAT TASTED LIKE MUD, FROM A JAR.

THERE WAS ALSO AN EXTRA-LARGE TUPPERWARE DISH

"HOW NICE" I SAID, JOKINGLY, "TUNA FISH ?"

NO, A HUNDRED HASHISH HOCKEY PUCKS. "WE'LL USE THESE PAPERS, THAT PIPE SUCKS."

OH, OKAY.

THEY TOLD ME SOME FRIENDS ROBBED AN ARMOURED VAN,

TOOK A MILLION FRANCS TO THE YUCATAN;

DID COCAINE IN SUCH MASS QUANTITY, IN A WEEK THEY WIRED ACROSS THE SEA

FOR MONEY TO GET BACK TO GAY PAREE.

SO BACK TO THE STREETS
AT HALF-PAST FOUR

I LEFT POOR CLAUDE
ON THE CRACKED-HOUSE FLOOR

WENT TO A BISTRO AND
ORDERED CANARD

"MONSIEUR!" I CRIED,
"THIS TASTES LIKE LARD!"

THIS CREATURE NEVER LAID ANY EGGS,
IN FACT-

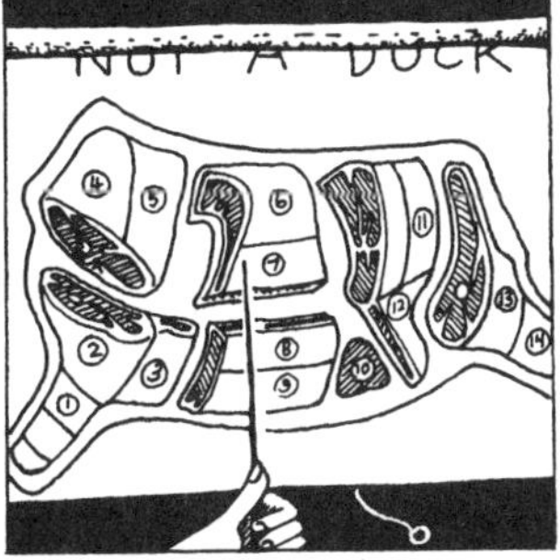

I'M SURE IT WALKED ON
FOUR LEGS!

IN PARIS MEN PISS JUST
WHEREVER THEY STAND

I ESCAPED TO A CLUB
TO SEE A BAND

A PERSPIRING DANCER TOOK MY HAND
FOR A KISS.

BUT I WAS WRONG, I KNOW THAT NOW.
HE WIPED MY CLEAN HAND
'CROSS HIS SWEATY BROW.

'TWAS MORE THAN MY STOMACH
WOULD ALLOW -
IT WAS GROSS.

WELL, THAT'S ENOUGH, I THOUGHT
FOR ONE DAY,
I WENT BACK TO THE STUDENT FOYER

MADE THE BED

BRUSHED MY TEETH AND
COMBED MY HAIR

WHEN I RETURNED
A YOUNG GERMAN BOY
WAS SLEEPING THERE.

"GET OUT OF MY BED!" I SAID,
IN ENGLISH.

NEXT MORNING OVER CUPS OF TEA

A FRESH, YOUNG AMERICAN
SAT DOWN NEXT TO ME.

SHE SAID, "HI, THERE,
WANNA GO SIGHTSEE?"

I SAID, "YOU'RE KIDDING".

Violet in
THE MAGIC LEMON
(a girly car story.)
©1988 Caryn Leschen
Long, long ago (last October) and far, far away (in Paris)-before I started painting animation cells for Fruity Marshmallow Krunchies- I met a lovely australian girl named Shari Lee- and her French car.
I always did like dancing fruits & vegetables.
My husband just went back to San Francisco & I fainted in front of the Louvre.
Yeh-I just dropped my x-boyfriend off at the airport & my car fainted in front of this hotel.
Shari and her boyfriend had just broken up, and her Citroën 2cv had just broken down, right in front of the Salade des Fruits Hotel.
So we drove this silly car all over Europe & on the way to Paris he tells me he's gotten my best girlfriend pregnant. She's gay! How...80's. Now he's gone back to Melbourne.
your card in the "Life's Path" position is "The Fool"
Shit- so is mine.
We had alot in common.
We both wore red lipstick and purple eyepencil. We even had the same birthday- the next Friday, uh, the thirteenth.
...so why don't we blow this chic crepe-stand and go to Barcelona to celebrate our birthdays?
Brilliant! Except I don't have enough money to take the train.
So we stood outside the hotel & tried to sell the Citroën which is "lemon" in French.
C'est une BELLE voiture! Et pour VOUS... 100 francs! *
zis car... does eet come weeth zee girl?
2cv
*it's a beautiful car! And for you...17 bucks!
Shari, are you sure it won't...wait! Omigod, it's started!
Don't turn it off! I'll get our things!!
RRRRRRR
Soon we were off to Barcelona! Soon we were off to Barcelona!
FRENCH L-MART
why didn't you tell me there was no gas in it?
GAZ
DAMN! There it goes again! My foot isn't even on the accelerator. This car is DRIVING ITSELF.
GOOD. Will you open this bottle of Petit Cru, then? My hands are all sticky from the pain chocolat!
Ahhh! The French pays du vin. I can smell the grapes ripening on the vine!
Shari that's because you spilled wine all over the front seat.
FRENCH KRISPIES

After dining on exotic whelk and pencilfish, the Birthday Girls took in one of Barcelona's Magic Bars.
FOOL
TAPA'S 250
FOR HOW MUCH?
Señoritas, come here! I am the Great Gregorio, warlock & gardener. I can guess your signs!
We figured any idiot could tell it was our birthdays.
THWOOP
BIRTHDAY GIRL
BIRTHDAY GIRL
You are TAURUS and YOU are LEO.
NO.
Pisces and Virgo!
nnnno.
Aries and Gemini?
NO!!
Gregorio's friend, Manolo, entertained us with a wierd gutteral noise he'd mastered with the back of his throat.
NO
GLLLLGLLL
Would you like to watch me magically balance this bottle on the edge of the table?
It was clearly time to take off in the Magic Lemon - but the CAR was GONE!!
magic bar
I guess it really was a magic bar!
yeah, it made our wheels disappear!
There was, however, still some magic left.
Hello, ladies! I am Pablo, a gorgeous Spanish cop that speaks perfect English. I will find your car for you.
Oh no! All that's left is this lousy tape deck!
REALLY? And I've been wanting to bring one to my poor sick mother in Madrid.
MARS
The next day at dawn, I boarded my bus for Italy.
oh, you can have it but it's terrible. When are you going to Madrid?
Tomorrow morning. Would you care to join me?
MILAN
ITALY
here are the keys to the Magic Lemon & an Australian dollar. Call me if you ever get to Australia.
PARIS
SF
BOSS
Violet, stop daydreaming! That lemon is not gonna PAINT ITSELF.
oh, really?
END.
©1988

DORI SEDA

Dori Seda was born June 6, 1951, in Elk Grove, Illinois. She earned a B.A. in art from Illinois State University in 1975 and moved to the San Francisco Bay Area in 1977. Her artistic efforts consisted of paintings and ceramics until 1980 when K. Lambert persuaded her to collaborate on a comic book story he had written. The result, "Bloods in Space," appeared in *Weirdo #2.* Encouraged by the reception it received, Dori began writing and drawing stories for *Weirdo, Wimmen's Comix,* and other publications, growing quickly in skill and renown. *Lonely Nights,* a comic book consisting entirely of her work, was published in 1986. A heavy smoker, she suffered from emphysema, a condition she never admitted to having. She died abruptly of heart and respiratory failure on February 26, 1988, after the onset of a severe case of flu. For an "alternate world" treatment of her life and personality, see "Dori Bangs" by Bruce Sterling (reprinted in *The Year's Best Science Fiction,* St. Martin's Press, 1990). She also appears in the Les Blank film, *Gap-toothed Women.*

The following dialogue is an excerpt of a conversation between Krystine Kryttre and Don Donahue, October 1990.

KRYTTRE: Wasn't it amazing to watch Dori construct her stories out of things that happened? She'd call me up on the phone and say, "Oh, oh! Biff made brains last night!" and a week later it's a script for a story. Even the most mundane things about her dog or about shirts for you. . . .

DONAHUE: That dog! He followed her home one night and she kept him. Her apartment was way too small for a dog that size.

KRYTTRE: They were *very* close, weren't they?

DONAHUE: Everybody was close to Tona in that apartment.

KRYTTRE: I never met Tona but I know his smell . . . the worst smell in the world. Nothing lives, breathes or crawls that has a smell quite like it. It wasn't a dog smell, it was musky, scrotty, stagnating, fermenting, feral. . . .

DONAHUE: That smell remains on every item that was ever in Dori's apartment for any length of time. I have Dori's vacuum cleaner that I never use because as the motor heats up all the dog smell comes out and fills the room . . . likewise her electric mixer.

KRYTTRE: Every time we'd go out it would be a major theatrical event. You couldn't go somewhere with Dori and not have everyone there looking at you. Whenever she would walk into a room, the party would start and things would get goofy.

DONAHUE: That bunny suit night was nerve-wracking for me because I thought I was going to have to fight somebody to defend her honor. The bunny suit had something like suspenders instead of a bra and her tits kept falling out. . . . Dori went to live with you for a month when she thought I had scabies.

KRYTTRE: Yes, she got all set up in my room, she had her little table and her kitties. I'd go to work in the morning and she'd still be asleep, and I'd get home at five and she'd be drawing and probably well into her third beer by then. . . . She'd be all happy and excited and go, "Krystine! Krystine! You're home, you're home! Look what I drew today!" She did a lot of work when she was staying with me. We'd sit down and draw together all day and talk about stuff. We'd both be in our little personal drawing trances but we'd be linked to each other too. If it wasn't for Dori I don't know what I'd be doing now. She gave me a really solid, positive encouragement. Dori was *absolutely* committed to being an underground cartoonist. Doing anything else simply wasn't worth her time.

Let's Eat Brains

a True Story Featuring

and

WHY DO YOU DRAW NATASHA SO BEAUTIFUL, AND ME SO FUNNY LOOKING?!!

BIFF

© 1987 DORI SEDA

NA-TA-SHA! IT SAYS HERE, IN ADELLE DAVIS' "LET'S COOK IT RIGHT," THAT BRAINS ARE THE RICHEST SOURCE OF B VITAMINS.
AND LISTEN TO ALL THESE YUMMY RE-CIPES..... "SAUTE'ED BRAINS WITH LEMON SAUCE," ..."CREAMED BRAINS,".... "BRAIN SALAD"...

YOU GIRLS JUST DON'T HAVE ANY SENSE OF ADVENTURE!!
HMMM... ALL I NEED IS SOME MASKING TAPE AND A MARKER.
Adelle Davis
LET'S COOK IT RIGHT
THUD!

Adelle Davis
LET'S EAT BRAINS
HEH-HEH

LATER...
TEE-HEE!
YOU'RE REAL FUNNY, DORI... I JUST LOOKED THROUGH YOUR COOKBOOK, AND LISTEN TO THIS! "BAKED BRAINS," ..."BROILED BRAINS"...
YOUR COOKBOOK SHOULD BE CALLED "THE JOY OF BRAINS!!"
JOY

THEN ONE EVENING BIFF CAME INTO MY STUDIO.
I'M MAKING DINNER TONIGHT, AND YOU AN' DON ARE INVITED!
HEY THANKS! WHAT TIME?
WAIT A SECOND... WHY IS BIFF BEING SO NICE TO ME?

UH-BIFF?... WHAT ARE YOU MAKING FOR DINNER?
BRAAAINS.
UH-THANKS, BUT I'LL PASS THIS TIME.

DORI!- WILL YOU COME DOWN HERE?! WE'RE HAVING A PARTY, AND THE BRAINS SMELL GREAT!!
OHHHKAAY...

I TRIED TO BE A SPORT ABOUT IT, BUT...
I'M SORRY... I JUST CAN'T EAT THIS.

BIFF!- MOST PEOPLE, WHEN THEY HAVE A DINNER PARTY, THEY COOK SOMETHING YUMMY... BUT YOU COOK SOMETHING THAT'S ABSOLUTELY DISGUSTING, AND THEN YOU DARE YOUR GUESTS TO EAT IT!!
SAUTÉED BRAINS WITH LEMON SAUCE AND CAPERS ARE YUMMY! - JUST TRY THEM!!.... ADELLE DAVIS CALLS BRAINS "SUPERIOR MEATS," 'CUZ OF ALL THE VITAMINS!!
YEAH-WELL, ADELLE DAVIS DIED OF CANCER!!
FUCK YOU, DORI!!!
YOU MUST WANT TO GET SMARTER, AND YOU THINK THE WAY TO DO IT IS TO EAT BRAINS! - WELL, THAT'S NOT HOW YA DO IT!!!
OH YEAH?- YOU DON'T HAVE ANY BRAINS, AND YOU DON'T NEED ANY BRAINS! ... ALL YOU EVER DO IS WRITE THOSE STUPID COMIC STORIES!!!
MMMM...
I LIKE THE WAY THE MEMBRANE PEELS OFF.
GREAT LEMON SAUCE, SCOOB.
DELICIOUS, BIFF!

BIFF'S DINNER PARTIES BECAME A WEEKLY EVENT AT THE WAREHOUSE, BUT I WAS NEVER INVITED AGAIN.
I REALLY LIKE IT WHEN BIFF DOES THE COOKING, BUT I WISH HE'D LEARN HOW TO MAKE SOMETHING ELSE.
DINNER'S READY FOR EVERYBODY BUT DORI!!
CHICKEN MARINATED IN WINE AND TARRAGON (SOMETHING NORMAL)

THEN BIFF'S PARENTS CAME TO VISIT....
THEY'RE REALLY YUMMY! ADELLE DAVIS SAYS THEY HAVE LOTS OF B VITAMINS, AND NATASHA AND I HAVE SO MUCH ENERGY AFTER WE EAT THEM!
BIFF!- YOU'RE NOT MAKING BRAINS FOR YOUR PARENTS?!!

YOU DON'T LIKE BRAINS EITHER? - I'M WITH YOU!
LET'S GO TO A RESTAURANT!!
DON'T LISTEN TO DORI! - SHE WON'T EVEN TRY BRAINS!! SHE'S JUST A TROUBLEMAKER!!

THAT NIGHT I HAD INSOMNIA.
MAYBE I'LL BE ABLE TO GO TO SLEEP IF I HAVE SOME SNACKY.

SHIT. NOTHING IN OUR REFRIGERATOR BUT BREWSKIS AND CAT FOOD.

HMMM...THEY LEFT SOME BRAINS ON THE STOVE. NOW MIGHT BE A GOOD TIME TO TRY SOME, WITHOUT BIFF AROUND TO GLOAT AT ME.

UHHH...MUSHY.

BLAAAAGHH!!!
The End

ANOTHER DISGUSTING TONA-TOONS STORY...
Cleanliness is next to Dogliness!!
SNORT!
Featuring
TONA
and his
ITCHY DOG-BUTT

BOY-IT'S BEEN A ROUGH DAY AT WORK, THE CAR BROKE DOWN...
I NEED A NICE COLD BREWSKI!

YEAH, TONA! I KNOW YOU WANT A DOG-WALK!!
HERE-HAVE SOME DOG FOOD... THAT OUGHTTA KEEP YOU ENTERTAINED FOR A FEW MINUTES AT LEAST.
SNORT!
DOG GRAVEL
RATTLE!

AHHHH....
OH-DRACULA! YA WANNA BE LOVAROONIE KITTY?
PURRR...

HEY!
FITZ ROWR!!!
BLOMP!

TONA - YOU'RE TOO BIG TO SIT ON MY LAP!!!
FITZ!

NOW I SUPPOSE YOU WANT A BUTT-RUB.
SCRATCH! SCRATCH!

YECCH! - TONA, YOUR ECZEMA IS GETTING PRETTY BAD.
GET OFF MY LAP- YOU'RE COVERING ME WITH ECZEMA FLAKES!!

WHAT'S THIS?
HA HA HA!
DAMMIT, TONA! YOU'VE ITCHED UP ANOTHER HOT SPOT!!

JUST WHAT I NEED... A DOG WITH DISGUSTING OPEN SORES ALL OVER HIS BODY!
YEAH, TONA - I'LL TAKE YOU FOR A DOG-WALK AS SOON AS I WASH YOUR ECZEMA FLAKES OFF MY HANDS!

TONA-STOP FLAUNTING THAT DISGUSTING OPEN SORE!!
DOES YOUR POOR DOGGY HAVE MANGE, DEAR?

BACK HOME AGAIN...

I BETTER GIVE YOU A BATH BEFORE MY NEIGHBORS REPORT ME TO THE S.P.C.A. FOR "DOG ABUSE."

I NEED A COUPLE MORE BREWSKIS FIRST.

OK, MISTER-NOT-VERY-PLEASANT... GET YOUR ITCHY DOG-BUTT IN HERE!!

OH NO.

FITZ! FITZ!

IT'S QUITE A FEAT FOR A SKINNY, DRUNK CARTOONIST TO DRAG A SOAPY, SLIPPERY, STRUGGLING, 100 LB. DOBERMAN INTO THE SHOWER.
COME ON, YOU JERK!!!
SHE'S GONNA KILL ME THIS TIME - I KNOW IT!!
SCRATCH!
MMMM... NICE BUTT-RUB, TONA...
GOOD-HE'S STOPPED FIGHTING.
AND WE'RE GONNA RINSE ALL THE HOT SPOTS, AND ALL THE ECZEMA OFF THE DOG-BUTT.
I REALLY DON'T FUCK MY DOG, BUT THIS IS PROBABLY EQUALLY AS DISGUSTING.
NOW LET'S GET THE WHOLE DOG IN HERE...
REEK!
REEK!
OK, TONA. ALL DONE.
YAAY!
SNORT!
SCRAMBLE!
I'M CLEAN!
MY BUTT DOESN'T ITCH!
I DON'T STINK ANYMORE!

REEK!
REEK!
I'M FILTHY.
I'M COVERED WITH DOG HAIR AND ECZEMA FLAKES.
I SMELL LIKE ITCHY DOG-BUTT.
MEOW?
CLOUD OF DOG-SMELL FILLING THE ENTIRE APARTMENT

REEK!
REEK!
REEK!
I NEED TO LAY DOWN, BUT I'M TOO DIRTY TO GET IN BED.
MEOW?

REEK!
REEK!
I'M FREEZING, BUT I'M TOO DIRTY TO PUT ON MY BATHROBE... 'GUESS I SHOULD TAKE A SHOWER.
CHATTER!

UGH!- THE WHOLE BATHROOM IS RUINED FOREVER.
SNORT!

'GUESS I'LL JUST WRAP MYSELF UP IN TONA'S DOG-BLANKET, AND HAVE ANOTHER BREWSKI...
REEK!
MEOW?

GOD, WHAT A HORRIBLE DAY.
PURRR...
The End

FASHION AS A LOSING BATTLE!

WHEN I WAS FIRST GOING OUT WITH DON, I THOUGHT HE WAS CUTE EXCEPT.....

OH, DORI DAHLING, THAT DRESS IS SIMPLY DEEVINE ON YOU!

THANKS! I SEWED THE SKIRT MYSELF.

WHY DOES DON ALWAYS WEAR THOSE PLAID FLANNEL SHIRTS EVERYWHERE HE GOES? HE LOOKS LIKE A LUMBERJACK!

SOMETIMES DON WOULD GET "DRESSED UP", AND WEAR A SPORT JACKET OVER HIS FLANNEL SHIRT.

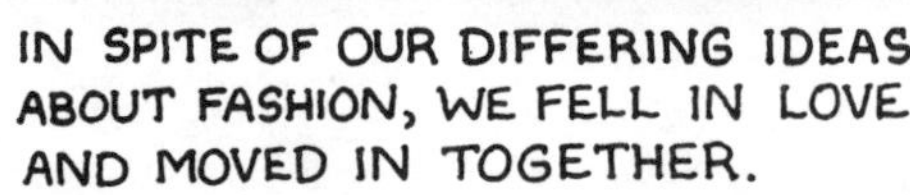

IN SPITE OF OUR DIFFERING IDEAS ABOUT FASHION, WE FELL IN LOVE AND MOVED IN TOGETHER.

IT'S GONNA BE SO WONDERFUL HAVING YOU WITH ME EVERY DAY!

YEAH... TOMORROW LET'S GO OUT AND BUY YOU SOME NEW CLOTHES!

DON WASN'T VERY RECEPTIVE TO THE "NEW IMAGE" I HAD IN MIND FOR HIM.

DON LIKED HIS NEW SWEATER AND PANTS A LOT.
HONEY, ARE YOU SLOPPING AROUND IN YOUR GOOD CLOTHES AGAIN?
WELL, I DON'T WANT THE WOMAN AT THE POST OFFICE TO THINK I'M A LUMBERJACK.
DON, THAT SWEATER LOOKS REALLY GOOD ON YOU.
LILY- THAT'S HIS GOOD SWEATER, AND HE WEARS IT EVERY DAY!

THREE MONTHS LATER...
GEE, THIS SWEATER MUST NOT HAVE BEEN MADE VERY WELL... IT'S GOT LITTLE FUZZY THINGS ALL OVER IT, AND THE SLEEVES ARE ALL STRETCHED OUT OF SHAPE.
THE SWEATER WAS MADE FINE - YOU JUST WORE IT TO DEATH!
NOW WHAT ARE YOU GOING TO WEAR TO THE PARTY TONIGHT?

OUR SECOND SHOPPING TRIP WAS LESS OF A STRUGGLE.
I GUESS YOU WERE RIGHT ABOUT PARTY SHIRTS!
SEE HONEY! YOU LOOK REAL NICE!
LET'S BUY TWO. -JUST PROMISE ME YOU WON'T WEAR THEM EVERY DAY, OK?

THEN WE WENT TO VISIT DON'S MOTHER, WHO HATES ME.
DORI BOUGHT YOU THAT SHIRT? HA! IT LOOKS LIKE A MATERNITY DRESS!
DORI DOESN'T KNOW HOW TO COOK A POT ROAST EITHER!
ALSO, DORI'S A HORRIBLE PERSON BECAUSE SHE DIDN'T COME WITH YOU TO VISIT ME ON EASTER, TWO YEARS AGO!

LAST WEEK WE WERE INVITED TO ANOTHER PARTY.
HEY- WHY AREN'T YOU WEARING ONE OF YOUR NEW SHIRTS?
BECAUSE THEY LOOK LIKE MATERNITY DRESSES.
THEY DO NOT!! BESIDES- IT'S THE WRONG KIND OF WEATHER FOR A FLANNEL SHIRT!!

YEAH... IT LOOKS LIKE IT MIGHT RAIN TONIGHT- MAYBE I SHOULD GO BACK IN AND GET MY SWEATER...
THE END

OF HUMAN BONDAGE AND DISCIPLINE
©1985 D. SOMERSET SEDA
IT'S A SATURDAY NIGHT, AND EVERYBODY'S OUT PARTYING... EXCEPT DORI, THE DEVOTED ARTIST, WHO IS VIRTUOUSLY AT HER DRAWING BOARD.
IRRESISTIBLE BITCH! I WISH I COULD RESIST! HURT ME! OWOWOW OW!
WHY AM I SO FAITHFUL, HONEY? WHY ARE YOU SO LOOSE?
'GUESS I NEED ANOTHER BREWSKI!
GEE... ONLY ONE BEER LEFT... MAYBE I SHOULD RUN TO THE LIQUOR STORE AND GET A COUPLE MORE BOTTLES!
DON'T BE A LIGHTWEIGHT! GET A COUPLE MORE SIX-PACKS!!
YA BETTER HURRY!-THE LIQUOR STORE'S GONNA CLOSE IN TEN MINUTES!
YOU'VE GOT A FULL CAN OF V-8 JUICE AND YOU'RE ALREADY DRUNK! BESIDES, YOU KNOW WHAT MISCHIEF YOU ALWAYS GET INTO WHEN YOU LISTEN TO THAT DEVIL-DORI!
THE ANGEL-DORI IS RIGHT! I REMEMBER A COUPLE OF YEARS AGO, BEFORE I CLEANED UP MY ACT...
WHY NOT PICK UP ANOTHER SIX-PACK WHILE YOU'RE AT IT?
I JUST CAN'T DRAW THE CASTRO THEATRE FROM MEMORY... MAYBE I SHOULD GO DOWN THERE RIGHT NOW AND MAKE A SKETCH.
MEOW?
...MAYBE I SHOULD PICK UP ANOTHER SIX-PACK WHILE I'M AT IT.
YEAH! AND YOU DON'T WANT TO GO OUT LOOKING LIKE THAT!.. PUT ON A LITTLE MAKE-UP!

LATER
YOU LOOK NICE! ARE YOU GOING TO A PARTY?
NO, I'M JUST ON MY WAY TO SKETCH THE CASTRO THEATRE.
?
YUCK! EVERY CREEP IN THE MISSION IS NOTICING ME... I SHOULDN'T HAVE PUT ON ALL THIS MAKE-UP.
SMACK!
A GARAGE SALE AT MIDNIGHT? I BETTER CHECK THIS OUT!
GARAGE SALE! BOOKS CLOTHING
"THE COMPLETE VAMPIRE?"... "TALES OF SATANISM?" WHAT AN ODD COLLECTION OF BOOKS.
...NOW THIS ONE'S A PERFECT CHRISTMAS PRESENT FOR MY BOY-FRIEND!
FAMOUS SEX CRIMES
I MUST HAVE THIS BOOK! BUT I ALREADY SPENT ALL MY MONEY ON BEER... WOULD YOU CONSIDER TRADING FOR A SIX-PACK?
NO PROBLEM! WOULD YOU LIKE TO JOIN US FOR BREAKFAST AT MUNCHKINS?
FAMOUS SEX CRIMES
NO, THANK YOU- ACTUALLY, I'M A CARTOONIST, AND I'M ON MY WAY TO SKETCH THE CASTRO THEATRE...
OOOOH! ARE YOU ANYBODY FAMOUS?
UH, NO.
THESE PEOPLE ARE WEIRD... GOD, LOOK AT THE TIME!

I'VE GOT JUST ENOUGH TIME TO GO HOME FOR MORE MONEY, AND GET BACK TO THE LIQUOR STORE BEFORE TWO O'CLOCK.
HEY! IF YOU DECIDE TO JOIN US, DON'T FORGET!-WE'LL BE AT MUNCHKINS!
FAMOUS SEX CRIMES
PUFF PUFF
I JUST MADE IT!
HEY DORI! LONG TIME, NO SEE!! I'LL WAIT FOR YOU OUTSIDE!
Liquors
GOOOD NIGHT!
HI FRED!
HEY! WOULD YA LIKE A LITTLE "NOSE CANDY?"
...I DON'T HAVE ANY MONEY, BUT I'VE GOT THIS SIX-PACK OF BEER!-HOW WOULD YOU LIKE TO COME OVER TO MY PLACE!
'SOUNDS GOOD, SWEETHEART.
WHEN YOU GET TO BE A FAMOUS CARTOONIST, DON'T EVER FORGET THE MISSION... THAT'S WHY THE ROLLING STONES GOT SO FAMOUS-THEY NEVER FORGOT THEIR ROOTS!
OH! HOW COULD I EVER FORGET THE MISSION!
ABANDONED DRAWING BOARD
SITTING UP ALL NIGHT TALKING GARBAGE
6:00 AM
OH SHIT.
OH BABY...
CHIRP! CHIRP!

YA GOTTA GET OUTTA HERE... I GOTTA BOYFRIEND!
YEAH?-WHERE IS HE NOW?
PISSED 'CUZ HE DIDN'T GET LAID.
SLAM!
THE CORNER STORE OPENS AT SIX.... MAYBE A FEW MORE BEERS WILL STEADY MY NERVES, AND I'LL STILL BE ABLE TO GET SOME DRAWING DONE...
HE THINKS I'M A DEGENERATE.
HOW'S YOUR DOG?
TWEET!
HOW DO I GET MYSELF INTO THESE SITUATIONS?
DAMN!- I CAN'T DRAW ANYTHING NOW. ...'MAY AS WELL GIVE UP AND GO TO BED.
PEOPLE USED TO WONDER WHY IT TOOK ME SIX MONTHS TO FINISH DRAWING ONE STORY, BUT THOSE DAYS ARE OVER! I'VE BECOME MORE RESPONSIBLE, AND MORE PROFESSIONAL...
YEAH, I KNOW ALL THAT- BUT A GIRL'S GOTTA HAVE A LITTLE FUN!!
YA KNOW, YOU MIGHT BE RIGHT. ...MAYBE I HAVE BEEN WORKING TOO HARD LATELY!
OH, DORI... YOU'RE JUST HOPELESS!!
THE END

CAROL TYLER

Born, November 1951

Like most kids who grew up in the fifties, I wore corduroy pants. I liked popsicles, too. My idea of a good time was hiding under a card table with a blanket draped over it where I would dream up innocuous scenarios of triumph over my siblings. As the fourth child in a Catholic family, I didn't feel very important. It's unfortunate that this pain thing happens in families. What saved me was knowing that love was quietly functioning somehow in our house. Besides, every day was zany with my inventive family, and we didn't plan it that way which made it even more delightful. I would say that life with the Tylers both added to and took the edge off my angst. They turned me into an artist.

In my teens, I decided not to invest much time or energy into the hair/nails/makeup thing. I figured that if I established **hag** as my fashion statement early on, it wouldn't be such a shock to then someday look in the mirror at, say, age forty and see a bag lady. Now that I'm thirty-nine, I wish I had at least used moisturizer! I suppose Lady Clairol products could help hide the gray, but I've never been able to figure out my specific blonde type. At least I've finally managed to make some beauty decisions that work for me (better late than never): The armpit hair stays. The legs will be shaved during shorts season only. And the boob locks are not as disgusting to me as they were in 1967. The baby didn't mind the hairy coconuts while nursing. But in high school it seemed to be the primary reason why I could never become an exotic dancer.

Back in the seventies this psychic told me I was an old soul with some kind of "finishing" destiny in this lifetime. This probably explains my recent compulsion to buy a decent filing cabinet. Anyway, as a youngster I was very devout. But then came Vatican II in 1964 and everything went haywire. I quit the church. In search of spiritual resolve after a twenty-five year absence, I attended mass just a few months ago. What a disappointment. Too many people smiling and no Latin buzz words! Where was the enigmatic tree I used to hang my spiritual bouquets upon? I'm so confused about this faith business and yet this psychic told me my destiny was "finishing." . . . Maybe she said "*fishing.*" . . . I don't know. The music was blaring pretty loud that night at the toga party.

Carol Tyler's
"DeTOUR of DUTY"
April 1989
FRAMING IS A MAN'S PROFESSION.
Goddam boxes are everywhere
WHY CAN'T I SLEEP?!
MY WORK HISTORY IS NOT THAT DIFFERENT FROM ANYONE ELSE'S....
TWO OVER EASY
BAUK! GUESS NOW THEY'RE SCRAMBLED!
HA HA THAT'S ME!
MY RESUME: CLERK, MAP TECNICIAN FOR ZONING DEPT.; DOMESTIC ENGINEER; DRYWALLER; ARCHIVIST; TOFU PRESSER FOR A GURU WHO DRINKS HIS OWN PISS; SPEEDY FLORAL DELIVERY TO FUNERAL PARLORS; LUMBER SORTER; BARTENDRESS; MEDICAL ILLUSTRATOR; POPCORN GIRL AT THE SHOW; MODEL; STEVEDORE;
DUMKOPF! WAS IST LOS MIT DU?
I'LL LOCK YOU IN DA KOOL-AH MIT DA LIMBOIG-AH!
Helga's HOUSE of CHEESE
FFT! FFT!
Y'KNOW YOU REALLY ARE LUCKY TO BE ANSWERING PHONES FOR ME, "MR. MUSIC" HIMSELF! I USED TO PACK 'EM IN UP THERE IN BUFFALO. JUST LIKE PRESLEY.
JUST WAIT!
ANY DAY NOW THAT PHONE'S GONNA RING. THIS TIME I'M GOIN' STRAIGHT TO THE TOP!
SUCKING ON A TOOTH PICK
Mike's MUSIC MACHINE
•WEDDINGS• •PARTIES• •SPECIAL EVENTS•
SO YOU'RE THE CENSUS TAKER— GLAD TO KNOW YA! AND I'M SURE HAPPY UNCLE SAM RECOGNIZES THE IMPORTANCE OF ENUMERATING ALL HOUSING UNITS, EVEN OUR TRAILERS HERE IN THESE TENNESSEE HILLS. CAN'T LETCHA LOOK AROUND, THO... UNLESS YOU DISROBE.
SHRINKING VIOLET
Lester's LAZY BONES 'Retirement' Nudist Camp.
LIKE A LOT OF GIRLS, MY FIRST JOB WAS BABYSITTING.
PUL-EEZE MOM?!
SURE I'LL GET THEM FOR YOU. BUT I WANT YOU TO START BEING RESPONSIBLE.
I WANT YOU TO GET A BABYSITTING JOB AND PAY ME BACK!
I PROMISE.
$6.5
WOOLWORTHS
LATEST BEATLE RECORDS
EARLY SEEDS OF MY CREDIT PROBLEMS
THE LANSKO'S HAD 6 KIDS WHO WERE BRATS. BUT IT WASN'T THEIR FAULT.
HI KIDS! YOUR MOM CALLED ME UP AND I'M GONNA SIT FOR YOU TONITE.
WE'RE NOT ALLOWED TO USE THE STOVE.
YOU COMIN' NOW? MOM'S NOT HERE AND WE'RE HUNGRY. WILL YA HEAT US UP SOME TOMATO SOUP?
OKEE DOKEE

THEIR MOM LEFT A LONG LIST OF CHORES FOR THEM TO DO AND I HAD TO ENFORCE IT... THEN PUT THEM TO BED.
SANDY YOU SPASTIK! NOW WE GOTTA WASH THE FLOOR AGAIN!
LET ME HAVE THAT BOWL!
NO! I'M NOT ALL DONE!

AT MIDNIGHT THE LANSKO'S WOULD RETURN FROM 6 HRS. OF SITTING IN THE TAVERN. I HAD TO REPORT EVERY ACTIVITY.
I SEE. SO THIS MAKES 2 WEEKS IN A ROW THAT JEFFY DIDN'T CLEAN OUT THE DOG PEN.
RICHARD! DON'T PICK HER UP LIKE THAT—
MR. LANSKO, LET ME DOWN!
BUT SHE'S SO LIGHT AND SO CUTE!
I THINK I'LL CARRY HER HOME LIKE THIS

AFTER TAKING ME HOME ON HIS SHOULDERS, MR. LANSKO WOULD THEN RETURN AND BEAT THE CRAP OUT OF WHOEVER DIDN'T FINISH THEIR CHORES (WAKING THEM FROM SLEEP!)
LETS SEE... 6 HRS. @ 50¢ per.
50, $1.00 50 $2.00 50
$3.00!
PAY HER, DEAR.
WE'D LIKE YA AGAIN NEXT WEEK
ONLY THIS TIME, WE'LL BE OUT TILL 2 AM.
AND IF THOSE LITTLE BRATS GIVE YOU ANY TROUBLE, YOU JUST LET ME KNOW!

ONE MONDAY I ACCIDENTLY TOOK THE WRONG BUS AND RAN INTO THE BROOD. I COULDN'T BELIEVE MY EYES.
I HAD NO IDEA! I'M SORRY!
RATFINK!
DAD ALMOST KILLED HIM!
JEFFY'S GOT A BROKEN ARM CUZ-ZA YOU!
I AUGHTA PULL YOUR PANTS DOWN AND SPANK YOU RIGHT HERE!

BUT MOM HAD TOLD ME TO DO WHAT MRS. LANSKO SAID 'CAUSE SHE WAS MY BOSS. I WAS MISERABLE. HOW ELSE WAS I GONNA PAY FOR MY RECORDS?
WAAA I HATE MYSELF!
Baby's good to me you know
She's happy as can be you know
she said so...
I'm in love with her and I feel FINE!
RF

I TOOK THE PROBLEM UP WITH MY REAL BOSS. HER SOLUTION WAS SIMPLE:
OH NO YA DON'T! IF YOU WANNA BEAT UP YOUR KIDS THAT'S YOUR BUSINESS.
BUTCHA AIN'T GONNA ABUSE MY KID IN THE PROCESS!
YOU'RE NOT OFF THE HOOK WITH THAT DEBT, Little Girl. ITS DISHES FOR A WEEK!
THANK YOU, MOTHER!
I WISH YOU COULD FIGHT ALL MY BATTLES!
THE END.

the RETURN of Mrs. KITE
1987-88
Carol Tyler
ITS CHICAGO, NOVEMBER, 1967— JUST ANOTHER TUESDAY NIGHT OR SO WE THOUGHT...
FOR THE TIMES CERTAINLY WERE 'A CHANGIN'. FOR US, THAT NIGHT IT GOT UNDER FULL SWING WITH:
Kleenex
WILL, DEAR— DID I EVER SHOW YOU THIS? ITS WATERFORD.
SURE, DOLL... ITS BEAUTIFUL. JUST LIKE YOU.
NOW... CAN WE GET TO THE BANK BEFORE IT CLOSES?
THIS'L BE MY LAST SAVINGS BOND, YOU KNOW.
DON'T WORRY, BABE. WHEN WE GET BACK TO MIAMI, I'LL GET A JOB.
PAT PAT
THE PLACE IS CRAWLIN' WITH JEWS. I'M SURE I CAN FIND SOME "FINE HOTEL" WORK.
WELL I WISH YOU WOULD— WE'VE GONE THRU AN AWFUL LOT OF MONEY THESE PAST FEW MONTHS
YOU REGRETTIN' IT?
UH (SIGH) I'M NOT SURE—
C'MON, STELLA! ITS ALL GONNA CHANGE I PROMISE YOU.

HALF HOUR LATER
I'D LIKE THAT IN FIFTIES AND HUNDREDS.
TELLER
THEN
WILL, DEAR— I'VE GOT IT!
HEY— DON'T BE FLASHIN' THAT MONEY AROUND. HERE, GIVE IT TO ME. NOW, YOU GO TO THE LITTLE GIRL'S ROOM WHILE I WATCH YOUR PURSE. WE'VE GOT A LONG FLIGHT AHEAD OF US.
MHM MHM!
STOP IT!
YOU ARE SO WONDER-FUL!
MMWUH
YECH
IN TWO MINUTES...
Ladies
YOU KNOW, I JUST CAN'T WAIT TO GET THERE & GET A HOT BATH...
!
Jesus Mary Joseph
MOMMY?
OH NO.. I'M AN ORPHAN AGAIN!!
UGH..

ACH! MEIN GOTT!
MAMA, LOOK
COME ON, HONEY. DON'T STARE! ITS JUST AN OLD SCRAGGLER WOMAN.

HEY! KNOCK KNOCK KNOCK KNOCK SOMEBODY COLL POL-LEESE!
AFE

ZEHR ISS A VOHMAN LAYHING HEOH!
HEY! OFFICER!
IS SHE YOUR SISTER?
NO, I AM PASSING LIKE YOU.
Wieboldts

ALL-RIGHT! LETS CLEAR IT OUT— WHAT HAPPENED?
VE DON'T KNOW. SHE JUSS FAINTED!
WHO IS SHE?
NOBODY KNOWS!
CHICAGO POLICE

NOTHING IN HERE BUT A SAFETY PIN...
YEAH, 1-9, THIS IS 1-8-3-7 WITH AN UNCONSCIOUS FEMALE, APPROX 80 YRS, IN NEED OF AN AMBULANCE CORNER LINCOLN-ADDISON, POSSIBLE JANE DOE, DO YOU READ?
POODR MISS-US.

MEANWHILE, OUT AT FOX LAKE...
IT WAS TWENTY YEARS AGO TODAY SGT. PEPPER TAUGHT THE BAND TO PLAY
THE WORLD'S GONE MAD!
IT SAYS HERE THAT IN 1947, 20 YEARS AGO, THE TAFT-HARTLEY ACT WAS PASSED OVER TRUMAN'S VETO IN JUNE, AND THAT IT WAS SO CONTROVERSIAL, IT WAS NICK-NAMED THE "Slave Labor" LAW.
GAHD! WHO CARES?! THAT WAS SO LONG AGO... DO YOU REMEMBER IT, MOM?
FREE LOVE
BRUM BRUM
GODDAMN FREE LOVE CHILDREN— TAKING PILLS TO GET HIGH! THEY SHOULD BE SHOT!
CLICK
MOM, CAN I WATCH TV?
Sears
I'M GOING UPSTAIRS!
6#!☆?;
SURE SON— AND GET THE WEATHER
HE'S GETTING MORE LIKE HIS MOTHER EVERY DAY.
YEAH: OLD and CRANKY
MOM, IS GRANDMA EVER COMING BACK?
I DON'T KNOW, HON.
I CAN'T BELIEVE SHE ELOPED WITH THAT WINO TENANT!
YEAH, YOUR FATHER WAS PRETTY UPSET...
HE'S STILL UPSET AND ITS BEEN ALMOST A YEAR.

I MEAN, CAN YOU IMAGINE SHOVELING HER WALKS IN SUB-ZERO WEATHER FOR 2 HRS...
AND THEN SEE YOUR MOTHER EMERGE WITH A MAN YOUNGER THAN YOU ARE...
MA! WHERE'YA GOIN?!
THEN THEY WALK PAST YOU, WITHOUT EVEN A SMILE, A HELLO, MUCH LESS A GLANCE...
NO GOOD-BYE....
Watchyer STEP, Doll.
GET INTO A WAITING CAB...
WITH A SUITCASE FULL OF CASH (WE FIND OUT LATER)...
AND FLY OFF TO FLORIDA.
BEARS
(WITH HIS BUDDIES THAT NIGHT)
I'LL KILL HIM!
MAYBE HE REALLY DOES TRULY LOVE HER— ALTHOUGH IT SEEMS HARD TO BELIEVE. CONSIDERING HER AGE.... AND ALL THAT MONEY—
SHE CAN DO WHAT SHE WANTS, CHARLIE. SHE'S AN ADULT.
SHE'S HEAD OF THE FAMILY—
SHE ONLY DID THIS TO GET MY GOAT.
NOW WAIT A MINUTE, CHUCK. YOUR MOTHER'S BEEN DESPERATELY LONELY SINCE SHE BECAME A WIDOW. WE ARE NOT TO JUDGE.
BULL-SHIT! THERE'S NO EXCUSE FOR DISHONORING PA!
SQUANDERING EVERYTHING HE BUILT UP...
MAKING A MOCKERY OUT OF THEIR MARRIAGE BY TAKING THE DRUNK'S NAME FOR CHRISSAKES...
("STELLA KITE."
aw TO HELL WITH HER— i'M GLAD SHE'S GONE.
PAIN IN THE NECK.
I AGREE
ER... UH...
WHAT ABOUT THIS NEW SEWER LINE THEY'RE PUTTIN' IN UP HERE, CHARLIE? BOY, AINT IT A DOOSIE
I WONDER IF SHE STILL HAS THOSE SHINY SLEEVES.
WHAT SHINY SLEEVES?

SHE USED TO WIPE HER NOSE ON HER SLEEVES.
THE SLEEVES OF HER DRESSES?!
EW GAHD! THAT IS SICK! I'LL DIE IF I TURN OUT LIKE THAT!
WHY DIDN'T SHE USE TISSUES?
TISSUE
SHE DID! BUT NOT TO WIPE HER NOSE WITH...
MA MAKES THOSE KLEENEX "CARNATIONS", YOU KNOW, WHERE YOU FOLD IT OVER AND OVER AND THEN PULL THE PETAL LAYERS OUT. AND YOU USE A BOBBY PIN FOR A STEM—
TISSUE
YOU'VE SEEN 'EM ALL OVER HER HOUSE—
POOR MIXED UP MA.... DROVE EVERYONE SHE LOVED OFF.
SHE ALWAYS SET A BEAUTIFUL TABLE, THOUGH.
AS LONG AS YOU DON'T OVERCOOK THE TURKEY WE'LL BE FINE
BREAD
DO YOU MISS HER, MOM?
I MISS HER LIKE A SORE THUMB.
Yipeee!
ITS 'SPOSED TO FREEZE TONITE!
CAN I GO SKATING TOMORROW
FLOUR
I WISH SHE'D COME BACK AND TELL MY FORTUNE—
FREEZE, HUH? WE'D BETTER PICK OUR MUMS!
CAN I GO OUTSIDE?
NO, YOU GET YOUR NIGHTIE ON.
BUT I NEED TO SEE SOMETHING
THE LAKE WON'T BE READY TILL CHRISTMAS. AND THATS 6 WKS. AWAY... FIRST THINGS FIRST, RIGHT MISS T?
WHAT MAKES YOU SO SPECIAL?
BECAUSE, BIRD BRAIN, IN CASE YOU HAVEN'T FIGURED IT OUT, SATURDAY IS MY BIRTHDAY—
SEEMS TO BE THE ONLY TIME ANYONE PAYS ATTENTION TO ME. EXCEPT WHEN I'M GETTING YELLED AT SO STOP PESTERING ME!

SOON...
GET IN THERE AND SHUT THE DOOR!
BUT I WANT TO WATCH THE WATER FREEZE.
GO IN THE HOUSE OR I'LL FREEZE YOUR BEHIND!
MOM, CAN I INVITE ONE OTHER PERSON TO THE PARTY?
BRR
ISN'T 20 ENOUGH?
WELL, YEAH. ITS JUST THAT LAURIE CAN'T COME UNLESS...
SHE GETS A RIDE WITH THIS TONY GUY.
WHO IS HE? DOES LAURIE'S MOTHER
WOOSH
KNOW? OOOH!
WOOSH
AAH! MY HAIR
HERE COMES OLD MAN WINTER BLOWIN' IN
SHE'D BETTER LET HIM DRIVE HER. ITS ONLY MY SWEET 16 PARTY, THE MOST IMPORTANT EVENT OF MY LIFE!
C'MON
WOOH! IT IS COLD OUT THERE!
STOMP STOMP
THIS MIGHT BE PUSHIN' IT, BUT I DON'T CARE! EVERYTHING'S GOTTA BE PERFECT.
CAN I, MOM? I MEAN, CAN LAURIE BRING TONY? SHE IS MY BEST FRIEND.
I DON'T KNOW. WE'LL SEE.
I'M THE COOLEST PERSON IN SCHOOL RIGHT NOW BECAUSE OF THIS PARTY—
WHAT A GREAT WAY TO WIN ED BACK FROM THAT THIEF BARBARA O'CONNOR!
AND I'LL BE "IN" FOR GOOD! INSTEAD OF THIS MARGINAL STATUS.
GO!
YOU'D BETTER GET ON UP AND FINISH YOUR HOMEWORK. ITS LATE. I'LL BRING UP YOUR FLOWERS WHEN I COME.
OK.
FIGHT
GO FIGHT WIN

FIGHT 2·3·4 TO NITE
BOMP BOMP
"WE'LL SEE."... GAHD- I HOPE I DIDN'T PISS HER OFF!
BOO! ha ha PEP SMARTY!
GO TO BED, MORON.
IN MY ROOM...
I think its time we STOP! hey what's that sound, everybody look what's goin' 'round
mar mar mar
IT WAS NICE OF LAURIE TO LEND ME HER LUCKY DRESS.
AND WHEN ED SEES ME IN THIS NUMBER, HE'LL WALTZ ACROSS THE ROOM, PICK ME UP, AND CARRY ME OFF TO FOREVER!
mar mar mar
AND BAB·O CAN DROP DEAD.
THANK GOD ITS SLEEVE-LESS. I WOULDN'T WANT 'EM TO GET SHINY!
CARMEL H.S.
MUM
paranoia strikes deep
Into your life it will creep
starts when you're always afraid
BEING 16 IS SO MUCH COOLER THAN BEING 15 - I GUESS I'D LET ED UNSNAP MY BRA IF IT CAME DOWN TO THAT.
OH NO YOU DON'T YOU'RE NOT WEARING THAT. YOUR FATHER'LL HAVE A HEART ATTACK!
MAH-M!
BUT... WHY?!
step outta LINE the man come and take you A-way
CARMEL H.S.
R-RING R-RING
I'D BETTER GET THAT PHONE
Hello
Yes..
I think its time we STOP!
PLUNK
HOW CAN YOU DO THIS TO ME, MOTHER!
YOU DON'T UNDERSTAND
OH MY GOD WHERE!
IT'LL TAKE US AN HOUR BUT WE'LL HURRY.
WELL
WHAT IS IT

CHUCK, THEY'VE FOUND YOUR MOTHER, SHE'S HAD A STROKE—
THEY DON'T EXPECT HER TO LIVE THRU THE NIGHT!

SHE WAS DOWN ON LINCOLN AVENUE UNCONSCIOUS.
THEY THINK SHE'D BEEN ROBBED.
OH FER CHRISSAKES!
HOW LONG HAS SHE BEEN BACK?!
LETS GET THE HELL OUTTA HERE!
JEZUZ WHERE ARE MY PANTS!
MO-M, WHAT'S WRONG?

OH HONEY- GRANDMA'S BACK BUT SHE'S VERY SICK...
YOU SAID MAYBE SHE... SHE WON'T LIVE TONIGHT.
THAT'S NOT FOR YOU TO THINK ABOUT OR WORRY ABOUT.
BUT MOM—
SHH! GO BY YOUR SISTER—
WAAA!
...I WONDER IF THEY'RE ALWAYS GOING TO BE SO JOYLESS. ..NEVER DO ANYTHING FUN.. NEVER LET ME DO ANYTHING EXCEPT HOW THEY WANT ME TO DO IT.
I CAN'T WAIT TO GET AWAY FROM THEM..
THEY'RE NUTS!
WHY IS HE CRYING? ITS ANNOYING ME.

OK, KIDS - I'LL CALL YOU AS SOON AS WE KNOW SOMETHING.
WHAT'S GOING ON?
YOUR GRANDMA IS IN THE HOSPITAL.
HERE?
LETS HIT THE ROAD

I'LL CALL YOU
GRAMMA'S GONNA DIE! SHE'S OLD!
No SHE'S NOT
STOP CRYING
SHE'LL BE OK...
SHE'D BETTER
HOW COULD YOU DO THIS TO ME "MRS. KITE"!
IF YOU DIE ON MY BIRTHDAY I'LL KILL YOU!
end.

un-covered property
©1987 Carol Tyler
A SHORT STUDY IN FAMILY DYNAMICS
FEATURING:
MOM and DAD
GINIA and JOE
(JIN-UH)
JIMMY and GU (SAY GUH)
(and me)

summer 1960

I'M WORKING WITH THE MEN.

HI! I'M WORKING.
OUTTA THE WAY, SQUIRT.
SCHEUMP

HEY! YOU FORGOT ONE.

HERE GU.

DAD, CAN I DIG FOR AWHILE?
HELL NO!

COME IN HERE A MINUTE, MISS
AW MOM, WHY? I'M HELPING!

DON'T GIVE ME A HARD TIME!
OK OK
YOU'RE GONNA GET IT NOW! YUK YUK YUK
SHUT UP Nerk-o

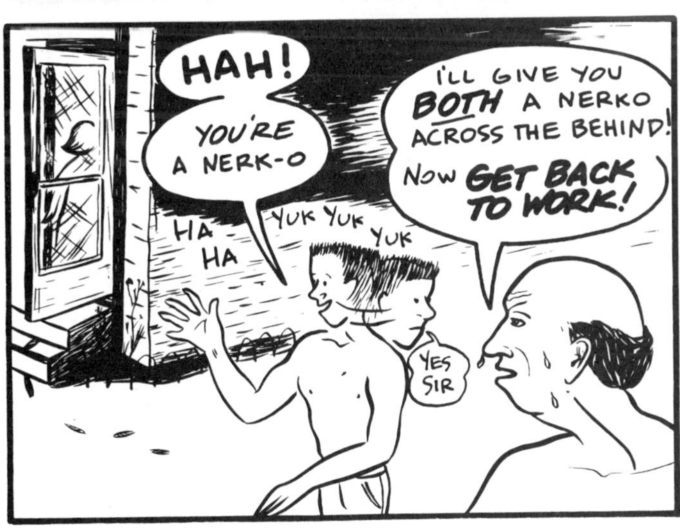
HAH!
YOU'RE A NERK-O
HA HA
YUK YUK YUK
I'LL GIVE YOU BOTH A NERKO ACROSS THE BEHIND!
Now GET BACK TO WORK!
YES SIR

MOM?
I'M IN HERE, HON!

THEN
SO FOR THE REST OF YOUR LIFE YOU CAN NEVER, EVER BE OUTSIDE WITHOUT YOUR SHIRT ON.
BUT I STILL DON'T KNOW WHY!?

THAT'S JUST THE WAY THINGS ARE, SWEETIE
ITS NOT FAIR
DAD AND JOE GET TO GO WITHOUT THEIR SHIRTS.

DAD AND JOE HAVE THEIR PROPERTY COVERED
YOU'RE A LADY LIKE MOMMY— AND LADIES COVER THEIR TOPS.
PUT THIS ON.
I DON'T WANT TO BE A LADY.

SO NOW, GO FIND YOUR SISTER, AND YOU FINISH THOSE DISHES.

AND DON'T WAKE THE BABY!
MOM? — WHAT ARE THEY DIGGING FOR ANYWAYS?
ITS A NEW WATER MAIN, SO WE WON'T HAVE TO USE THE HAND PUMP.

SOON, UPSTAIRS...
I'll send you all my love
every day in a letter
CANDIES

Sealed With a Kiss
mmm

Sealed With A Kiss
BOY DO I FEEL STUPID—
THAT'S BECAUSE YOU **ARE** STUPID.
PLOP

Sealed With A Kiss

HOW COME GIRLS HAVE TO WEAR SHIRTS?
Wha Wha Wha
GETCHER FEET OFF.
LIFE

OH NEVERMIND.
OK, I'LL TELL YOU....
ITS *MEN.*

IT DRIVES THEM WILD TO SEE A GIRL WITHOUT HER SHIRT ON.
ITS TRUE—
YOU CAN EVEN MAKE A GUY CHANGE HIS **MIND**— ONE LOOK AT YOUR NAKED "THINGS" AND HE'S LIKE A PUPPY.
REALLY?
THEY SAY.

MUST BE, BECAUSE YOU ALWAYS HEAR THEM HOLLERIN': "KEEP YOUR SHIRT ON" .... CAUSE THEY DON'T WANT TO BE ACTING LIKE HOUND DOGS. I GUESS.

LOOKY. ITS MARILYN, MAKIN' SOME GUY THINK TWICE!
VA VA VOOM!
HA HA HA HA HA HA

AAAh OOOOh
HA HA HA
ARF ARF
HA HA HA
HA HA
HA HA THAT'S A REGULAR OL' KNEE SLAPPER!
CAN I please HAVE A PIECE OF CANDY?

NO!
AND WE'VE PROBABLY JUST SINNED, TOO. WE'D BETTER SAY A ROSARY.
St. Thers
BUT WE'RE SPOSED TA DO DISHES.

AFTER WE'RE DONE.
Glory Bead to the FATHER, and to the SON, and to the HOLY GHOST...
Father
Son
H.G.
CANDY

EEK!
MY CANDY! I'll GET YOU, RUNT—
AMBUSH!
WHAT THE?!..
POK
POK
POK
OW

A LITTLE BIT LATER
BUT I'M TIRED OF PUMPING.
KEEP IT UP OR I'LL TELL MOM HOW YOU WASTED FOOD.

CANDY DOESN'T COUNT AS FOOD.
YES IT DOES NERKO...
WHO'S THAT GUY?

MOM! WHO'S THAT?
I'M SORRY MR. TYLER, BUT THIS AREA IS NOT ZONED FOR THAT KIND OF HOOK-UP.
SNIF SNIF

UH OH... I BET HE'S FROM COUNTY CODES...
THINK FAST.
WHAT THE HELL D'YA MEAN? I GOT MY PERMIT—

I DUG UP MY WHOLE DAMN YARD!
OH NO
PLEASE
MISTER...

!
WE'VE JUST GOTTA HAVE THAT WATERMAIN!
THE END

사랑스러운 나의친구 미쓰 리

甜心李小姐

Sweet Miss LEE

NOTE: JUST TO KEEP YOU ON YOUR TOES, THE TRANSLATIONS HAVE THEIR OWN MEANING, AND ARE NOT MERELY A RE-PRESENTATION OF THE ENGLISH. HA HA!

SPECIAL THANKS TO: HYE KWON AND PROF. EUGENE KIM FOR THEIR HELP WITH THE KOREAN LANGUAGE AND TO EMMA AT SING HING FOR HER HELP WITH THE CHINESE CHARACTERS.

TRUE STORY!

Carol Tyler Nov. 1988

SHE KEPT TO HERSELF MOSTLY, REVERENTLY ATTENDING TO HER ROOM.
THE PLACE WAS LIKE A SANCTUARY. THE FLOORS WERE SPOTLESS. SHE ALWAYS REMOVED HER SHOES BEFORE ENTERING.

WE GOT ALONG GREAT!
YOU BE LAUR-O I BE HAH-DEE.
OK, OLLIE! HA HA HA
LEE SEEMED VERY PEACEFUL EXCEPT WHEN A PHONE CALL CAME IN FOR HER. APPARENTLY SHE WAS ESCAPING AN ARRANGED MARRIAGE TO SOME LOCAL KOREAN BIG SHOT.
I THINK ITS FOR YOU, LEE
전화를 받아
FBI SCAM... bla..bla..bla.. SOVIET THREAT.. bla.. bla bla.. FARM CRISIS.. bla bla.
NO! NO!
I AM NOT HERE!

SUMMER CAME AND WE OPENED ALL THE WINDOWS. JUNE BROUGHT FORTH GREENERY AND A NEW LOVE FOR LEE.
REE?
TEE HEE
XIANG, TOO, WAS YOUNG AND INNOCENT. A DELIGHTFUL COUNTERPART TO SWEET MISS LEE.
(ONCE, I WAS CRUISIN' BACK THRU THE APARTMENT CAUSE I FORGOT SOMETHING AND I CAUGHT THEM HOLDING HANDS— THEY WERE QUITE EMBARRASSED.)

THE ONLY PROBLEM WAS, XIANG WAS ON SCHOLARSHIP FROM COMMUNIST CHINA. A ROMANTIC INTERLUDE SUCH AS THIS WAS FORBIDDEN BY HIS SPONSOR (ESPECIALLY WITH A WESTERNER!).
DEAR LOVE... WITH EACH MINUTE MY PASSION GROWS FOR YOU... BUT IT IS DANGEROUS TO SEE YOU. IF I AM FOUND OUT, I WILL BE SENT HOME IN DISGRACE!
IN ORDER TO BE TOGETHER, XIANG WOULD HAVE TO MAP OUT AN ELABORATE SMOKE SCREEN. ONCE INSIDE THE APARTMENT THEY COULD RELAX.
XO
X
10 PACES BEHIND
ONE BLOCK OVER
HA HA HA
我爱妳
(AND THEY NEVER DID ANYTHING BUT HOLD HANDS)

I TRIED TO ADVANCE THE COURSE OF TRUE LOVE
IF YOU WANT, MIKE AND I WILL LEAVE THIS WEEKEND SO THAT YOU GUYS CAN BE ALONE—
FOR WHAT?
!?
YOU KNOW... ROMANCE?
OH NO. MUSN'T RISK CHILDREN.
HOW ABOUT A DIAPHRAGM?
IN CUNT? YOU PUT THAT IN CUNT? HA HA HA!
BRASH AMERICAN
HOWEVER, IT WAS GOVERNMENT THAT HAD FINAL SAY IN THIS RELATIONSHIP.
MR. XIANG WILL NOT BE PERMITTED TO RETURN. HE SENDS THIS NOTE.
我永遠不会忘記妳
FRAIL AND DISTRAUGHT, LITTLE LEE WAS WITHERING AWAY LIKE THE AUTUMN LEAVES.
I MADE SOME HOME-MADE SOUP. WOULD YOU LIKE SOME? PLEASE COME EAT WITH ME—
NO SANK YOU. I WILL NOT EAT.
XIANG! I CAN'T LIVE WITHOUT YOU.
THEN, ON THE DECEMBER NIGHT WHEN MARTIAL LAW WAS DECLARED IN POLAND, HE CAME POUNDING ON THE DOOR.
YOU MUST LET HIM IN.
ITS OK
WHO ARE YOU?
I AM MR. SIN AND I HAVE COME TO CLAIM MY BRIDE.
IT WAS HORRIBLE TO SEE THE MELTING SNOW-MUD SPLOTCHES OF MR.SIN'S PATH AS HE PUMPED ACROSS HER HAND-BUFFED FLOOR.
너는 내여자야, 내아내가 될 운명 이라구!
YES, MR. SIN, I AM YOURS.
HE SCOWLED AT ME AND THEN FIRMLY SHUT THE DOOR. IT MADE ME FEEL SO UNCOMFORTABLE THAT I LEFT.
LATER, I CAME HOME TO THE OPPRESSIVE SOUND OF MR. SIN'S STRIDOR. IT WAS KEEPING ME AWAKE, BUT THERE WAS NOTHING I COULD DO.
ICK.
AAGH UGH AAGH UGH I HAVE WAITED SO LONG FOR YOU
BY NOON, SIN HAD MOVED ALL OF HER STUFF OUT, AND WE SAID GOODBYE. BUT SHE HAD ONE FINAL TASK AND RETURNED TO HER ROOM.
XIANG! I WASH THIS FLOOR WITH MY TEARS!
비 가오면 언제나 생각 나는 그 사람,
IT WAS A SAD PARTING FOR ME TOO, LEE. I WISH I KNEW WHERE YOU WERE.
THE END.

BIBLIOGRAPHY

M. K. Brown: "White Girl Sings the Blues," *National Lampoon* (1989); "Coping With Chain-Saw Massacres," *National Lampoon* (1986); "I Can't Work Today," *Wimmen's Comix* #9 (Last Gasp, 1984); "Easy Home Auto," *National Lampoon* (1988); "They Came From Space," *Arcade* #6 (Print Mint, 1976); "Odd Moon Rising," *National Lampoon* (1987); "Guide Dogs," *National Lampoon* (1987); "Let's Do the White Girl Twist," *National Lampoon* (1986); "Free Glue Sample," *National Lampoon* (1987); "Right Brain/Wrong Brain," *National Lampoon* (1986); "Marriage/Mirage," *Mother Jones* (1979);"Singles Bar," *National Lampoon* (1979); "Espeakink Spanich en Macy's," *National Lampoon* (1986).

Julie Doucet: "Heavy Flow," *Weirdo* #26 (Last Gasp, 1989); "Vive la Différence," *Weirdo* #27 (Last Gasp, 1990); "Magic Necklace," *Weirdo* #27 (Last Gasp, 1990); "My Conscience is Bugging Me," *Drawn & Quarterly* #2 (1990); "So Why I Had That Stupid Dream," *Rip Off Comics* #28 (Rip Off Press, 1990).

Mary Fleener: "The Jelly," *Slutburger Stories* (Rip Off Press, 1990); "Slug Fest," *Rip Off Comics* (Rip Off Press, 1989); "Skulls 'n Stiffs," *Heck!* (Rip Off Press, 1989).

Phoebe Gloeckner: "Periodic Fantasy," *Weirdo* #24 (Last Gasp, 1988); "Magda Meets the Little Men in the Woods," *Wimmen's Comix* #14 (Rip Off Press, 1989); "Quaker School Q-ties," *Weirdo* #26 (Last Gasp, 1989); "An Evening in Prague," *Young Lust* #7 (Last Gasp, 1990); "The Sad Tale of the Visible Woman and Her Invisible Man," *Wimmen's Comix* #16 (Rip Off Press, 1990).

Aline Kominsky-Crumb: "Merci Areevwahr Ameriker," *Weirdo* #27 (Last Gasp, 1990); "Nose Job," *Wimmen's Comix* #15 (Rip Off Press, 1989); "Arnie's Girl," *Weirdo* #26 (Last Gasp, 1989); "Moo Goo Gai Pan," *Weirdo* #20 (Last Gasp, 1989); "Le Bunché de Paree Turns 40," *Weirdo* #24 (Last Gasp, 1988).

Krystine Kryttre: "Bimbos From Hell," *Weirdo* #22 (Last Gasp, 1987); "Father Phlem," *Sexy Stories From World's Religions* (Last Gasp, 1990); "On Being Too Intense," *Tits & Clits* #7 (Nanny Goat Productions, 1987); "Dolores Park," Weirdo #26 (Last Gasp, 1989); "Horny Blows It," *Snake Eyes* #1 (Fantagraphics, 1990); "Nihilist Romance," *Deadbeat Magazine* (Frank Deadbeat, 1986); "The Next 5 Miles," *Death Warmed Over* (Cat-Head Comics, 1990).

Carol Lay: "The Prince and the Art Girl," *Weirdo* #27 (Last Gasp, 1990); "Grunge 361," *Good Girls* #4 (Fantagraphics, 1989); "Face the Facts of Love," *El Vibora* (Ediciones La Cupula, 1983).

Caryn Leschen: "Disastrous Relationshipsland," *Wimmen's Comix* #14 (Rip Off Press, 1989); "The Toilets of Europe," *Wimmen's Comix* #10 (Last Gasp, 1985); "The Magic Lemon," *Wimmen's Comix* #13 (Renegade Press, 1988); "Be Yourself," *Wimmen's Comix* #11 (Renegade Press, 1987); "Violet in Paris," *Wimmen's Comix* #9 (Last Gasp, 1984).

Carel Moiseiwitsch: "Tammy Faye Bakker and Her Hoppin', Shoppin' Demons," *Weirdo* #25 (Last Gasp, 1989); "High on PMS," *Weirdo, #22 (Last Gasp, 1989); "Mean Woman Blues," Rock & Roll Quarterly* (The Village Voice, 1988); "Little Fight in Mexico," *Rip Off Comix* #26 (Rip Off Press, 1990); "More Guys than Gals are Forced into Sex," *LA Weekly* (1989); "Declaration of Independence," *Village Voice* (1988); "Beastly Woman," *Sortez la Chienne #3* (Summer 1988); "Wonder Calavera—Woman Revolucionaria," *Pop-Duet* (Summer 1987); "Car Woman," "Femme Fatale," "Siren," And "Guilt Without Sex," (all *Rotating Bodies* (*Peterade Press*, 1988).

Penny Moran Van Horn: "The Pickup," (previously unpublished); "Texas Characters (Miz Flak)," *Weirdo* #27 (Last Gasp, 1990); "A Bird in the Beard," *Weirdo* #26 (Last Gasp, 1986); "Ten Dollars for Two Minutes," Weirdo #19 (Last Gasp, 1986); "Catholic School," *Wimmen's Comix* #15 (Rip Off Press, 1989); "Domestic Bliss," *The Daily Texan* (University of Texas, Austin, 1990).

Diane Noomin: "I Had to Advertise for Love," *Young Lust* #7 (Last Gasp, 1990); "Lesbo A GoGo," *Real Girl* #1 (Fantagraphics, 1990); "Life in the Bagel Belt," *True Glitz* (Rip Off Press, 1990); "Coming of Age in Canarsie," *Wimmen's Comix* #15 (Rip Off Press, 1989); "Meet Marvin Mensch," *Wimmen's Comix* #16 (Rip Off Press, 1990); "Don't Ask," *Wimmen's Comix* #14 (Rip Off Press, 1989); "Rubberware," *Wimmen's Comix* #10 (Last Gasp, 1985); "The C Word," *Choices* (Angry Isis Press, 1990); "Utterly Private Eye," *Wimmen's Comix* #9 (Last Gasp, 1984).

Dori Seda: "Of Human Bondage and Discipline," *Lonely Nights* (Last Gasp, 1985); "Let's Eat Brains," *Weirdo* #22 (Last Gasp, 1987); "Cleanliness Is Next to Dogliness," *Weirdo* #18 (Last Gasp, 1986); "Fashion as a Losing Battle," *Wimmen's Comix* #11 (Renegade Press, 1987).

Leslie Sternbergh: "Girls, Girls, Girls" (script: Joyce Brabner), *Tits 'n Clits* #7 (Nanny Goat Productions, 1988); "Ave. B Girls Paperdolls," *STOP Magazine* v. 2 (Cessna/Scharff, 1990); "Killer Shoes," *Wimmen's Comix* #11 (Renegade Press, 1987); "Dinner at Ben's," *Weirdo* #26 (Last Gasp, 1989); "I Was a Broadway B Girl (For a Day)," *Wimmen's Comix* #9 (Last Gasp, 1984).

Carol Tyler: "Sweet Miss Lee," *Wimmen's Comix* #14 (Rip Off Press, 1989); "Return of Mrs. Kite," *Weirdo* #22 (Last Gasp, 1988); "Uncovered Property," *Weirdo* #20 (Last Gasp, 1987); "Detour of Duty," *Street Music* #4 (Fantagraphics Books, 1989), "Anatomy of a New Mom," *Weirdo* #25 (Last Gasp, 1989).

DIRECTORY OF PUBLISHERS

Last Gasp
2180 Bryant Street
San Francisco, CA 94110

Fantagraphics Books
7563 Lake City Way
Seattle, WA 98115

El Vibora
Pza. Beatas 3
08003 Barcelona
Spain

Rip Off Press
P.O. Box 4686
Auburn, CA 95604

The Print Mint
830 Folger Avenue
Berkeley, CA 94710

Renegade Press
3908 E. 4th Street
Long Beach, CA 90814

Drawn & Quarterly
95 Bernard Street, West
Montreal, Quebec
Canada H2T 2J9

STOP Magazine
235 E. 26th Street
Studio C
New York, N.Y. 10010

Mother Jones Magazine
1663 Mission Street
San Francisco, CA

National Lampoon
1 Park Avenue
New York, N.Y. 10016

Angry Isis Press
1982 15th Street
San Francisco, CA 94110

Nanny Goat Productions
P.O. Box 845
Laguna Beach, CA 92652

The Daily Texan
University of Texas
Austin, TX

Cat-Head Comics
P.O. Box 576
Hudson, MA

Frank Deadbeat
1943 Page Street #2
San Francisco, CA 94117

Pop Tart
Peterade Press
3505 Commercial St.
Vancouver, BC
Canada V5N 4E8

Sortez La Chienne
48 Rue Gambetta
56000 Lille
France